UNIDROIT

International Institute for the Unification of Private Law

PRINCIPLES

OF

INTERNATIONAL

COMMERCIAL

CONTRACTS

Rome 1994

Suggested form of citation:

UNIDROIT Principles Art. 1.6(2)

Published by the
International Institute for the Unification of Private Law
(Unidroit), Via Panisperna, 28 - 00184 Rome -
Fax: +39 6 / 6994 1394

ISBN: 88 - 86449 - 00 - 3

FOREWORD

It is with the utmost pleasure that the International Institute for the Unification of Private Law (UNIDROIT) announces the completion of the drawing up of the UNIDROIT Principles of International Commercial Contracts. This achievement represents the outcome of many years of intensive research and deliberations involving the participation of a large number of eminent lawyers from all five continents of the world.

Tribute must first be paid to the members of the Working Group primarily entrusted with the preparation of the UNIDROIT Principles and, among them, especially to the Rapporteurs for the different chapters. Without their personal commitment and unstinting efforts, so ably coordinated throughout by Michael Joachim Bonell, this ambitious project could not have been brought to its successful conclusion.

We must also express gratitude for the most valuable input given by the numerous practising lawyers, judges, civil servants and academics from widely differing legal cultures and professional backgrounds, who became involved in the project at various stages of the drafting process and whose constructive criticism was of the greatest assistance.

In this moment of great satisfaction for the Institute we cannot but evoke the memory of Mario Matteucci, who for so many years served UNIDROIT as Secretary-General and then as President and whose belief in the Principles as a vital contribution to the process of international unification of law was a source of constant inspiration to us all.

Malcolm Evans　　　　　　　　　　　　　　　　*Riccardo Monaco*
Secretary-General　　　　　　　　　　　　　　　　　　　*President*

INTRODUCTION

Efforts towards the international unification of law have hitherto essentially taken the form of binding instruments, such as supranational legislation or international conventions, or of model laws. Since these instruments often risk remaining little more than a dead letter and tend to be rather fragmentary in character, calls are increasingly being made for recourse to non-legislative means of unification or harmonisation of law.

Some of those calls are for the further development of what is termed "international commercial custom", for example through model clauses and contracts formulated by the interested business circles on the basis of current trade practices and relating to specific types of transactions or particular aspects thereof.

Others go even further and advocate the elaboration of an international restatement of general principles of contract law.

UNIDROIT's initiative for the elaboration of "Principles of International Commercial Contracts" goes in that direction.

It was as long ago as 1971 that the Governing Council decided to include this subject in the Work Programme of the Institute. A small Steering Committee, composed of Professors René David, Clive M. Schmitthoff and Tudor Popescu, representing the civil law, the common law and the socialist systems, was set up with the task of conducting preliminary inquiries into the feasibility of such a project.

It was not until 1980, however, that a special Working Group was constituted for the purpose of preparing the various draft chapters of the Principles. The Group, which included representatives of all the major legal systems of the world, was composed of leading experts in the field of contract law and international trade law. Most of them were academics, some high ranking judges or civil servants, who all sat in a personal capacity.

The Group appointed from among its members Rapporteurs for the different chapters of the Principles, who were entrusted with the task of submitting successive drafts together with Comments. These were then discussed by the Group and circulated to a wide range of experts, including UNIDROIT's extensive network of correspondents. In addition, the Governing Council offered its advice on the policy to be followed, especially in those cases where the Group had found it difficult to reach a consensus. The necessary editorial work was entrusted to an Editorial Committee, assisted by the Secretariat.

For the most part the UNIDROIT Principles reflect concepts to be found in many, if not all, legal systems. Since however the Principles are intended to provide a system of rules especially tailored to the needs of international commercial transactions, they also embody what are perceived to be the best solutions, even if still not yet generally adopted.

The objective of the UNIDROIT Principles is to establish a balanced set of rules designed for use throughout the world irrespective of the legal traditions and the economic and political conditions of the countries in which they are to be applied. This goal is reflected both in their formal presentation and in the general policy underlying them.

As to their formal presentation, the UNIDROIT Principles deliberately seek to avoid the use of terminology peculiar to any given legal system. The international character of the Principles is also stressed by the fact that the comments accompanying each single provision systematically refrain from referring to national laws in order to explain the origin and rationale of the solution retained. Only where the rule has been taken over more or less literally from the world wide accepted United Nations Convention on Contracts for the International Sale of Goods (CISG) is explicit reference made to its source.

With regard to substance, the UNIDROIT Principles are sufficiently flexible to take account of the constantly changing circumstances brought about by the technological and economic developments affecting cross-border trade practice. At the same time they attempt to ensure fairness in international commercial relations by expressly stating the general duty of the parties to act in accordance with good faith and fair dealing and, in a number of specific instances, imposing standards of reasonable behaviour.

Naturally, to the extent that the UNIDROIT Principles address issues also covered by CISG, they follow the solutions found in that Convention, with such adaptations as were considered appropriate to reflect the particular nature and scope of the Principles[*].

---

[*] See especially Arts. 1.8, 1.9, 2.2, in conjunction with 5.7 and 7.2.2.

Introduction

In offering the UNIDROIT Principles to the international legal and business communities, the Governing Council is fully conscious of the fact that the Principles, which do not involve the endorsement of Governments, are not a binding instrument and that in consequence their acceptance will depend upon their persuasive authority. There are a number of significant ways in which the UNIDROIT Principles may find practical application, the most important of which are amply explained in the Preamble.

The Governing Council is confident that those to whom the UNIDROIT Principles are addressed will appreciate their intrinsic merits and derive full advantage from their use.

THE GOVERNING COUNCIL OF UNIDROIT

Rome, May 1994

THE UNIDROIT GOVERNING COUNCIL

MEMBERS OF THE WORKING GROUP

Michael Joachim BONELL — Professor of Law, University of Rome I "La Sapienza"; *Chairman of the Working Group; Rapporteur on Chapter 1 (including the Preamble), Chapter 2 and Chapter 4*

Patrick BRAZIL — Attorney, Canberra; former Secretary, Attorney-General's Department; former member of the UNIDROIT Governing Council

Paul-André CREPEAU — Director, Centre de recherche en droit privé et comparé du Québec; Professor of Law, McGill University, Montreal

Samuel K. DATE-BAH — Professor of Law, University of Accra; Special Adviser (Legal), Commonwealth Secretariat, London

Adolfo DI MAJO — Professor of Law, University of Rome I "La Sapienza"

Ulrich DROBNIG — Director, Max-Planck-Institut für ausländisches und internationales Privatrecht, Hamburg; *Rapporteur on Chapter 7, Section 2 and Co-Rapporteur on Chapter 3*

E. Allan FARNSWORTH — Professor of Law, Columbia University in the City of New York School of Law; Member of the UNIDROIT Governing Council; *Chairman of the Editorial Committee*

Marcel FONTAINE — Professor of Law, Centre de droit des Obligations, Université Catholique de Louvain, Louvain-la-Neuve; *Rapporteur on Chapter 5 and on Chapter 6, Section 1 (excluding Articles 6.1.14 to 6.1.17)*

Michael P. FURMSTON — Professor of Law, University of Bristol; *Rapporteur on Chapter 7, Section 1 (excluding Articles 7.1.4 and 7.1.6)*

Alejandro GARRO — Lecturer at the Columbia University in the City of New York School of Law; former Attorney, Buenos Aires

Arthur S. HARTKAMP — Advocate-General at the Supreme Court of the Netherlands, The Hague; Professor of Law, Utrecht University; member of the UNIDROIT Governing Council

Hisakazu HIROSE — Professor of Law, University of Tokyo, Komaba

HUANG Danhan — Professor of Law, University of International Business and Economics; former Deputy Director of the Department of Treaties and Law at the Ministry of Foreign Economic Relations and Trade of the People's Republic of China, Beijing

Alexander S. KOMAROV — President of the Court of International Commercial Arbitration at the Russian Federation Chamber of Commerce and Industry; Head of Law Department, All-Russian Academy of Foreign Trade, Moscow

Ole LANDO — Professor of Law, Institute of European Market Law, Copenhagen School of Economics and Business Administration; *Rapporteur on Chapter 7, Section 3, Co-Rapporteur on Chapter 3*

Dietrich MASKOW — Attorney, Berlin; Former Director, Institut für ausländisches Recht und Rechtsvergleichung der DDR; *Rapporteur on Articles 6.1.14 to 6.1.17 and on Chapter 6, Section 2*

Denis TALLON — Professor of Law; Former Director, Institut de droit comparé de Paris, Université de droit, d'économie et de sciences sociales (Paris 2); *Rapporteur on Article 7.1.6 and on Chapter 7, Section 4*

Secretary to the Working Group was Lena PETERS of the UNIDROIT Secretariat

Initially the Working Group also included C. Massimo Bianca (University of Rome I "La Sapienza"); Jerzy Rajski (University of Warsaw; Co-Rapporteur on the preliminary drafts of Chapters 5 and 6); Tony Wade (The Asser Institute at The Hague); Wang Zhenpu (Deputy Director of the Department of Treaties and Law at the Ministry of Foreign Economic Relations and Trade of the People's Republic of China).

OTHER PARTICIPANTS IN THE PROJECT

The following also participated in one capacity or another in the project: José M. Abascal Zamora (Panamerican University of Mexico City); Enrique Aimone Gibson (Catholic University of Valparaìso); Joseph 'Bayo Ajala (former Solicitor-General of the Federation of Nigeria and Director-General Federal Ministry of Justice); Bernard Audit (University of Paris II Panthéon-Assas); Luiz O. Baptista (President of the Bar Association of São Paolo); Jorge Barrera Graf (Universidad Nacional Autónoma de México); Henry T. Bennett (former Deputy Secretary of the Attorney-General's Department, Canberra); Eric E. Bergsten (Pace University; former Secretary to the United Nations Commission on International Trade Law); George Berlioz (Attorney in Paris); Piero Bernardini (Attorney in Rome; former Head of the Legal Office of the Ente Nazionale Idrocarburi (ENI)); Richard Buxbaum (University of California at Berkeley); Franz Bydlinski (University of Vienna); Amelia Boss (Temple University); Andrzej Calus (Warsaw School of Economics); John W. Carter (University of Sydney); James Richard Crawford (University of Cambridge); Ronald C.C. Cuming (University of Saskatchewan); Giorgio De Nova (University of Milan); Louis Del Duca (Dickinson School of Law); Arturo Diaz Bravo (Attorney in Mexico City); Aubrey L. Diamond (University of London); Alfred Duchek (Generalanwalt at the Austrian Federal Ministry of Justice); Fritz Enderlein (Attorney in Berlin; former Director of the Institut für ausländisches Recht und Rechtsvergleichung in Potsdam-Babelsberg); John Goldring (University of Wollongong); James Gordley (University of California at Berkeley); Anita Hill (University of Oklahoma); Fernando Hinestrosa (University of Bogotà); Kurt Grönfors (University of Gothenburg); Lars Hjerner (University of Stockholm); Richard Hyland (Rutgers University at Camden), *Rapporteur on Article 7.1.4*; Rafael Illescas Ortiz (University Carlos III of Madrid); Philippe Kahn (Director of the Centre de recherche sur le droit des marchés et des investissements internationaux, Dijon); Koh Kheng-Lian (University of Singapore); Lodvik Kopac (Attorney in Prague; former Deputy Director at the Federal Ministry of Foreign Trade of the CSSR); Ernest Krings (Advocate-General at the Supreme Court of Belgium); Pierre Lalive (University of Geneva); Hans Leser (University of Marburg); Berardino Libonati (University of Rome I

"La Sapienza"); Giovanni Longo (Secretary-General of the Supreme Court of Italy); Kéba Mbaye (former Vice-President of the International Court of Justice); Luis Moisset de Espanés (University of Còrdova); José C. Moreira Alves (former President of the Supreme Court of Brazil); Barry Nicholas (University of Oxford); Tinuade Oyekunle (Attorney in Lagos; former Director International and Comparative Law Division, Nigerian Federal Ministry of Justice); Grace Orleans (Acting Solicitor-General, Ghana); Alfred E. von Overbeck (University of Fribourg); Luiz G. Paes de Barros Leães (University of São Paolo); Gonzalo Parra Aranguren (University of Caracas); Michel Pelichet (Deputy Secretary-General of the Hague Conference on Private International Law); Pietro Perlingieri (University of Naples); Allan Philip (President of the Comité Maritime International); László Réczei (Professor of Law, University of Budapest; former Ambassador); Pietro Rescigno (University of Rome I "La Sapienza"); Julio C. Rivera (University of Buenos Aires); Walter Rolland (University of Halle; former Ministerialdirektor at the Federal Ministry of Justice); Eero Routamo (University of Helsinki); Arthur Rosett (University of California Los Angeles); Rodolfo Sacco (University of Turin); Claude Samson (University of Laval); Benito Sansò (University of Caracas); David Sassoon (Attorney in Tel Aviv); Peter Schlechtriem (University of Freiburg); Kurt Siehr (University of Zurich); José Luis Siqueiros (Professor of Law; Attorney in Mexico City); Sir Thomas Smith (University of Edinburgh); T. Bradbrooke Smith (former Assistant Deputy Attorney General at the Department of Justice, Ottawa); Kazuaki Sono (Hokkaido University of Sapporo; former Secretary, United Nations Commission on International Trade Law; former Legal Consultant of the World Bank); Jean-Georges Sauveplanne (University of Utrecht); Nagendra Singh (former President of the International Court of Justice); Sandro Schipani (University of Rome II "Tor Vergata"); Giuseppe Sperduti (University of Rome I "La Sapienza"); Sompong Sucharitkul (former Ambassador and former Thai member of the International Law Commission); Guido Tedeschi (Hebrew University, Jerusalem); Evelio Verdera y Tuells (University of Madrid "La Complutense"); Michael Will (University of Geneva); Hernany Veytia Palomino (Panamerican University of Mexico City); Jelena Vilus (University of Belgrade); Peter Winship (Southern Methodist University, Dallas).

CONTENTS

Contents

PREAMBLE

(Purpose of the Principles)

These Principles set forth general rules for international commercial contracts.

They shall be applied when the parties have agreed that their contract be governed by them.

They may be applied when the parties have agreed that their contract be governed by "general principles of law", the "*lex mercatoria*" or the like.

They may provide a solution to an issue raised when it proves impossible to establish the relevant rule of the applicable law.

They may be used to interpret or supplement international uniform law instruments.

They may serve as a model for national and international legislators.

COMMENT

The Principles set forth general rules which are basically conceived for "international commercial contracts".

1. "International" contracts

The international character of a contract may be defined in a great variety of ways. The solutions adopted in both national and international legislation range from a reference to the place of business or habitual residence of the parties in different countries to the adoption of more general criteria such as the contract having "significant connections with more than one State", "involving a choice between the laws of different States", or "affecting the interests of international trade".

The Principles do not expressly lay down any of these criteria. The assumption, however, is that the concept of "international" contracts should be given the broadest possible interpretation, so as ultimately to exclude only those situations where no international element at all is involved, i.e. where all the relevant elements of the contract in question are connected with one country only.

2. "Commercial" contracts

The restriction to "commercial" contracts is in no way intended to take over the distinction traditionally made in some legal systems between "civil" and "commercial" parties and/or transactions, i.e. to make the application of the Principles dependent on whether the parties have the formal status of "merchants" (*commerçants, Kaufleute*) and/or the transaction is commercial in nature. The idea is rather that of excluding from the scope of the Principles so-called "consumer transactions" which are within the various legal systems being increasingly subjected to special rules, mostly of a mandatory character, aimed at protecting the consumer, i.e. a party who enters into the contract otherwise than in the course of its trade or profession.

The criteria adopted at both national and international level also vary with respect to the distinction between consumer and non-consumer contracts. The Principles do not provide any express definition, but the assumption is that the concept of "commercial" contracts should be understood in the broadest possible sense, so as to include not only trade transactions for the supply or exchange of goods or services, but also other types of economic transactions, such as investment and/or concession agreements, contracts for professional services, etc.

3. The Principles and domestic contracts between private persons

Notwithstanding the fact that the Principles are conceived for international commercial contracts, there is nothing to prevent private persons from agreeing to apply the Principles to a purely domestic contract. Any such agreement would however be subject to the mandatory rules of the domestic law governing the contract.

4. The Principles as rules of law governing the contract

a. *Express choice by the parties*

As the Principles represent a system of rules of contract law which are common to existing national legal systems or best adapted to the special requirements of international commercial transactions, there might be good reasons for the parties to choose them expressly as the rules applicable to their contract, in the place of one or another particular domestic law.

Parties who wish to adopt the Principles as the rules applicable to their contract would however be well advised to combine the reference to the Principles with an arbitration agreement.

The reason for this is that the freedom of choice of the parties in designating the law governing their contract is traditionally limited to national laws. Therefore, a reference by the parties to the Principles will normally be considered to be a mere agreement to incorporate them in the contract, while the law governing the contract will still have to be determined on the basis of the private international law rules of the forum. As a result, the Principles will bind the parties only to the extent that they do not affect the rules of the applicable law from which the parties may not derogate.

The situation may be different if the parties agree to submit disputes arising from their contract to arbitration. Arbitrators are not necessarily bound by a particular domestic law. This is self-evident if they are authorised by the parties to act as *amiable compositeurs* or *ex aequo et bono*. But even in the absence of such an authorisation there is a growing tendency to permit the parties to choose "rules of law" other than national laws on which the arbitrators are to base their decisions. See in particular Art. 28(1) of the *1985 UNCITRAL Model Law on International Commercial Arbitration*; see also Art. 42(1) of the *1965 Convention on the Settlement of Investment Disputes between States and Nationals of other States (ICSID Convention)*.

In line with this approach, the parties would be free to choose the Principles as the "rules of law" according to which the arbitrators would decide the dispute, with the result that the Principles would apply to the exclusion of any particular national law, subject only to the application of those rules of domestic law which are mandatory irrespective of which law governs the contract (see Art. 1.4).

In disputes falling under the ICSID Convention, the Principles might even be applicable to the exclusion of any domestic rule of law.

b. *The Principles applied as lex mercatoria*

Parties to international commercial contracts who cannot agree on the choice of a particular domestic law as the law applicable to their contract sometimes provide that it shall be governed by the "general principles of law", by the "usages and customs of international trade", by the *lex mercatoria*, etc.

Hitherto, such reference by the parties to not better identified principles and rules of a supranational or transnational character has been criticised, among other grounds, because of the extreme vagueness of such concepts. In order to avoid, or at least considerably to reduce, the uncertainty accompanying the use of such vague concepts for the determination of their content, it might be advisable to have recourse to a systematic and well-defined set of rules such as the Principles.

5. The Principles as a substitute for the domestic law otherwise applicable

The Principles may however become relevant even where the contract is governed by a particular domestic law. This is the case whenever it proves extremely difficult if not impossible to establish the relevant rule of that particular domestic law with respect to a specific issue and a solution can be found in the Principles. The reasons for such a difficulty generally lie in the special character of the legal sources and/or the cost of access to them.

Recourse to the Principles as a substitute for the domestic law otherwise applicable is of course to be seen as a last resort; on the other hand it may be justified not only in the event of the absolute impossibility of establishing the relevant rule of the applicable law, but also whenever the research involved would entail disproportionate efforts and/or costs. The current practice of courts in such situations is that of applying the *lex fori*. Recourse to the Principles would have the advantage of avoiding the application of a law which will in most cases be more familiar to one of the parties.

6. The Principles as a means of interpreting and supplementing existing international instruments

Any legislation, whether of international or national origin, raises questions concerning the precise meaning of its individual provisions. Moreover, such legislation is by its very nature unable to anticipate all the problems to which it will be applied. When applying domestic statutes it is possible to rely on long established principles and criteria of interpretation to be found within each legal system. The situation is far more uncertain with respect to instruments which, although formally incorporated into the various national legal systems, have been prepared and agreed upon at international level.

According to the traditional view recourse should, even in such cases, be had to the principles and criteria provided in domestic law, be it the law of the forum or that which would, according to the relevant rules of private international law, be applicable in the absence of the uniform law.

At present, both courts and arbitral tribunals tend more and more to abandon such a "conflictual" method and seek instead to interpret and supplement international instruments by reference to autonomous and internationally uniform principles. This approach, which has indeed been expressly sanctioned in the most recent conventions (see, e.g., Art. 7 of the *1980 UN Convention on Contracts for the International Sale of Goods (CISG)*), is based on the assumption that uniform law, even after its incorporation into the various national legal systems, only formally becomes an integrated part of the latter, whereas from a substantive point of view it does not lose its original character of a special body of law autonomously developed at international level and intended to be applied in a uniform manner throughout the world.

Until now, such autonomous principles and criteria for the interpretation and supplementing of international instruments have had to be found in each single case by the judges and arbitrators themselves on the basis of a comparative survey of the solutions adopted in the different national legal systems. The Principles could considerably facilitate their task in this respect.

7. The Principles as a model for national and international legislators

In view of their intrinsic merits the Principles may in addition serve as a model to national and international law-makers for the drafting of legislation in the field of general contract law or with respect to special types of transactions. At a national level, the Principles may be particularly useful to those countries which lack a developed body of legal rules relating to contracts and which intend to update their law, at least with respect to foreign economic relationships, to current international standards. Not too different is the situation of those countries with a well-defined legal system, but which after the recent dramatic changes in their socio-political structure have an urgent need to rewrite their laws, in particular those relating to economic and business activities.

At an international level the Principles could become an important term of reference for the drafting of conventions and model laws.

So far the terminology used to express the same concept differs considerably from one instrument to another, with the obvious risk of misunderstandings and misinterpretations. Such inconsistencies could be avoided if the terminology of the Principles were to be adopted as an international uniform glossary.

CHAPTER 1

GENERAL PROVISIONS

ARTICLE 1.1
(Freedom of contract)

The parties are free to enter into a contract and to determine its content.

COMMENT

1. Freedom of contract as a basic principle in the context of international trade

The principle of freedom of contract is of paramount importance in the context of international trade. The right of business people to decide freely to whom they will offer their goods or services and by whom they wish to be supplied, as well as the possibility for them freely to agree on the terms of individual transactions, are the cornerstones of an open, market-oriented and competitive international economic order.

2. Economic sectors where there is no competition

There are of course a number of possible exceptions to the principle laid down in the present article.

As concerns the freedom to conclude contracts with any other person, there are economic sectors which States may decide in the public interest to exclude from open competition. In such cases the goods or services in question can only be requested from the one available supplier, which will usually be a public body, and which may or may not be under a duty to conclude a contract with whoever makes a request, within the limits of the availability of the goods or services.

3. Limitation of party autonomy by mandatory rules

With respect to the freedom to determine the content of the contract, in the first instance the Principles themselves contain provisions from which the parties may not derogate. See Art. 1.5.

Moreover, there are both public and private law rules of mandatory character enacted by States (e.g. anti-trust, exchange control or price laws; laws imposing special liability regimes or prohibiting grossly unfair contract terms, etc.), which may prevail over the rules contained in the Principles. See Art. 1.4.

ARTICLE 1.2

(No form required)

Nothing in these Principles requires a contract to be concluded in or evidenced by writing. It may be proved by any means, including witnesses.

COMMENT

1. Contracts as a rule not subject to formal requirements

This article states the principle that as a rule the conclusion of a contract is not subject to any requirement as to form. Although the article mentions only the requirement of writing, it may be extended to other requirements as to form. The rule also covers the subsequent modification or termination of a contract by agreement of the parties.

The principle, which is to be found in many, although not in all, legal systems, seems particularly appropriate in the context of international trade relationships where, thanks to modern means of communication, many transactions are concluded at great speed and are not paper-based.

The first sentence of the article takes into account the fact that some legal systems regard formal requirements as matters relating to substance, while others impose them for evidentiary purposes only. The second sentence is intended to make it clear that to the extent that the principle of freedom of form applies, it implies the admissibility of oral evidence in judicial proceedings.

2. Possible exceptions under the applicable law

The principle of freedom of form may of course be overridden by the applicable law. See Art. 1.4. National laws as well as international instruments may impose special requirements as to form with respect either to the contract as a whole or to individual terms (e.g. arbitration agreements; jurisdiction clauses).

3. Form requirements agreed by the parties

Moreover, the parties may themselves agree on a specific form for the conclusion, modification or termination of their contract. In this context see Arts. 2.13, 2.17 and 2.18.

ARTICLE 1.3

(Binding character of contract)

A contract validly entered into is binding upon the parties. It can only be modified or terminated in accordance with its terms or by agreement or as otherwise provided in these Principles.

COMMENT

1. The principle *pacta sunt servanda*

This article lays down another basic principle of contract law, that of *pacta sunt servanda*.

The binding character of a contractual agreement obviously presupposes that an agreement has actually been concluded by the parties and that the agreement reached is not affected by any ground of invalidity. The rules governing the conclusion of contractual agreements are laid down in Chapter 2 of the Principles, while the grounds of invalidity are dealt with in Chapter 3. Additional requirements for the valid conclusion of contracts may be found in the applicable national or international mandatory rules.

2. Exceptions

A corollary of the principle of *pacta sunt servanda* is that a contract may be modified or terminated whenever the parties so agree. Modification or termination without agreement are on the contrary the exception and can therefore be admitted only when in conformity with the terms of the contract or when expressly provided for in the Principles. See Arts. 3.10(2), 3.10(3), 3.13, 5.8, 6.1.16, 6.2.3, 7.1.7, 7.3.1 and 7.3.3.

3. Effects on third persons not dealt with

While as a rule a contract produces effects only between the parties, there may be cases where it also affects third persons. Thus, a seller may under some domestic laws be under a contractual duty to protect the physical integrity and property not only of the buyer but also of accompanying persons during their presence on the seller's premises; equally, the consignee of a cargo may be entitled to sue the carrier for non-performance of a contractual duty undertaken by the latter in its contract of carriage with the sender. By stating the principle of the binding force of the contract between the parties, this article does not intend to prejudice any effect which that contract may have vis-à-vis third persons under the applicable law.

Similarly the Principles do not deal with the effects of avoidance and termination of a contract on the rights of third persons.

ARTICLE 1.4

(Mandatory rules)

Nothing in these Principles shall restrict the application of mandatory rules, whether of national, international or supranational origin, which are applicable in accordance with the relevant rules of private international law.

COMMENT

1. Mandatory rules prevail

Given the particular nature of the Principles, they cannot be expected to prevail over applicable mandatory rules, whether of national, international or supranational origin. In other words, mandatory provisions, whether enacted by States autonomously or to implement international conventions, or adopted by supranational organisations, cannot be overruled by the Principles.

2. Mandatory rules applicable in the event of mere incorporation of the Principles in the contract

In cases where the parties' reference to the Principles is considered to be only an agreement to incorporate them in the contract, the Principles will first of all encounter the limit of the mandatory rules of the law governing the contract, i.e. they will bind the parties only to the extent that they do not affect the rules of the applicable law from which parties may not contractually derogate. In addition, the mandatory rules of the forum, and possibly also those of third States, will likewise prevail, provided that they claim application whatever the law governing the contract and, in the case of the rules of third States, there is a close connection between those States and the contract in question.

3. Mandatory rules applicable if the Principles are the law governing the contract

Yet, even where, as may be the case if the dispute is brought before an arbitral tribunal, the Principles are applied as the law governing the contract, they cannot prejudice the application of those mandatory rules which claim application irrespective of which law is applicable to the contract (*lois d'application nécessaire*). Examples of such mandatory rules, the application of which cannot be excluded simply by choosing another law, are to be found in the field of foreign exchange regulations (see Art. VIII(2)(b) of the *Agreement of the International Monetary Fund, (Bretton Woods Agreement)*), import-export licences (see Arts. 6.1.14 - 6.1.17 of these Principles on public permission requirements), regulations pertaining to restrictive trade practices, etc.

4. Recourse to the rules of private international law relevant in each individual case

Both courts and arbitral tribunals differ considerably in the way in which they determine the mandatory rules applicable to international commercial contracts. For this reason the present article deliberately refrains from entering into the merit of the various questions involved, in particular whether in addition to the mandatory rules of the forum and of the *lex contractus* those of third States are also to be taken into account and if so, to what extent and on the basis of which criteria. These questions are to be settled in accordance with the rules of private international law which are relevant in each particular case (see, for instance, Art. 7 of the *1980 Rome Convention on the Law applicable to Contractual Obligations*).

ARTICLE **1.5**

(Exclusion or modification by the parties)

The parties may exclude the application of these Principles or derogate from or vary the effect of any of their provisions, except as otherwise provided in the Principles.

COMMENT

1. The non-mandatory character of the Principles

The rules laid down in the Principles are in general of a non-mandatory character, i.e. the parties may in each individual case either simply exclude their application in whole or in part or modify their content so as to adapt them to the specific needs of the kind of transaction involved.

2. Exclusion or modification may be express or implied

The exclusion or modification of the Principles by the parties may be either express or implied. There is an implied exclusion or modification when the parties expressly agree on contract terms which are inconsistent with provisions of the Principles and it is in this context irrelevant whether the terms in question have been negotiated individually or form part of standard terms incorporated by the parties in their contract.

If the parties expressly agree to the application of some only of the chapters of the Principles (e.g. "As far as the performance and non-performance of this contract is concerned, the UNIDROIT Principles shall apply"), it is presumed that the chapters concerned will be applied together with the general provisions of Chapter 1.

3. Mandatory provisions to be found in the Principles

A few provisions of the Principles are of a mandatory character, i.e. their importance in the system of the Principles is such that parties should not be permitted to exclude or to derogate from them as they wish. It is true that given the particular nature of the Principles the non-observance of this precept may have no consequences. On the other hand, it should be noted that the provisions in question reflect standards of behaviour and rules which are of a mandatory character under most domestic laws also.

Those provisions of the Principles which are mandatory are normally expressly indicated as such. This is the case with Art. 1.7 on good faith and fair dealing, with the provisions of Chapter 3 on substantive validity, except in so far as they relate or apply to mistake and to initial impossibility (see Art. 3.19), with Art. 5.7(2) on price determination and with Art. 7.4.13(2) on agreed payment for non-performance. Exceptionally, the mandatory character of a provision is only implicit and follows from the content and purpose of the provision itself (see Art. 7.1.6).

ARTICLE 1.6

(Interpretation and supplementation of the Principles)

(1) In the interpretation of these Principles, regard is to be had to their international character and to their purposes including the need to promote uniformity in their application.

(2) Issues within the scope of these Principles but not expressly settled by them are as far as possible to be settled in accordance with their underlying general principles.

COMMENT

1. Interpretation of the Principles as opposed to interpretation of the contract

The Principles, like any other legal text, be it of a legislative or of a contractual nature, may give rise to doubts as to the precise meaning of their content. The interpretation of the Principles is however different from that of the individual contracts to which they apply. Even if the Principles are considered to bind the parties only at contractual level, i.e. their application is made dependent on their incorporation in individual contracts, they remain an autonomous set of rules worked out with a view to their application in a uniform manner to an indefinite number of contracts of different types entered into in various parts of the world. As a consequence they must be interpreted in a different manner from the terms of each individual contract. The rules for the interpretation of the latter are laid down in Chapter 4 of the Principles. The present article deals rather with the manner in which the Principles are to be interpreted.

2. Regard to the international character of the Principles

The first criterion laid down by this article for the interpretation of the Principles is that regard is to be had to their "international character". This means that their terms and concepts are to be interpreted autonomously, i.e. in the context of the Principles themselves and not by reference to the meaning which might traditionally be attached to them by a particular domestic law.

Such an approach becomes necessary if it is recalled that the Principles are the result of thorough comparative studies carried out by lawyers coming from totally different cultural and legal backgrounds. When drafting the individual provisions, these experts had to find sufficiently neutral legal language on which they could reach a common understanding. Even in the exceptional cases where terms or concepts peculiar to one or more national laws are employed, the intention was never to use them in their traditional meaning.

3. Purposes of the Principles

By stating that in the interpretation of the Principles regard is to be had to their purposes, this article makes it clear that they are not to be construed in a strict and literal sense but in the light of the purposes and the rationale underlying the individual provisions as well as the Principles as a whole. The purpose of the individual provisions can be ascertained both from the text itself and from the comments thereon. As to the purposes of the Principles as a whole, this article, in view of the fact that the Principles' main objective is to provide a uniform framework for international commercial contracts, expressly refers to the need to promote uniformity in their application, i.e. to ensure that in practice they are to the greatest possible extent interpreted and applied in the same way in different countries. As to other purposes, see the remarks contained in the Introduction. See further Art. 1.7 which, although addressed to the parties, may also be seen as an expression of the underlying purpose of the Principles as such to promote the observance of good faith and fair dealing in contractual relations.

4. Supplementation of the Principles

A number of issues which would fall within the scope of the Principles are not settled expressly by them. In order to determine whether an issue is one that falls within the scope of the Principles even though it is not expressly settled by them, or whether it actually falls outside their scope, regard is to be had first to what is expressly stated either in the text or in the comments (see e.g. Art. 3.1, comment 3 on Art. 1.3 and comment 4 on Art. 1.4). A useful additional guide in this respect is the subject-matter index of the Principles.

The need to promote uniformity in the application of the Principles implies that when such gaps arise a solution should be found, whenever possible, within the system of the Principles itself before resorting to domestic laws.

The first step is to attempt to settle the unsolved question through an application by analogy of specific provisions. Thus, Art. 6.1.6 on place of performance should also govern restitution. Similarly, the rules laid down in Art. 6.1.9 with respect to the case where a monetary obligation is expressed in a currency other than that of the place for payment may also be applied when the monetary obligation is expressed by reference to units of account such as the Special Drawing Right (SDR) or the European Currency Unit (ECU). If the issue cannot be solved by a mere extension of specific provisions dealing with analogous cases, recourse must be made to their underlying general principles, i.e. to the principles and rules which may be applied on a much wider scale because of their general character. Some of these fundamental principles are expressly stated in the Principles (see, e.g., Arts. 1.1, 1.3, 1.5 and 1.7). Others have to be extracted from specific provisions, i.e. the particular rules contained therein must be analysed in order to see whether they can be considered an expression of a more general principle, and as such capable of being applied also to cases different from those specifically regulated.

Parties are of course always free to agree on a particular national law to which reference should be made for the supplementing of the Principles. A provision of this kind could read "This contract is governed by the UNIDROIT Principles supplemented by the law of country X", or "This contract shall be interpreted and executed in accordance with the UNIDROIT Principles. Questions not expressly settled therein shall be settled in accordance with the law of country X".

ARTICLE 1.7

(Good faith and fair dealing)

(1) Each party must act in accordance with good faith and fair dealing in international trade.

(2) The parties may not exclude or limit this duty.

COMMENT

1. "Good faith and fair dealing" as a fundamental idea underlying the Principles

There are a number of provisions throughout the different chapters of the Principles which constitute a direct or indirect application of the principle of good faith and fair dealing. See, for instance, Articles 2.4(2)(b), 2.15, 2.16, 2.18, 2.20, 3.5, 3.8, 3.10, 4.1(2), 4.2(2), 4.6, 4.8, 5.2, 5.3, 6.1.3, 6.1.5, 6.1.16(2), 6.1.17(1), 6.2.3(3)(4), 7.1.2, 7.1.6, 7.1.7, 7.2.2(b)(c), 7.4.8 and 7.4.13. This means that good faith and fair dealing may be considered to be one of the fundamental ideas underlying the Principles. By stating in general terms that each party must act in accordance with good faith and fair dealing para. (1) of this article makes it clear that even in the absence of special provisions in the Principles the parties' behaviour throughout the life of the contract, including the negotiation process, must conform to good faith and fair dealing.

Illustrations

1. A grants B forty-eight hours as the time within which B may accept its offer. When B, shortly before the expiry of the deadline, decides to accept, it is unable to do so: it is the weekend, the fax at A's office is disconnected and there is no telephone answering machine which can take the message. When on the following Monday A refuses B's acceptance A acts contrary to good faith since when it fixed the time-limit for acceptance it was for A to ensure that messages could be received at its office throughout the forty-eight hour period.

2. A contract for the supply and installation of a special production line contains a provision according to which A, the seller, is obliged to communicate to B, the purchaser, any improvements made by A to the technology of that line. After a year B learns of an important improvement of which it had not been informed. A is not excused by the fact that the production of that particular type of production line is no longer its responsibility but that of C, a wholly-owned affiliated company of A. It would be against good faith for A to invoke the separate entity of C, which was specifically set up to take over this production in order to avoid A's contractual obligations vis-à-vis B.

3. A, an agent, undertakes on behalf of B, the principal, to promote the sale of B's goods in a given area. Under the contract A's right to compensation arises only after B's approval of the contracts procured by A. While B is free to decide whether or not to approve the contracts procured by A, a systematic and unjustified refusal to approve any contract procured by A would be against good faith.

4. Under a line of credit agreement between A, a bank, and B, a customer, A suddenly and inexplicably refuses to make further advances to B whose business suffers heavy losses as a consequence. Notwithstanding the fact that the agreement contains a term permitting A to accelerate payment "at will", A's demand for payment in full without prior warning and with no justification would be against good faith.

2. "Good faith and fair dealing in international trade"

The reference to "good faith and fair dealing in international trade" first makes it clear that in the context of the Principles the two concepts are not to be applied according to the standards ordinarily adopted within the different national legal systems. In other words, such domestic standards may be taken into account only to the extent that they are shown to be generally accepted among the various legal systems. A further implication of the formula used is that good faith and fair dealing must be construed in the light of the special conditions of international trade. Standards of business practice may indeed vary considerably from one trade sector to another, and even within a given trade sector they may be more or less stringent depending on the socio-economic environment in which the enterprises operate, their size and technical skill, etc.

It should be noted that the provisions of the Principles and/or the comments thereto at times refer only to "good faith" or to "good faith and fair dealing". Such references should always be understood as a reference to "good faith and fair dealing in international trade" as specified in this article.

Illustrations

5.   Under a contract for the sale of high-technology equipment the purchaser loses the right to rely on any defect in the goods if it does not give notice to the seller specifying the nature of the defect without undue delay after it has discovered or ought to have discovered the defect. A, a buyer operating in a country where such equipment is commonly used, discovers a defect in the equipment after having put it into operation, but in its notice to B, the seller of the equipment, A gives misleading indications as to the nature of the defect. A loses its right to rely on the defect since a more careful examination of the defect would have permitted it to give B the necessary specifications.

6.   The facts are the same as in Illustration 5, the difference being that A operates in a country where this type of equipment is so far almost unknown. A does not lose its right to rely on the defect because B, being aware of A's lack of technical knowledge, could not reasonably have expected A properly to identify the nature of the defect.

3. The mandatory nature of the principle of good faith and fair dealing

The parties' duty to act in accordance with good faith and fair dealing is of such a fundamental nature that the parties may not contractually exclude or limit it (para. (2)). As to specific applications of the general prohibition to exclude or limit the principle of good faith and fair dealing between the parties, see Arts. 3.19, 7.1.6 and 7.4.13.

On the other hand, nothing prevents parties from providing in their contract for a duty to observe more stringent standards of behaviour.

ARTICLE 1.8

(Usages and practices)

(1) The parties are bound by any usage to which they have agreed and by any practices which they have established between themselves.

(2) The parties are bound by a usage that is widely known to and regularly observed in international trade by parties in the particular trade concerned except where the application of such a usage would be unreasonable.

COMMENT

1. Practices and usages in the context of the Principles

This article lays down the principle according to which the parties are in general bound by practices and usages which meet the requirements set forth in the article. Furthermore, these same requirements must be met by practices and usages for them to be applicable in the cases and for the purposes expressly indicated in the Principles. See, for instance, Arts. 2.6(3), 4.3, and 5.2.

2. Practices established between the parties

A practice established between the parties to a particular contract is automatically binding, except where the parties have expressly excluded its application. Whether a particular practice can be deemed to be "established" between the parties will naturally depend on the circumstances of the case, but behaviour on the occasion of only one previous transaction between the parties will not normally suffice.

Illustration

> 1. A, a supplier, has repeatedly accepted claims from B, a customer, for quantitative or qualitative defects in the goods as much as two weeks after their delivery. When B gives another notice of defects only after a fortnight, A cannot object that it is too late since the two-weeks' notice amounts to a practice established between A and B which will as such be binding on A.

3. Agreed usages

By stating that the parties are bound by usages to which they have agreed, para. (1) of this article merely applies the general principle of freedom of contract laid down in Art. 1.1. Indeed, the parties may either negotiate all the terms of their contract, or for certain questions simply refer to other sources including usages. The parties may stipulate the application of any usage, including a usage developed within a trade sector to which neither party belongs, or a usage relating to a different type of contract. It is even conceivable that the parties will agree on the application of what are sometimes misleadingly called usages, i.e. a set of rules issued by a particular trade association under the title of "Usages", but which only in part reflects established general lines of conduct.

4. Other applicable usages

Para. (2) lays down the criteria for the identification of usages applicable in the absence of a specific agreement by the parties. The fact that the usage must be "widely known to and regularly observed [...] by parties in the particular trade concerned" is a condition for the application of any usage, be it at international or merely at national or local level. The additional qualification "in international trade" is intended to avoid usages developed for, and confined to, domestic transactions also being invoked in transactions with foreigners.

Illustration

> 2. A, a real estate agent, invokes a particular usage of the profession in its country vis-à-vis B, a foreign customer. B is not bound by such a usage if that usage is of a local nature and relates to a trade which is predominantly domestic in character.

Only exceptionally may usages of a purely local or national origin be applied without any reference thereto by the parties. Thus, usages existing on certain commodity exchanges or at trade exhibitions or ports should be applicable provided that they are regularly followed with respect to foreigners as well. Another exception concerns the case of a businessperson who has already entered into a number of similar contracts in a foreign country and who should therefore be bound by the usages established within that country for such contracts.

Illustrations

3.   A, a terminal operator, invokes a particular usage of the port where it is located vis-à-vis B, a foreign carrier. B is bound by this local usage if the port is normally used by foreigners and the usage in question has been regularly observed with respect to all customers, irrespective of their place of business and of their nationality.

4.   A, a sales agent from country X, receives a request from B, one of its customers in country Y, for the customary 10% discount upon payment of the price in cash. A may not object to the application of such a usage on account of its being restricted to country Y if A has been doing business in that country for a certain period of time.

5. Application of usage unreasonable

A usage may be regularly observed by the generality of business people in a particular trade sector but its application in a given case may nevertheless be unreasonable. Reasons for this may be found in the particular conditions in which one or both parties operate and/or the atypical nature of the transaction. In such cases the usage will not be applied.

Illustration

5.   A usage exists in a commodity trade sector according to which the purchaser may not rely on defects in the goods if they are not duly certified by an internationally recognised inspection agency. When A, a buyer, takes over the goods at the port of destination, the only internationally recognised inspection agency operating in that port is on strike and to call another from the nearest port would be excessively costly. The application of the usage in this case would be unreasonable and A may rely on the defects it has discovered even though they have not been certified by an internationally recognised inspection agency.

6. Usages prevail over the Principles

Both courses of dealing and usages, once they are applicable in a given case, prevail over conflicting provisions contained in the Principles. The reason for this is that they bind the parties as implied terms of the contract as a whole or of single statements or other conduct on the part of one of the parties. As such, they are superseded by any express term stipulated by the parties but, in the same way as the latter, they prevail over the Principles, the only exception being those provisions which are specifically declared to be of a mandatory character. See comment 3 on Art. 1.5.

ARTICLE 1.9

(Notice)

(1) Where notice is required it may be given by any means appropriate to the circumstances.

(2) A notice is effective when it reaches the person to whom it is given.

(3) For the purpose of paragraph (2) a notice "reaches" a person when given to that person orally or delivered at that person's place of business or mailing address.

(4) For the purpose of this article "notice" includes a declaration, demand, request or any other communication of intention.

COMMENT

1. Form of notice

This article first lays down the principle that notice or any other kind of communication of intention (declarations, demands, requests, etc.) required by individual provisions of the Principles are not subject to any particular requirement as to form, but may be given by any means appropriate in the circumstances. Which means are appropriate will depend on the actual circumstances of the case, in particular on the availability and the reliability of the various modes of communication, and the importance and/or urgency of the message to be delivered. Thus, if the postal service is unreliable, it might be more appropriate to use fax, telex or other forms of electronic communication for a communication which has to be made in writing, or the telephone if an oral communication is sufficient. In choosing the means of communication the sender must as a rule take into account the situation which exists both in its own and in the addressee's country.

2. Receipt principle

With respect to all kinds of notices the Principles adopt the so-called "receipt" principle, i.e. they are not effective unless and until they reach the person to whom they are given. For some communications this is expressly stated in the provisions dealing with them: see Arts. 2.3(1), 2.3(2), 2.5, 2.6(2), 2.8(1) and 2.10. The purpose of para. (2) of the present article is to indicate that the same will also be true in the absence of an express statement to this effect: see Arts. 2.9, 2.11, 3.13, 3.14, 6.1.16, 6.2.3, 7.1.5, 7.1.7, 7.2.1, 7.2.2, 7.3.2 and 7.3.4.

3. Dispatch principle to be expressly stipulated

The parties are of course always free expressly to stipulate the application of the dispatch principle. This may be appropriate in particular with respect to the notice a party has to give in order to preserve its rights in cases of the other party's actual or anticipated non-performance when it would not be fair to place the risk of loss, mistake or delay in the transmission of the message on the former. This is all the more true if the difficulties which may arise at international level in proving effective receipt of a notice are borne in mind.

4. "Reaches"

It is important in relation to the receipt principle to determine precisely when the communications in question "reach" the addressee. In an attempt to define the concept, para. (3) of this article draws a distinction between oral and other communications. The former "reach" the addressee if they are made personally to it or to another person authorised by it to receive them. The latter "reach" the addressee as soon as they are delivered either to the addressee personally or to its place of business or mailing address. The particular communication in question need not come into the hands of the addressee. It is sufficient that it be handed over to an employee of the addressee authorised to accept it, or that it be placed in the addressee's mailbox, or received by the addressee's fax, telex or computer.

ARTICLE **1.10**

(Definitions)

In these Principles
– "court" includes an arbitral tribunal;
– where a party has more than one place of business the relevant "place of business" is that which has the closest relationship to the contract and its performance, having regard to the circumstances known to or contemplated by the parties at any time before or at the conclusion of the contract;
– "obligor" refers to the party who is to perform an obligation and "obligee" refers to the party who is entitled to performance of that obligation.
– "writing" means any mode of communication that preserves a record of the information contained therein and is capable of being reproduced in tangible form.

COMMENT

1. Courts and arbitral tribunals

The importance of the Principles for the purpose of the settlement of disputes by means of arbitration has already been stressed (see above the comments on the Preamble). In order however to avoid undue heaviness of language, only the term "court" is used in the text of the Principles, on the understanding that it covers arbitral tribunals as well as courts.

2. Party with more than one place of business

For the purpose of the application of the Principles a party's place of business is of relevance in a number of contexts such as the place for the delivery of notices (Art. 1.9(3)); a possible extension of the time of acceptance because of a holiday falling on the last day (Art. 2.8(2)); the place of performance (Art. 6.1.6) and the determination of the party who should apply for a public permission (Art. 6.1.14(a)).

With reference to a party with multiple places of business (normally a central office and various branch offices) the present article lays down the rule that the relevant place of business should be considered to be that which has the closest relationship to the contract and to its performance. Nothing is said with respect to the case where the place of the conclusion of the contract and that of performance differ, but in such a case the latter would seem to be the more relevant one. In the determination of the place of business which has the closest relationship to a given contract and to its performance, regard is to be had to the circumstances known to or contemplated by both parties at any time before or at the conclusion of the contract. Facts known only to one of the parties or of which the parties became aware only after the conclusion of the contract cannot be taken into consideration.

3. "Obligor" - "obligee"

Where necessary, to better identify the party performing and the party receiving performance of obligations the terms "obligor" and "obligee" are used, irrespective of whether the obligation is non-monetary or monetary.

4. "Writing"

In some cases the Principles refer to a "writing" or a "contract in writing". See Arts. 1.2, 2.9(2), 2.12, 2.17 and 2.18. The Principles define this formal requirement in functional terms. Thus, a writing includes not only a telegram and a telex, but also any other mode of communication that preserves a record and can be reproduced in tangible form. This formal requirement should be compared with the more flexible form of a "notice". See Art. 1.9(1).

CHAPTER 2

FORMATION

ARTICLE 2.1

(Manner of formation)

A contract may be concluded either by the acceptance of an offer or by conduct of the parties that is sufficient to show agreement.

COMMENT

1. Offer and acceptance

Basic to the Principles is the idea that the agreement of the parties is, in itself, sufficient to conclude a contract (see Art. 3.2). The concepts of offer and acceptance have traditionally been used to determine whether, and if so when, the parties have reached agreement. As this article and this chapter make clear, the Principles retain these concepts as essential tools of analysis.

2. Conduct sufficient to show agreement

In commercial practice contracts, particularly when related to complex transactions, are often concluded after prolonged negotiations without an identifiable sequence of offer and acceptance. In such cases it may be difficult to determine if and when a contractual agreement has been reached. According to this article a contract may be held to be concluded even though the moment of its formation cannot be determined, provided that the conduct of the parties is sufficient to show agreement. In order to determine whether there is sufficient evidence of the parties' intention to be bound by a contract, their conduct has to be interpreted in accordance with the criteria set forth in Art. 4.1 *et seq.*

Illustration

> A and B enter into negotiations with a view to setting up a joint
> venture for the development of a new product. After prolonged
> negotiations without any formal offer or acceptance and with some
> minor points still to be settled, both parties begin to perform. When
> subsequently the parties fail to reach an agreement on these minor
> points, a court or arbitral tribunal may decide that a contract was
> nevertheless concluded since the parties had begun to perform,
> thereby showing their intention to be bound by a contract.

ARTICLE 2.2

(Definition of offer)

**A proposal for concluding a contract con-
stitutes an offer if it is sufficiently definite and
indicates the intention of the offeror to be bound
in case of acceptance.**

COMMENT

In defining an offer as distinguished from other communications
which a party may make in the course of negotiations initiated with a
view to concluding a contract, this article lays down two requirements:
the proposal must (i) be sufficiently definite to permit the conclusion of
the contract by mere acceptance and (ii) indicate the intention of the
offeror to be bound in case of acceptance.

1. Definiteness of an offer

Since a contract is concluded by the mere acceptance of an offer,
the terms of the future agreement must already be indicated with
sufficient definiteness in the offer itself. Whether a given offer meets
this requirement cannot be established in general terms. Even essential
terms, such as the precise description of the goods or the services to
be delivered or rendered, the price to be paid for them, the time or
place of performance, etc., may be left undetermined in the offer
without necessarily rendering it insufficiently definite: all depends on
whether or not the offeror by making the offer, and the offeree by
accepting it, intends to enter into a binding agreement, and whether or
not the missing terms can be determined by interpreting the

language of the agreement in accordance with Arts. 4.1 *et seq.,* or supplied in accordance with Arts. 4.8 or 5.2. Indefiniteness may moreover be overcome by reference to practices established between the parties or to usages (see Art. 1.8), as well as by reference to specific provisions to be found elsewhere in the Principles (e.g. Arts. 5.6 (Determination of quality of performance), 5.7 (Price determination), 6.1.1 (Time of performance), 6.1.6 (Place of performance), and 6.1.10 (Currency not expressed)).

Illustration

> 1.   A has for a number of years annually renewed a contract with B for technical assistance for A's computers. A opens a second office with the same type of computers and asks B to provide assistance also for the new computers. B accepts and, despite the fact that A's offer does not specify all the terms of the agreement, a contract has been concluded since the missing terms can be taken from the previous contracts as constituting a practice established between the parties.

2. Intention to be bound

The second criterion for determining whether a party makes an offer for the conclusion of a contract, or merely opens negotiations, is that party's intention to be bound in the event of acceptance. Since such an intention will rarely be declared expressly, it often has to be inferred from the circumstances of each individual case. The way in which the proponent presents the proposal (e.g. by expressly defining it as an "offer" or as a mere "declaration of intent") provides a first, although not a decisive, indication of possible intention. Of even greater importance are the content and the addressees of the proposal. Generally speaking, the more detailed and definite the proposal, the more likely it is to be construed as an offer. A proposal addressed to one or more specific persons is more likely to be intended as an offer than is one made to the public at large.

Illustrations

> 2.   After lengthy negotiations the Executive Directors of two companies, A and B, lay down the conditions on which B will acquire 51% of the shares in company C which is totally owned by A. The "Memorandum of Agreement" signed by the negotiators contains a final clause stating that the agreement is not binding until approved by A's Board of Directors. There is no contract before such approval is given by them.

3.   A, a government agency, advertises for bids for the setting up
of a new telephone network. Such an advertisement is merely an
invitation to submit offers, which may or may not be accepted by
A. If, however, the advertisement indicates in detail the technical
specifications of the project and states that the contract will be
awarded to the lowest bid conforming to the specifications, it may
amount to an offer with the consequence that the contract will be
concluded once the lowest bid has been identified.

A proposal may contain all the essential terms of the contract but
nevertheless not bind the proponent in case of acceptance if it makes
the conclusion of the contract dependent on the reaching of agreement
on some minor points left open in the proposal. See Art. 2.13.

ARTICLE 2.3

(Withdrawal of offer)

**(1) An offer becomes effective when it
reaches the offeree.**

**(2) An offer, even if it is irrevocable, may
be withdrawn if the withdrawal reaches the offeree before or at the same time as the offer.**

COMMENT

1. When an offer becomes effective

Para. (1) of this article, which is taken literally from Art. 15 CISG,
provides that an offer becomes effective when it reaches the offeree
(see Art. 1.9(2)). For the definition of "reaches" see Art. 1.9(3). The
time at which the offer becomes effective is of importance as it
indicates the precise moment as from which the offeree can accept it,
thus definitely binding the offeror to the proposed contract.

2. Withdrawal of an offer

There is, however, a further reason why it may in practice be
important to determine the moment at which the offer becomes
effective. Indeed, up to that time the offeror is free to change its mind
and to decide not to enter into the agreement at all, or to replace the
original offer by a new one, irrespective of whether or not the original

offer was intended to be irrevocable. The only condition is that the offeree is informed of the offeror's altered intentions before or at the same time as the offeree is informed of the original offer. By expressly stating this, para. (2) of the present article makes it clear that a distinction is to be drawn between "withdrawal" and "revocation" of an offer: before an offer becomes effective it can always be withdrawn whereas the question of whether or not it may be revoked (see Art. 2.4) arises only after that moment.

ARTICLE 2.4

(Revocation of offer)

(1) Until a contract is concluded an offer may be revoked if the revocation reaches the offeree before it has dispatched an acceptance.

(2) However, an offer cannot be revoked

(a) if it indicates, whether by stating a fixed time for acceptance or otherwise, that it is irrevocable; or

(b) if it was reasonable for the offeree to rely on the offer as being irrevocable and the offeree has acted in reliance on the offer.

COMMENT

The problem of whether an offer is or is not revocable is traditionally one of the most controversial issues in the context of the formation of contracts. Since there is no prospect of reconciling the two basic approaches followed in this respect by the different legal systems, i.e. the common law approach according to which an offer is as a rule revocable, and the opposite approach followed by the majority of civil law systems, the only remaining possibility is that of selecting one approach as the main rule, and the other as the exception.

1. Offers as a rule revocable

Para. (1) of this article, which is taken literally from Art. 16 CISG, states that until the contract is concluded offers are as a rule revocable. The same paragraph, however, subjects the revocation of an offer to the condition that it reach the offeree before the offeree has dispatched an acceptance. It is thus only when the offeree orally accepts the offer, or when the offeree may indicate assent by performing an act without giving notice to the offeror (see Art. 2.6(3)), that the offeror's right to revoke the offer continues to exist until such time as the contract is concluded. Where, however, the offer is accepted by a written indication of assent, so that the contract is concluded when the acceptance reaches the offeror (see Art. 2.6(2)), the offeror's right to revoke the offer terminates earlier, i.e. when the offeree dispatches the acceptance. Such a solution may cause some inconvenience to the offeror who will not always know whether or not it is still possible to revoke the offer. It is, however, justified in view of the legitimate interest of the offeree in the time available for revocation being shortened.

2. Irrevocable offers

Para. (2) provides for two important exceptions to the general rule as to the revocability of offers: (i) where the offer contains an indication that it is irrevocable and (ii) where the offeree, having other good reasons to treat the offer as being irrevocable, has acted in reliance on that offer.

a. *Indication of irrevocability contained in the offer*

The indication that the offer is irrevocable may be made in different ways, the most direct and clear of which is an express statement to that effect by the offeror (e.g. "This is a firm offer"; "We shall stand by our offer until we receive your answer"). It may, however, simply be inferred from other statements by, or conduct of, the offeror. The indication of a fixed time for acceptance may, but need not necessarily, amount by itself to an implicit indication of an irrevocable offer. The answer must be found in each case through a proper interpretation of the terms of the offer in accordance with the various criteria laid down in the general rules on interpretation in Chapter 4. In general, if the offeror operates within a legal system where the fixing of a time for acceptance is considered to indicate irrevocability, it may be assumed that by specifying such a fixed time the offeror intends to make an irrevocable offer. If, on the other hand, the offeror operates in a legal system where the fixing of a time for acceptance is not sufficient to indicate irrevocability, the offeror will not normally have had such an intention.

Illustrations

1. A, a travel agency, informs a client of a cruise in its brochure for the coming New Year holidays. It urges the client to book within the next three days, adding that after that date there will probably be no more places left. This statement by itself will not be considered to indicate that the offer is irrevocable during the first three days.

2. A invites B to submit a written offer of the terms on which B is prepared to construct a building. B presents a detailed offer containing the statement "Price and other conditions are not good after 1 September". If A and B operate within a legal system where such a statement is considered to be an indication that the offer is irrevocable until the specified date, B can expect the offer to be understood as being irrevocable. The same may not necessarily be the case if the offeree operates in a legal system where such a statement is not considered as being sufficient to indicate that the offer is irrevocable.

b. *Reliance by offeree on irrevocability of offer*

The second exception to the general rule regarding the revocability of offers, i.e. where "it was reasonable for the offeree to rely on the offer as being irrevocable", and "the offeree has acted in reliance on the offer", is an application of the general principle of good faith and fair dealing laid down in Art. 1.7. The reliance of the offeree may have been induced either by the conduct of the offeror, or by the nature of the offer itself (e.g. an offer whose acceptance requires extensive and costly investigation on the part of the offeree or an offer made with a view to permitting the offeree in turn to make an offer to a third party). The acts which the offeree must have performed in reliance on the offer may consist in making preparations for production, buying or hiring of materials or equipment, incurring expenses etc., provided that such acts could have been regarded as normal in the trade concerned, or should otherwise have been foreseen by, or known to, the offeror.

Illustrations

3. A, an antique dealer, asks B to restore ten paintings on condition that the work is completed within three months and that the price does not exceed a specific amount. B informs A that, so as to know whether or not to accept the offer, B finds it necessary to begin work on one painting and will then give a definite answer

within five days. A agrees, and B, relying on A's offer, begins work immediately. A may not revoke the offer during those five days.

4. A seeks an offer from B for incorporation in a bid on a project to be assigned within a stated time. B submits an offer on which A relies when calculating the price of the bid. Before the expiry of the date, but after A has made the bid, B informs A that it is no longer willing to stand by its offer. B's offer is irrevocable until the stated date since in making its bid A relied on B's offer.

ARTICLE 2.5

(Rejection of offer)

An offer is terminated when a rejection reaches the offeror.

COMMENT

1. Rejection may be express or implied

An offer may be rejected either expressly or impliedly. A frequent case of implied rejection is a reply to an offer which purports to be an acceptance but which contains additions, limitations or other modifications (see Art. 2.11(1)).

In the absence of an express rejection the statements by, or the conduct of, the offeree must in any event be such as to justify the belief of the offeror that the offeree has no intention of accepting the offer. A reply on the part of the offeree which merely asks whether there would be a possible alternative (e.g. "Is there any chance of the price being reduced?", or "Could you deliver a couple of days earlier?") would not normally be sufficient to justify such a conclusion.

It should be recalled that a rejection will bring about the termination of any offer, irrespective of whether it was revocable or irrevocable according to Art. 2.4.

Illustration

A receives an offer from B stating that the offer will be firm for two weeks. A replies by return of post asking for partially different conditions which B does not accept. A may no longer accept the original offer even though there are still several days left before the expiry of the two week period since by making a counter-offer A implicitly rejected the original offer.

2. Rejection only one cause of termination of an offer

Rejection by the offeree is only one of the causes of termination of an offer. Other causes are dealt with in Arts. 2.4(1) and 2.7.

ARTICLE 2.6

(Mode of acceptance)

(1) A statement made by or other conduct of the offeree indicating assent to an offer is an acceptance. Silence or inactivity does not in itself amount to acceptance.

(2) An acceptance of an offer becomes effective when the indication of assent reaches the offeror.

(3) However, if, by virtue of the offer or as a result of practices which the parties have established between themselves or of usage, the offeree may indicate assent by performing an act without notice to the offeror, the acceptance is effective when the act is performed.

COMMENT

1. Indication of assent to an offer

For there to be an acceptance the offeree must in one way or another indicate "assent" to the offer. The mere acknowledgement of receipt of the offer, or an expression of interest in it, is not sufficient. Furthermore, the assent must be unconditional, i.e. it cannot be made dependent on some further step to be taken by either the offeror (e.g. "Our acceptance is subject to your final approval") or the offeree (e.g. "We hereby accept the terms of the contract as set forth in your Memorandum and undertake to submit the contract to our Board for approval within the next two weeks"). Finally, the purported acceptance must contain no variation of the terms of the offer or at least none which materially alters them (see Art. 2.11).

2. Acceptance by conduct

Provided that the offer does not impose any particular mode of acceptance, the indication of assent may either be made by an express statement or be inferred from the conduct of the offeree. Para. (1) of this article does not specify the form such conduct should assume: most often it will consist in acts of performance, such as the payment of an advance on the price, the shipment of goods or the beginning of work at the site, etc.

3. Silence or inactivity

By stating that "[s]ilence or inactivity does not in itself amount to acceptance", para. (1) makes it clear that as a rule mere silence or inactivity on the part of the offeree does not allow the inference that the offeree assents to the offer. The situation is different if the parties themselves agree that silence shall amount to acceptance, or if there exists a course of dealing or usage to that effect. In no event, however, is it sufficient for the offeror to state unilaterally in its offer that the offer will be deemed to have been accepted in the absence of any reply from the offeree. Since it is the offeror who takes the initiative by proposing the conclusion of the contract, the offeree is free not only to accept or not to accept the offer, but also simply to ignore it.

Illustrations

> 1.   A requests B to set out the conditions for the renewal of a contract for the supply of wine, due to expire on 31 December. In its offer B includes a provision stating that "if we have not heard from you at the latest by the end of November, we will assume that you have agreed to renew the contract on the conditions as indicated above". A finds the proposed conditions totally unacceptable and does not even reply. The former contract expires on the fixed date without a new contract having been agreed between the parties.

> 2.   Under a long-term agreement for the supply of wine B regularly met A's orders without expressly confirming its acceptance. On 15 November A orders a large stock for New Year. B does not reply, nor does it deliver at the requested time. B is in breach since, in accordance with the practice established between the parties, B's silence in regard to A's order amounts to an acceptance.

4. When acceptance becomes effective

According to para. (2) an acceptance becomes effective at the moment the indication of assent reaches the offeror (see Art. 1.9(2)). For the definition of "reaches" see Art. 1.9(3). The reason for the adoption of the "receipt" principle in preference to the "dispatch" principle is that the risk of transmission is better placed on the offeree than on the offeror, since it is the former who chooses the means of communication, who knows whether the chosen means of communication is subject to special risks or delay, and who is consequently best able to take measures to ensure that the acceptance reaches its destination.

As a rule, an acceptance by means of mere conduct likewise becomes effective only when notice thereof reaches the offeror. It should be noted, however, that special notice to this effect by the offeree will be necessary only in cases where the conduct will not of itself give notice of acceptance to the offeror within a reasonable period of time. In all other cases, e.g. where the conduct consists in the payment of the price, or the shipment of the goods by air or by some other rapid mode of transportation, the same effect may well be achieved simply by the bank or the carrier informing the offeror of the funds transfer or of the consignment of the goods.

An exception to the general rule of para. (2) is to be found in the cases envisaged in para. (3), i.e. where "by virtue of the offer or as a result of practices which the parties have established between themselves or of usage, the offeree may indicate assent by performing an act without notice to the offeror". In such cases the acceptance is effective at the moment the act is performed, irrespective of whether or not the offeror is promptly informed thereof.

Illustrations

3.   A asks B to write a special program for the setting up of a data bank. Without giving A notice of acceptance, B begins to write the program and, after its completion, insists on payment in accordance with the terms set out in A's offer. B is not entitled to payment since B's purported acceptance of A's offer never became effective as B never notified A of it.

4.   The facts are the same as in Illustration 3, the difference being that in the offer B is informed of A's absence for the following two weeks, and that if B intends to accept the offer B should begin writing the program immediately so as to save time. The contract is concluded once B begins to perform, even if B fails to inform A thereof either immediately or at a later stage.

This article corresponds to paras. (1), (2) first part and (3) of Art. 18 CISG.

ARTICLE 2.7

(Time of acceptance)

An offer must be accepted within the time the offeror has fixed or, if no time is fixed, within a reasonable time having regard to the circumstances, including the rapidity of the means of communication employed by the offeror. An oral offer must be accepted immediately unless the circumstances indicate otherwise.

COMMENT

With respect to the time within which an offer must be accepted, this article, which corresponds to the second part of para. (2) of Art. 18 CISG, distinguishes between oral and written offers. Oral offers must be accepted immediately unless the circumstances indicate otherwise. As to written offers, all depends upon whether or not the offer indicated a fixed time for acceptance: if it did, the offer must be accepted within that time, while in all other cases the indication of assent must reach the offeror "within a reasonable time having regard to the circumstances, including the rapidity of the means of communication employed by the offeror".

It is important to note that the rules laid down in this article also apply to situations where, in accordance with Art. 2.6(3), the offeree may indicate assent by performing an act without notice to the offeror: in these cases it is the act of performance which has to be accomplished within the respective periods of time.

For the determination of the precise starting point of the period of time fixed by the offeror, and the calculation of holidays occurring during that period of time, see Art. 2.8; as to cases of late acceptance and of delay in transmission, see Art. 2.9.

ARTICLE 2.8

(Acceptance within a fixed period of time)

(1) A period of time for acceptance fixed by the offeror in a telegram or a letter begins to run from the moment the telegram is handed in for dispatch or from the date shown on the letter or, if no such date is shown, from the date shown on the envelope. A period of time for acceptance fixed by the offeror by means of instantaneous communication begins to run from the moment that the offer reaches the offeree.

(2) Official holidays or non-business days occurring during the period for acceptance are included in calculating the period. However, if a notice of acceptance cannot be delivered at the address of the offeror on the last day of the period because that day falls on an official holiday or a non-business day at the place of business of the offeror, the period is extended until the first business day which follows.

COMMENT

The offeror may fix a deadline within which the offeree must accept the offer. As long as this is done by indicating a precise date (e.g. "In case you intend to accept my offer, please do so no later than 1 March"), no special problems arise. If, on the other hand, the offeror merely indicates a period of time (e.g. "You have ten days to accept this offer"), the problem may arise as to when the period starts to run as well as as to the effect of holidays occurring during, or at the expiry of, that period. The present article, which corresponds to Art. 20 CISG, is intended to provide an answer to these two questions when nothing is said in the offer itself.

ARTICLE 2.9

(Late acceptance. Delay in transmission)

(1) A late acceptance is nevertheless effective as an acceptance if without undue delay the offeror so informs the offeree or gives notice to that effect.

(2) If a letter or other writing containing a late acceptance shows that it has been sent in such circumstances that if its transmission had been normal it would have reached the offeror in due time, the late acceptance is effective as an acceptance unless, without undue delay, the offeror informs the offeree that it considers the offer as having lapsed.

COMMENT

1. Late acceptance normally ineffective

According to the principle laid down in Art. 2.7 for an acceptance to be effective it must reach the offeror within the time fixed by the latter or, if no time is fixed, within a reasonable time. This means that as a rule an acceptance which reaches the offeror thereafter is without effect and may be disregarded by the offeror.

2. Offeror may nevertheless "accept" late acceptance

Para. (1) of this article, which corresponds to Art. 21 CISG, states that the offeror may nevertheless consider a late acceptance as having arrived in time and thus render it effective, provided that the offeror "without undue delay [...] so informs the offeree or gives notice to that effect". If the offeror takes advantage of this possibility, the contract is to be considered as having been concluded as soon as the late acceptance reaches the offeror and not when the offeror informs the offeree of its intention to consider the late acceptance effective.

Illustration

1. A indicates 31 March as the deadline for acceptance of its offer. B's acceptance reaches A on 3 April. A, who is still interested in the contract, intends to "accept" B's late acceptance, and immediately informs B of its intention. Notwithstanding the fact that this notice only reaches B on 5 April the contract is concluded on 3 April.

3. Acceptance late because of delay in transmission

As long as the acceptance is late because the offeree did not send it in time, it is natural to consider it as having no effect unless the offeror expressly indicates otherwise. The situation is different when the offeree has replied in time, but the acceptance reaches the offeror late because of an unexpected delay in transmission. In such a case the reliance of the offeree on the acceptance having arrived in time deserves protection, with the consequence that the late acceptance is considered to be effective unless the offeror objects without undue delay. The only condition required by para. (2) is that the letter or other writing containing the late acceptance shows that it has been sent in such circumstances that, had its transmission been normal, it would have reached the offeror in due time.

Illustration

> 2.   The facts are the same as in Illustration 1, the difference being that B, knowing that the normal time for transmission of letters by mail to A is three days, sends its letter of acceptance on 25 March. Owing to a strike of the postal service in A's country the letter, which shows the date of its mailing on the envelope, only arrives on 3 April. B's acceptance, though late, is nevertheless effective unless A objects without undue delay.

ARTICLE **2.10**

(Withdrawal of acceptance)

An acceptance may be withdrawn if the withdrawal reaches the offeror before or at the same time as the acceptance would have become effective.

COMMENT

With respect to the withdrawal of an acceptance the present article lays down the same principle as that contained in Art. 2.3 concerning the withdrawal of an offer, i.e. that the offeree may change its mind and withdraw the acceptance provided that the withdrawal reaches the offeror before or at the same time as the acceptance.

It should be noted that while the offeror is bound by the offer and may no longer change its mind once the offeree has dispatched the acceptance (see Art. 2.4(1)), the offeree looses its freedom of choice only at a later stage, i.e. when the notice of acceptance reaches the offeror.

This article corresponds to Art. 22 CISG.

ARTICLE 2.11
(Modified acceptance)

(1) A reply to an offer which purports to be an acceptance but contains additions, limitations or other modifications is a rejection of the offer and constitutes a counter-offer.

(2) However, a reply to an offer which purports to be an acceptance but contains additional or different terms which do not materially alter the terms of the offer constitutes an acceptance, unless the offeror, without undue delay, objects to the discrepancy. If the offeror does not object, the terms of the contract are the terms of the offer with the modifications contained in the acceptance.

COMMENT

1. Acceptance with modifications normally to be considered a counter-offer

In commercial dealings it often happens that the offeree, while signifying to the offeror its intention to accept the offer ("acknowledgement of order"), nevertheless includes in its declaration terms additional to or different from those of the offer. Para. (1) of this article provides that such a purported acceptance is as a rule to be considered a rejection of the offer and that it amounts to a counter-offer by the offeree, which the offeror may or may not accept either expressly or impliedly, e.g. by an act of performance.

2. Modifications which do not alter the nature of the acceptance

The principle according to which the acceptance must be the mirror image of the offer implies that even unimportant differences between the offer and the acceptance permit either party at a later stage to question the existence of the contract. In order to avoid such a result, which a party may well seek merely because market conditions have changed unfavourably, para. (2) provides for an exception to the general rule laid down in para. (1) by stating that if the additional or modified terms contained in the acceptance do not "materially" alter the terms of the offer, the contract is concluded with those modifications unless the offeror objects without undue delay.

What amounts to a "material" modification cannot be determined in the abstract but will depend on the circumstances of each case. Additional or different terms relating to the price or mode of payment, place and time of performance of a non-monetary obligation, the extent of one party's liability to the other or the settlement of disputes, will normally, but need not necessarily, constitute a material modification of the offer. An important factor to be taken into account in this respect is whether the additional or different terms are commonly used in the trade sector concerned and therefore do not come as a surprise to the offeror.

Illustrations

1. A orders a machine from B to be tested on A's premises. In its acknowledgement of order B declares that it accepts the terms of the offer, but adds that it wishes to be present at the testing of the machine. The additional term is not a "material" modification of the offer and will therefore become part of the contract unless A objects without undue delay.

2. The facts are the same as in Illustration 1, the difference being that in its acknowledgement of order B adds an arbitration clause. Unless the circumstances indicate otherwise, such a clause amounts to a "material" modification of the terms of the offer, with the result that B's purported acceptance would constitute a counter-offer.

3. A orders a stated quantity of wheat from B. In its acknowledgement of order B adds an arbitration clause which is standard practice in the commodity sector concerned. Since A cannot be surprised by such a clause, it is not a "material" modification of the terms of the offer and, unless A objects without undue delay, the arbitration clause becomes part of the contract.

ARTICLE 2.12

(Writings in confirmation)

If a writing which is sent within a reasonable time after the conclusion of the contract and which purports to be a confirmation of the contract contains additional or different terms, such terms become part of the contract, unless they materially alter the contract or the recipient, without undue delay, objects to the discrepancy.

COMMENT

1. "Writings in confirmation"

This article deals with the situation where a contract has already been concluded either orally or by the exchange of written communications limited to the essential terms of the agreement, and one party subsequently sends the other a document intended simply to confirm what has already been agreed upon, but which in fact contains terms which are additional to or different from those previously agreed by the parties. In theory, this situation clearly differs from that envisaged in Art. 2.11, where a contract has not yet been concluded and the modifying terms are contained in the offeree's purported acceptance. Yet, since in practice it may be very difficult if not impossible to distinguish between the two situations, the present article adopts with respect to modifying terms contained in a writing in confirmation the same solution as that envisaged in Art. 2.11. In other words, just as for the modifications contained in an acknowledgement of order, it is provided that terms additional to or different from those previously agreed by the parties contained in a writing in confirmation become part of the contract, provided that they do not "materially" alter the agreement and that the recipient of the document does not object to them without undue delay.

It goes without saying that also in the context of writings in confirmation the question of which of the new terms "materially" alter the terms of the previous agreement can be answered definitely only in the light of the circumstances of each individual case. On the other hand, the present article clearly does not apply to cases where the party sending the writing in confirmation expressly invites the other party to return it duly counter-signed for acceptance. In such circumstances it is irrelevant whether the writing contains modifications, and if so whether or not these modifications are "material" since the writing must in any case be expressly accepted by the addressee if there is to be a contract.

Illustrations

    1.   A orders by telephone a machine from B, who accepts the order. The following day A receives a letter from B confirming the terms of their oral agreement but adding that B wishes to be present at the testing of the machine on A's premises. The additional term is not a "material" modification of the terms previously agreed between the parties and will therefore become part of the contract unless A objects without undue delay.

    2.   The facts are the same as in Illustration 1, the difference being that the modification contained in B's writing in confirmation consists in the addition of an arbitration clause. Unless the circumstances indicate otherwise such a clause amounts to a "material" modification of the terms previously agreed between the parties with the result that it will not become part of the contract.

    3.   A orders by telex a stated quantity of wheat and B accepts immediately by telex. Later on the same day B sends a letter to A confirming the terms of their agreement but adding an arbitration clause which is standard practice in the commodity sector concerned. Since A cannot be surprised by such a clause, it is not a "material" modification of the terms previously agreed and, unless A objects without undue delay, the arbitration clause becomes part of the contract.

2. Writing in confirmation to be sent within a reasonable time after conclusion of the contract

The rule according to which silence on the part of the recipient amounts to acceptance of the content of the writing in confirmation, including any non-material modifications of the terms previously agreed, presupposes that the writing is sent "within a reasonable time after the conclusion of the contract". Any writing of this kind sent after a period of time which, in the circumstances, appears to be unreasonably long, loses any significance, and silence on the part of the recipient may therefore no longer be interpreted as acceptance of its content.

3. Invoices

For the purposes of this article, the term "writing in confirmation" is to be understood in a broad sense, i.e. as covering also those cases where a party uses the invoice or another similar document relating to performance to specify the conditions of the contract concluded either orally or by informal correspondence, provided that such use is customary in the trade sector and/or country concerned.

ARTICLE 2.13

(Conclusion of contract dependent on agreement on specific matters or in a specific form)

Where in the course of negotiations one of the parties insists that the contract is not concluded until there is agreement on specific matters or in a specific form, no contract is concluded before agreement is reached on those matters or in that form.

COMMENT

1. Conclusion of contract dependent on agreement on specific matters

As a rule, a contract is concluded if the parties reach agreement on the terms which are essential to the type of transaction involved, while minor terms which the parties have not settled may subsequently be implied either in fact or by law. See comment 1 on Art. 2.2 and also Arts. 4.8 and 5.2.

Illustration

> 1. A agrees with B on all the terms which are essential to their intended contract for the distribution of A's goods. When the question subsequently arises of who should bear the costs of the publicity campaign, neither party may claim that no contract has come into existence by reason of the silence of the contract on this point, as the missing term is not essential to the type of transaction in question and will be implied in fact or by law.

Parties may, however, in a given case consider specific matters to be of such importance that they do not intend to enter into a binding agreement unless these matters are settled in a satisfactory manner. If the parties, or one only of them, make such an intention explicit, the contract as such does not come into existence without agreement on those matters. By using the word "insists", the present article makes it clear that it is not sufficient for the parties to manifest their intention to this effect simply in passing, but that it must be done unequivocally.

Illustration

> 2. The facts are the same as in Illustration 1, the difference being that during the negotiations B repeatedly declares that the question of who should bear the cost of the publicity campaign must be settled expressly. Notwithstanding their agreement on all the essential terms of the contract, no contract has come into existence between A and B since B had insisted that the conclusion of the contract was dependent on agreement regarding that specific term.

2. Conclusion of contract dependent on agreement in a specific form

In commercial practice, particularly when transactions of considerable complexity are involved, it is quite frequent that after prolonged negotiations the parties sign an informal document called "Preliminary Agreement", "Memorandum of Understanding", "Letter of Intent" or the like, containing the terms of the agreement so far reached, but at the same time state their intention to provide for the execution of a formal document at a later stage ("Subject to Contract", "Formal Agreement to follow"). In some cases the parties consider their contract as already being concluded and the execution of the formal document only as confirmation of the already complete agreement. If, however, both parties, or only one of them, make it clear that they do not intend to be bound unless the formal document has been drawn up, there will be no contract until that time even if the parties have agreed on all the relevant aspects of their transaction.

Illustrations

> 3. After prolonged negotiations A and B sign a "Memorandum of Understanding" containing the terms of an agreement for a joint venture for the exploration and exploitation of the continental shelf of country X. The parties agree that they will at a later stage draw up the agreement in formal documents to be signed and exchanged

at a public ceremony. If the "Memorandum" already contains all the relevant terms of the agreement and the subsequent documents are intended merely to permit the agreement to be properly presented to the public, it may be taken that the contract was already concluded when the first written document was signed.

4. The facts are the same as in Illustration 3, the difference being that the "Memorandum of Understanding" contains a clause such as "Not binding until final agreement is executed" or the like. Until the signing and the exchange of the formal documents there is no binding contract.

ARTICLE 2.14

(Contract with terms deliberately left open)

(1) If the parties intend to conclude a contract, the fact that they intentionally leave a term to be agreed upon in further negotiations or to be determined by a third person does not prevent a contract from coming into existence.

(2) The existence of the contract is not affected by the fact that subsequently

(a) the parties reach no agreement on the term; or

(b) the third person does not determine the term,

provided that there is an alternative means of rendering the term definite that is reasonable in the circumstances, having regard to the intention of the parties.

COMMENT

1. Contract with terms deliberately left open

A contract may be silent on one or more issues because the parties simply did not think of them during the negotiations. Provided that the parties have agreed on the terms essential to the type of transaction concerned, a contract will nonetheless have been concluded and the missing terms will be supplied on the basis of Arts. 4.8 or 5.2. See comment 1 on Art. 2.2. Quite different is the case dealt with in the present article: here the parties intentionally leave open one or more terms because they are unable or unwilling to determine them at the time of the conclusion of the contract, and refer for their determination to an agreement to be made by them at a later stage, or to a third person.

This latter situation, which is especially frequent in, although not confined to, long-term transactions, gives rise in essence to two problems: first, whether the fact that the parties have intentionally left terms open prevents a contract from coming into existence and second, if this is not the case, what will happen to the contract if the parties subsequently fail to reach agreement or the third person fails to make the determination.

2. Open terms not in themselves an impediment to valid conclusion of contract

Para. (1) states that if the parties intended to conclude a contract, the fact that they have intentionally left a term to be agreed upon in further negotiations or to be determined by a third person does not prevent a contract from coming into existence.

In cases where it is not expressly stated, the parties' intention to conclude a contract notwithstanding the terms left open may be inferred from other circumstances, such as the non-essential character of the terms in question, the degree of definiteness of the agreement as a whole, the fact that the open terms relate to items which by their very nature can be determined only at a later stage, the fact that the agreement has already been partially executed, etc.

Illustration

> 1. A, a shipping line, enters into a detailed agreement with B, a terminal operator, for the use of B's container terminal. The agreement fixes the minimum volume of containers to be discharged or loaded annually and the fees payable, while the fees for additional containers are left to be determined if and when the minimum volume is reached. Two months later A learns that B's competitor would offer better conditions and refuses to perform, claiming that the agreement with B never resulted in a binding contract because the question of the fees had not been settled. A is liable for non-performance because the detailed character of the agreement as well as the fact that both A and B began performance immediately indicate clearly that their intention was to enter into a binding agreement.

3. Failure of mechanism provided for by parties for determination of open terms

If the parties are unable to reach agreement on the open terms or the third person does not determine them, the question arises as to whether or not the contract comes to an end. According to para. (2) of this article the existence of the contract is not affected "provided that there is an alternative means of rendering the term definite that is reasonable in the circumstances, having regard to the intention of the parties". A first alternative exists whenever the missing term may be supplied on the basis of Art. 5.2; if the parties have deferred the determination of the missing term to a third person to be nominated by an instance such as the President of the Tribunal, or of the Chamber of Commerce, etc., it may also consist in the appointment of a new third person. The cases in which a given contract may be upheld by resorting to such alternative means will, however, be quite rare in practice. Few problems should arise as long as the term to be implemented is of minor importance. If, on the other hand, the term in question is essential to the type of transaction concerned, there must be clear evidence of the intention of the parties to uphold the contract: among the factors to be taken into account in this connection are whether the term in question relates to items which by their very nature can be determined only at a later stage, whether the agreement has already been partially executed, etc.

Illustration

2. The facts are the same as in Illustration 1, the difference being that when the minimum volume of containers to be loaded or unloaded is reached the parties fail to agree on the fees payable in respect of the additional containers. A stops performing, claiming that the contract has come to an end. A is liable for non-performance, since the fact that the parties have started performing without making future agreement on the missing term a condition for the continuation of their business relationship is sufficient evidence of their intention to uphold the contract even in the absence of such agreement. The fees for the additional containers will be determined according to the criteria laid down in Art. 5.7.

ARTICLE 2.15

(Negotiations in bad faith)

(1) **A party is free to negotiate and is not liable for failure to reach an agreement.**

(2) **However, a party who negotiates or breaks off negotiations in bad faith is liable for the losses caused to the other party.**

(3) **It is bad faith, in particular, for a party to enter into or continue negotiations when intending not to reach an agreement with the other party.**

COMMENT

1. Freedom of negotiation

As a rule, parties are not only free to decide when and with whom to enter into negotiations with a view to concluding a contract, but also if, how and for how long to proceed with their efforts to reach an agreement. This follows from the basic principle of freedom of contract enunciated in Art. 1.1, and is essential in order to guarantee healthy competition among business people engaged in international trade.

2. Liability for negotiating in bad faith

A party's right freely to enter into negotiations and to decide on the terms to be negotiated is, however, not unlimited, and must not conflict with the principle of good faith and fair dealing laid down in Art. 1.7. One particular instance of negotiating in bad faith which is expressly indicated in para. (3) of this article is that where a party enters into negotiations or continues to negotiate without any intention of concluding an agreement with the other party. Other instances are where one party has deliberately or by negligence misled the other party as to the nature or terms of the proposed contract, either by actually misrepresenting facts, or by not disclosing facts which, given the nature of the parties and/or the contract, should have been disclosed. As to the duty of confidentiality, see Art. 2.16.

A party's liability for negotiating in bad faith is limited to the losses caused to the other party (para. (2)). In other words, the aggrieved party may recover the expenses incurred in the negotiations and may also be compensated for the lost opportunity to conclude another contract with a third person (so-called reliance or negative interest), but may generally not recover the profit which would have resulted had the original contract been concluded (so-called expectation or positive interest).

Illustrations

1. A learns of B's intention to sell its restaurant. A, who has no intention whatsoever of buying the restaurant, nevertheless enters into lengthy negotiations with B for the sole purpose of preventing B from selling the restaurant to C, a competitor of A's. A, who breaks off negotiations when C has bought another restaurant, is liable to B, who ultimately succeeds in selling the restaurant at a lower price than that offered by C, for the difference in price.

2. A, who is negotiating with B for the promotion of the purchase of military equipment by the armed forces of B's country, learns that B will not receive the necessary export licence from its own governmental authorities, a pre-requisite for permission to pay B's fees. A does not reveal this fact to B and finally concludes the contract, which, however, cannot be enforced by reason of the missing licences. A is liable to B for the costs incurred after A had learned of the impossibility of obtaining the required licences.

3. A enters into lengthy negotiations for a bank loan from B's branch office. At the last minute the branch office discloses that it had no authority to sign and that its head office had decided not to approve the draft agreement. A, who could in the meantime have obtained the loan from another bank, is entitled to recover the expenses entailed by the negotiations and the profits it would have made during the delay before obtaining the loan from the other bank.

3. Liability for breaking off negotiations in bad faith

The right to break off negotiations also is subject to the principle of good faith and fair dealing. Once an offer has been made, it may be revoked only within the limits provided for in Art. 2.4. Yet even before this stage is reached, or in a negotiation process with no ascertainable sequence of offer and acceptance, a party may no longer be free to break off negotiations abruptly and without justification. When such a point of no return is reached depends of course on the circumstances of the case, in particular the extent to which the other party, as a result of the conduct of the first party, had reason to rely on the positive outcome of the negotiations, and on the number of issues relating to the future contract on which the parties have already reached agreement.

Illustration

> 4. A assures B of the grant of a franchise if B takes steps to gain experience and is prepared to invest US$ 150,000. During the next two years B makes extensive preparations with a view to concluding the contract, always with A's assurance that B will be granted the franchise. When all is ready for the signing of the agreement, A informs B that the latter must invest a substantially higher sum. B, who refuses, is entitled to recover from A the expenses incurred with a view to the conclusion of the contract.

ARTICLE 2.16
(Duty of confidentiality)

Where information is given as confidential by one party in the course of negotiations, the other party is under a duty not to disclose that information or to use it improperly for its own purposes, whether or not a contract is subsequently concluded. Where appropriate, the remedy for breach of that duty may include compensation based on the benefit received by the other party.

COMMENT

1. Parties in general not under a duty of confidentiality

Just as there exists no general duty of disclosure, so parties, when entering into negotiations for the conclusion of a contract, are normally under no obligation to treat the information they have exchanged as confidential. In other words, since a party is normally free to decide which facts relevant to the transaction under negotiation to disclose, such information is as a rule to be considered non-confidential, i.e. information which the other party may either disclose to third persons or use for purposes of its own should no contract be concluded.

Illustration

> 1. A invites B and C, producers of air-conditioning systems, to submit offers for the installation of such a system. In their offers B and C also provide some technical details regarding the functioning of their respective systems, with a view to enhancing the merits of their products. A decides to reject B's offer and to continue negotiations only with C. A is free to use the information contained in B's offer in order to induce C to propose more favourable conditions.

2. Confidential information

A party may have an interest in certain information given to the other party not being divulged or used for purposes other than those for which it was given. As long as that party expressly declares that such information is to be considered confidential, the situation is clear, for by receiving the information the other party implicitly agrees to treat it as confidential. The only problem which may arise is that if the period during which the other party is not to disclose the information is too long, this might contravene the applicable laws prohibiting restrictive trade practices. Yet even in the absence of such an express declaration the receiving party may be under a duty of confidentiality. This is the case where, in view of the particular nature of the information or the professional qualifications of the parties, it would be contrary to the general principle of good faith and fair dealing for the receiving party to disclose it, or to use it for its own purposes after the breaking off of negotiations.

Illustrations

> 2. The facts are the same as in Illustration 1, the difference being that in its offer B expressly requests A not to divulge certain technical specifications contained therein. A may not use this information in its negotiations with C.

> 3. A is interested in entering into a joint venture agreement with B or C, the two leading car manufacturers in country X. Negotiations progress with B in particular, and A receives fairly detailed information relating to B's plans for a new car design. Although B does not expressly request A to treat this information as confidential, because it is for a new car design A may be under a duty not to disclose it to C, nor is A allowed to use those plans for its own production process should the negotiations not result in the conclusion of a contract.

3. Damages recoverable

The breach of confidentiality implies first liability in damages. The amount of damages recoverable may vary, depending on whether or not the parties entered into a special agreement for the non-disclosure of the information. Even if the injured party has not suffered any loss, it may be entitled to recover from the non-performing party the benefit the latter received by disclosing the information to third persons or by using it for its own purposes. If necessary, for example when the information has not yet been disclosed or has been disclosed only partially, the injured party may also seek an injunction in accordance with the applicable law.

ARTICLE 2.17

(Merger clauses)

A contract in writing which contains a clause indicating that the writing completely embodies the terms on which the parties have agreed cannot be contradicted or supplemented by evidence of prior statements or agreements. However, such statements or agreements may be used to interpret the writing.

COMMENT

If the conclusion of a contract is preceded by more or less extended negotiations, the parties may wish to put their agreement in writing and declare that document to constitute their final agreement. This can be achieved by an appropriately drafted "merger" or "integration" clause (e.g. "This contract contains the entire agreement between the parties"). However, the effect of such a clause is not to deprive prior statements or agreements of any relevance: they may still be used as a means of interpreting the written document. See also Art. 4.3(a).

A merger clause of course covers only prior statements or agreements between the parties and does not preclude subsequent informal agreements between them. The parties are, however, free to extend an agreed form even to future amendments. See Art. 2.18.

This article indirectly confirms the principle set out in Art. 1.2 in the sense that, in the absence of a merger clause, extrinsic evidence supplementing or contradicting a written contract is admissible.

ARTICLE **2.18**

(Written modification clauses)

A contract in writing which contains a clause requiring any modification or termination by agreement to be in writing may not be otherwise modified or terminated. However, a party may be precluded by its conduct from asserting such a clause to the extent that the other party has acted in reliance on that conduct.

COMMENT

Parties concluding a written contract may wish to ensure that any modification or termination by agreement will also be in writing and to this end include a special clause in the contract. This article states that as a rule such a clause renders any oral modification or termination ineffective, thus rejecting the idea that such oral modification or termination of the contract may be seen as an implied abrogation of the written modification clause.

The article however provides for an exception to the general rule by specifying that a party may be precluded by its conduct from invoking the written modification clause to the extent that the other party has acted in reliance on that conduct.

Illustration

A, a contractor, contracts with B, a school board, for the construction of a new school building. The contract provides that the second floor of the building is to have sufficient bearing capacity to support the school library. Notwithstanding a written modification clause in the same contract, the parties orally agree that the second floor of the building should be of non-bearing construction. A completes construction according to the modification, and B, who has observed the progress of the construction without making any objections, only at this point objects to how the second floor has been constructed. A court may decide that B is not entitled to invoke the written modification clause as A reasonably relied on the oral modification, and is therefore not liable for non-performance.

ARTICLE **2.19**

(Contracting under standard terms)

(1) Where one party or both parties use standard terms in concluding a contract, the general rules on formation apply, subject to Articles 2.20 - 2.22.

(2) Standard terms are provisions which are prepared in advance for general and repeated use by one party and which are actually used without negotiation with the other party.

COMMENT

1. Contracting under standard terms

This article is the first of four articles (Arts. 2.19 - 2.22) which deal with the special situation where one or both parties use standard terms in concluding a contract.

2. Notion of "standard terms"

"Standard terms" are to be understood as those contract provisions which are prepared in advance for general and repeated use by one party and which are actually used without negotiation with the other party (para. (2)). What is decisive is not their formal presentation (e.g. whether they are contained in a separate document or in the contract document itself; whether they have been issued on pre-printed forms or whether they are only on computer, etc.), nor who prepared them (the party itself, a trade or professional association, etc.), nor their volume (whether they consist of a comprehensive set of provisions covering almost all the relevant aspects of the contract, or of only one or two provisions regarding, for instance, exclusion of liability and arbitration). What is decisive is the fact that they are drafted in advance for general and repeated use and that they are actually used in a given case by one of the parties without negotiation with the other party. This latter requirement obviously relates only to the standard terms as such, which the other party must accept as a whole, while the other terms of the same contract may well be the subject of negotiation between the parties.

3. General rules on formation apply

Usually, the general rules on formation apply irrespective of whether or not one or both parties use standard terms (para. (1)). It follows that standard terms proposed by one party bind the other party only on acceptance, and that it depends upon the circumstances of the case whether the two parties must refer to the standard terms expressly or whether the incorporation of such terms may be implied. Thus, standard terms contained in the contract document itself will normally be binding upon the mere signature of the contract document as a whole, at least as long as they are reproduced above that signature and not, for instance, on the reverse side of the document. On the other hand, standard terms contained in a separate document will normally have to be referred to expressly by the party intending to use them. Implied incorporation may be admitted only if there exists a practice established between the parties or usage to that effect. See Art. 1.8.

Illustrations

1. A intends to conclude an insurance contract with B covering the risk of liability for accidents of A's employees at work. The parties sign a model contract form presented by B after filling in the blank spaces relating, among other matters, to the premium and to the maximum amount insured. By virtue of its signature, A is bound not only by the terms which it has individually negotiated with B, but also by the General Conditions of the National Insurers' Association, which are printed on the form.

2. A normally concludes contracts with its customers on the basis of its own standard terms which are printed as a separate document. When making an offer to B, a new customer, A fails to make an express reference to the standard terms. B accepts the offer. The standard terms are not incorporated in the contract unless A can prove that B knew or ought to have known of A's intention to conclude the contract only on the basis of its own standard terms, e.g. because the same standard terms had regularly been adopted in previous transactions.

3. A intends to buy grain on the commodity exchange in London. In the contract concluded between A and B, a broker on that exchange, no express reference is made to the standard terms which normally govern brokerage contracts concluded at the exchange in

question. The standard terms are nevertheless incorporated in the contract because their application to the kind of contract in question amounts to a usage.

ARTICLE 2.20

(Surprising terms)

(1) No term contained in standard terms which is of such a character that the other party could not reasonably have expected it, is effective unless it has been expressly accepted by that party.

(2) In determining whether a term is of such a character regard shall be had to its content, language and presentation.

COMMENT

1. Surprising terms in standard terms not effective

A party which accepts the other party's standard terms is in principle bound by them irrespective of whether or not it actually knows their content in detail or fully understands their implications. An important exception to this rule is, however, laid down in this article which states that, notwithstanding its acceptance of the standard terms as a whole, the adhering party is not bound by those terms which by virtue of their content, language or presentation are of such a character that it could not reasonably have expected them. The reason for this exception is the desire to avoid a party which uses standard terms taking undue advantage of its position by surreptitiously attempting to impose terms on the other party which that party would scarcely have accepted had it been aware of them. For other articles intended to protect the economically weaker or less experienced party, see Arts. 3.10 and 4.6.

2. Terms "surprising" by virtue of their content

A particular term contained in standard terms may come as a surprise to the adhering party first by reason of its content. This is the case whenever the content of the term in question is such that a reasonable person of the same kind as the adhering party would not have expected it in the type of standard terms involved. In determining whether or not a term is unusual, regard must be had on the one hand to the terms which are commonly to be found in standard terms generally used in the trade sector concerned, and on the other to the individual negotiations between the parties. Thus, for example, a term excluding or limiting the contractual liability of the proponent may or may not be considered to be "surprising", and in consequence ineffective in a particular case, its effectiveness depending on whether or not terms of that kind are common in the trade sector concerned, and are consistent with the way in which the parties conducted their negotiations.

Illustration

> 1. A, a travel agency, offers package tours for business trips. The terms of the advertisement give the impression that A is acting as a tour operator who undertakes full responsibility for the various services comprising the package. B books a tour on the basis of A's standard terms. Notwithstanding B's acceptance of the terms as a whole, A may not rely on a term stating that, with respect to the hotel accommodation, it is acting merely as an agent for the hotelkeeper, and therefore declines any liability.

3. Terms "surprising" by virtue of their language or presentation

Other reasons for a particular term contained in standard terms being surprising to the adhering party may be the language in which it is couched, which may be obscure, or the way in which it is presented typographically, for instance in minute print. In order to determine whether or not this is the case, regard is to be had not so much to the formulation and presentation commonly used in the type of standard terms involved, but more to the professional skill and experience of persons of the same kind as the adhering party. Thus, a particular wording may be both obscure and clear at the same time, depending on whether or not the adhering party belongs to the same professional category as the party using the standard terms.

The language factor may also play an important role in the context of international transactions. If the standard terms are drafted in a foreign language it cannot be excluded that some of its terms, although fairly clear in themselves, will turn out to be surprising for the adhering party who could not reasonably have been expected fully to appreciate all their implications.

Illustrations

> 2.   A, an insurance company operating in country X, is an affiliate of B, a company incorporated in country Y. A's standard terms comprise some 50 terms printed in small type. One of the terms designates the law of country Y as the applicable law. Unless this term is presented in bold letters or in any other way apt to attract the attention of the adhering party, it will be without effect since customers in country X would not reasonably expect to find a choice-of-law clause designating a foreign law as the law governing their contracts in the standard terms of a company operating in their own country.

> 3.   A, a commodity dealer operating in Hamburg, uses in its contracts with its customers standard terms containing, among others, a provision stating "Hamburg - Freundschaftliche Arbitrage". In local business circles this clause is normally understood as meaning that possible disputes are to be submitted to a special arbitration governed by particular rules of procedure of local origin. In contracts with foreign customers this clause may be held to be ineffective, notwithstanding the acceptance of the standard terms as a whole, since a foreign customer cannot reasonably be expected to understand its exact implications, and this irrespective of whether or not the clause has been translated into its own language.

4. Express acceptance of "surprising" terms

The risk of the adhering party being taken by surprise by the kind of terms so far discussed clearly no longer exists if in a given case the other party draws the adhering party's attention to them and the adhering party accepts them. The present article therefore provides that a party may no longer rely on the "surprising" nature of a term in order to challenge its effectiveness, once it has expressly accepted the term.

ARTICLE 2.21

(Conflict between standard terms and non-standard terms)

In case of conflict between a standard term and a term which is not a standard term the latter prevails.

COMMENT

Standard terms are by definition prepared in advance by one party or a third person and incorporated in an individual contract without their content being discussed by the parties (see Art. 2.19(2)). It is therefore logical that whenever the parties specifically negotiate and agree on particular provisions of their contract, such provisions will prevail over conflicting provisions contained in the standard terms since they are more likely to reflect the intention of the parties in the given case.

The individually agreed provisions may appear in the same document as the standard terms, but may also be contained in a separate document. In the first case they may easily be recognised on account of their being written in characters different from those of the standard terms. In the second case it may be more difficult to distinguish between the provisions which are standard terms and those which are not, and to determine their exact position in the hierarchy of the different documents. To this effect the parties often include a contract provision expressly indicating the documents which form part of their contract and their respective weight.

Special problems may however arise when the modifications to the standard terms have only been agreed upon orally, without the conflicting provisions contained in the standard terms being struck out, and those standard terms contain a provision stating the exclusive character of the writing signed by the parties, or that any addition to or modification of their content must be in writing. For these cases see Arts. 2.17 and 2.18.

ARTICLE 2.22

(Battle of forms)

Where both parties use standard terms and reach agreement except on those terms, a contract is concluded on the basis of the agreed terms and of any standard terms which are common in substance unless one party clearly indicates in advance, or later and without undue delay informs the other party, that it does not intend to be bound by such a contract.

COMMENT

1. Parties using different standard terms

It is quite frequent in commercial transactions for both the offeror when making the offer, and the offeree when accepting it, each to refer to its own standard terms. In the absence of express acceptance by the offeror of the offeree's standard terms, the problem arises as to whether a contract is concluded at all and if so, which, if either, of the two conflicting sets of standard terms should prevail.

2. "Battle of forms" and general rules on offer and acceptance

If the general rules on offer and acceptance were to be applied, there would either be no contract at all since the purported acceptance by the offeree would, subject to the exception provided for in Art. 2.11(2), amount to a counter-offer, or if the two parties have started to perform without objecting to each other's standard terms, a contract would be considered to have been concluded on the basis of those terms which were the last to be sent or to be referred to (the "last shot").

3. The "knock-out" doctrine

The "last shot" doctrine may be appropriate if the parties clearly indicate that the adoption of their standard terms is an essential condition for the conclusion of the contract. Where, on the other hand, the parties, as is very often the case in practice, refer to their standard terms more or less automatically, for example by exchanging printed order and acknowledgement of order forms with the respective terms on the reverse side, they will normally not even be aware of the conflict between their respective standard terms. There is in such cases no reason to allow the parties subsequently to question the very existence of the contract or, if performance has commenced, to insist on the application of the terms last sent or referred to.

It is for this reason that the present article provides, notwithstanding the general rules on offer and acceptance, that if the parties reach an agreement except on their standard terms, a contract is concluded on the basis of the agreed terms and of any standard terms which are common in substance ("knock-out" doctrine).

Illustration

1.   A orders a machine from B indicating the type of machine, the price and terms of payment, and the date and place of delivery. A uses an order form with its "General Conditions for Purchase" printed on the reverse side. B accepts by sending an acknowledgement of order form on the reverse side of which appear its own "General Conditions for Sale". When A subsequently seeks to withdraw from the deal it claims that no contract was ever concluded as there was no agreement as to which set of standard terms should apply. Since, however, the parties have agreed on the essential terms of the contract, a contract has been concluded on those terms and on any standard terms which are common in substance.

A party may, however, always exclude the operation of the "knock-out" doctrine by clearly indicating in advance, or by later and without undue delay informing the other, that it does not intend to be bound by a contract which is not based on its own standard terms. What will in practice amount to such a "clear" indication cannot be stated in absolute terms but the inclusion of a clause of this kind in the standard terms themselves will not normally be sufficient since what is necessary is a specific declaration by the party concerned in its offer or acceptance.

Illustrations

2.   The facts are the same as in Illustration 1, the difference being that A claims that the contract was concluded on the basis of its standard terms since they contain a clause which states that "Deviating standard terms of the party accepting the order are not valid if they have not been confirmed in writing by us". The result will be the same as in Illustration 1, since merely by including such a clause in its standard terms A does not indicate with sufficient clarity its determination to conclude the contract only on its own terms.

3.   The facts are the same as in Illustration 1, the difference being that the non-standard terms of A's offer contain a statement to the effect that A intends to contract only on its own standard terms. The mere fact that B attaches its own standard terms to its acceptance does not prevent the contract from being concluded on the basis of A's standard terms.

CHAPTER 3

VALIDITY

ARTICLE 3.1

(Matters not covered)

These Principles do not deal with invalidity arising from
    (a) lack of capacity;
    (b) lack of authority;
    (c) immorality or illegality.

COMMENT

This article makes it clear that not all the grounds of invalidity of a contract to be found in the various national legal systems fall within the scope of the Principles. This is in particular the case of lack of capacity, lack of authority and immorality or illegality. The reason for their exclusion lies both in the inherent complexity of questions of status, agency and public policy and the extremely diverse manner in which they are treated in domestic law. In consequence, matters such as *ultra vires*, the authority of an agent to bind its principal as well as the authority of directors to bind their company, and the illegal or immoral content of contracts will continue to be governed by the applicable law.

ARTICLE 3.2

(Validity of mere agreement)

A contract is concluded, modified or terminated by the mere agreement of the parties, without any further requirement.

COMMENT

The purpose of this article is to make it clear that the mere agreement of the parties is sufficient for the valid conclusion, modification or termination by agreement of a contract, without any of the further requirements which are to be found in some domestic laws.

1. No need for consideration

In common law systems, consideration is traditionally seen as a prerequisite for the validity or enforceability of a contract as well as for its modification or termination by the parties.

However, in commercial dealings this requirement is of minimal practical importance since in that context obligations are almost always undertaken by both parties. It is for this reason that Art. 29(1) CISG dispenses with the requirement of consideration in relation to the modification and termination by the parties of contracts for the international sale of goods. The fact that the present article extends this approach to the conclusion, modification and termination by the parties of international commercial contracts in general can only bring about greater certainty and reduce litigation.

2. No need for *cause*

This article also excludes the requirement of *cause* which exists in some civil law systems and is in certain respects functionally similar to the common law "consideration".

Illustration

> 1. At the request of its French customer A, bank B in Paris issues a guarantee on first demand in favour of C, a business partner of A in England. Neither B nor A can invoke the possible absence of consideration or *cause* for the guarantee.

It should be noted however that this article is not concerned with the effects which may derive from other aspects of *cause*, such as its illegality. See comment 2 on Art. 3.3.

3. All contracts consensual

Some civil law systems have retained certain types of "real" contract, i.e. contracts concluded only upon the actual handing over of the goods concerned. Such rules are not easily compatible with modern business perceptions and practice and are therefore also excluded by the present article.

Illustration

> 2. Two French businessmen, A and B, agree with C, a real estate developer, to lend C 300,000 French francs on 2 July. On 25 June, A and B inform C that, unexpectedly, they need the money for their own business. C is entitled to receive the loan, although the loan is generally considered a "real" contract in France.

ARTICLE 3.3

(Initial impossibility)

(1) The mere fact that at the time of the conclusion of the contract the performance of the obligation assumed was impossible does not affect the validity of the contract.

(2) The mere fact that at the time of the conclusion of the contract a party was not entitled to dispose of the assets to which the contract relates does not affect the validity of the contract.

COMMENT

1. Performance impossible from the outset

Contrary to a number of legal systems which consider a contract of sale void if the specific goods sold have already perished at the time of conclusion of the contract, para. (1) of this article, in conformity with the most modern trends, states in general terms that the mere fact that at the time of the conclusion of the contract the performance of the obligation assumed was impossible does not affect the validity of the contract.

A contract is valid even if the assets to which it relates have already perished at the time of contracting, with the consequence that initial impossibility of performance is equated with impossibility occurring after the conclusion of the contract. The rights and duties of the parties arising from one party's (or possibly even both parties') inability to perform are to be determined according to the rules on non-performance. Under these rules appropriate weight may be attached, for example, to the fact that the obligor (or the obligee) already knew of the impossibility of performance at the time of contracting.

The rule laid down in para. (1) also removes possible doubts as to the validity of contracts for the delivery of future goods.

If an initial impossibility of performance is due to a legal prohibition (e.g. an export or import embargo), the validity of the contract depends upon whether under the law enacting the prohibition the latter is intended to invalidate the contract or merely to prohibit its performance.

Para. (1) moreover departs from the rule to be found in some civil law systems according to which the object (*objet*) of a contract must be possible.

The paragraph also deviates from the rule of the same systems which requires the existence of a *cause*, since, in a case of initial impossibility, the *cause* for a counter-performance is lacking. See Art. 3.2.

2. Lack of legal title or power

Para. (2) of this article deals with cases where the party promising to transfer or deliver assets was not entitled to dispose of the assets because it lacked legal title or the right of disposition at the time of the conclusion of the contract.

Some legal systems declare a contract of sale concluded in such circumstances to be void. Yet, as in the case with initial impossibility, and for even more cogent reasons, para. (2) of this article considers such a contract to be valid. Indeed, a contracting party may, and often does, acquire legal title to, or the power of disposition over, the assets in question after the conclusion of the contract. Should this not occur, the rules on non-performance will apply.

Cases where the power of disposition is lacking must be distinguished from those of lack of capacity. The latter relate to certain disabilities of a person which may affect all or at least some types of contract concluded by it, and falls outside the scope of the Principles. See Art. 3.1(a).

ARTICLE 3.4

(Definition of mistake)

Mistake is an erroneous assumption relating to facts or to law existing when the contract was concluded.

COMMENT

1. Mistake of fact and mistake of law

This article equates a mistake relating to facts with a mistake relating to law. Identical legal treatment of the two types of mistake seems justified in view of the increasing complexity of modern legal systems. For cross-border trade the difficulties caused by this complexity are exacerbated by the fact that an individual transaction may be affected by foreign and therefore unfamiliar legal systems.

2. Decisive time

The article indicates that the mistake involves an erroneous assumption relating to the factual or legal circumstances that exist at the time of the conclusion of the contract.

The purpose of fixing this time element is to distinguish cases where the rules on mistake with their particular remedies apply from those relating to non-performance. Indeed, a typical case of mistake may, depending on the point of view taken, often just as well be seen as one involving an obstacle which prevents or impedes the performance of the contract. If a party has entered into a contract under a misconception as to the factual or legal context and therefore misjudged its prospects under that contract, the rules on mistake will apply. If, on the other hand, a party has a correct understanding of the surrounding circumstances but makes an error of judgment as to its prospects under the contract, and later refuses to perform, then the case is one of non-performance rather than mistake.

ARTICLE 3.5

(Relevant mistake)

(1) A party may only avoid the contract for mistake if, when the contract was concluded, the mistake was of such importance that a reasonable person in the same situation as the party in error would only have concluded the contract on materially different terms or would not have concluded it at all if the true state of affairs had been known, and

(a) the other party made the same mistake, or caused the mistake, or knew or ought to have known of the mistake and it was contrary to reasonable commercial standards of fair dealing to leave the mistaken party in error; or

(b) the other party had not at the time of avoidance acted in reliance on the contract.

(2) However, a party may not avoid the contract if

(a) it was grossly negligent in committing the mistake; or

(b) the mistake relates to a matter in regard to which the risk of mistake was assumed or, having regard to the circumstances, should be borne by the mistaken party.

COMMENT

This article states the conditions necessary for a mistake to be relevant with a view to avoidance of the contract. The introductory part of para. (1) determines the conditions under which a mistake is sufficiently serious to be taken into account; sub-paras. (a) and (b) of para. (1) add the conditions regarding the party other than the mistaken party; para. (2) deals with the conditions regarding the mistaken party.

1. Serious mistake

To be relevant, a mistake must be serious. Its weight and importance are to be assessed by reference to a combined objective/subjective standard, namely what "a reasonable person in the same situation as the party in error" would have done if it had known the true circumstances at the time of the conclusion of the contract. If it would not have contracted at all, or would have done so only on materially different terms, hen, and only then, is the mistake considered to be serious.

In this context the introductory part of para. (1) relies on an open-ended formula, rather than indicating specific essential elements of the contract to which the mistake must relate. This flexible approach allows full account to be taken of the intentions of the parties and the circumstances of the case. In ascertaining the parties' intentions, the rules of interpretation laid down in Chapter 4 must be applied. General commercial standards and relevant usages will be particularly important.

Normally in commercial transactions certain mistakes, such as those concerning the value of goods or services or mere expectations or motivations of the mistaken party, are not considered to be relevant. The same is true of mistakes as to the identity of the other party or its personal qualities, although special circumstances may sometimes render such mistakes relevant (e.g. when services to be rendered require certain personal qualifications or when a loan is based upon the credit-worthiness of the borrower).

The fact that a reasonable person would consider the circumstances erroneously assumed to be essential is however not sufficient, since additional requirements concerning both the mistaken and the other party must be met if a mistake is to become relevant.

2. Conditions concerning the party other than the mistaken party

A mistaken party may avoid the contract only if the other party satisfies one of four conditions laid down in para. (1).

The first three conditions indicated in sub-para. (a) have in common the fact that the other party does not deserve protection because of its involvement in one way or another with the mistaken party's error.

The first condition is that both parties laboured under the same mistake.

Illustration

> 1.   A and B, when concluding a contract for the sale of a sports car, were not and could not have been aware of the fact that the car had in the meantime been stolen. Avoidance of the contract is admissible.

However, if the parties erroneously believe the object of the contract to be in existence at the time of the conclusion of the contract, while in reality it had already been destroyed, Art. 3.3 has to be taken into account.

The second condition is that the error of the mistaken party is caused by the other party. This is the case whenever the error can be traced to specific representations made by the latter party, be they express or implied, negligent or innocent, or to conduct which in the circumstances amounts to a representation. Even silence may cause an error. A mere "puff" in advertising or in negotiations will normally be tolerated.

If the error was caused intentionally, Art. 3.8 applies.

The third condition is that the other party knew or ought to have known of the error of the mistaken party and that it was contrary to reasonable commercial standards of fair dealing to leave the mistaken party in error. What the other party ought to have known is what should have been known to a reasonable person in the same situation as that party. In order to avoid the contract the mistaken party must also show that the other party was under a duty to inform it of its error.

The fourth condition is laid down in sub-para. (b) and is that the party other than the mistaken party had not, up to the time of avoidance, acted in reliance on the contract. For the time of avoidance, see Arts. 3.15 and 1.9.

3. Conditions concerning the mistaken party

Para. (2) of the present article mentions two cases in which the mistaken party may not avoid the contract.

The first of these, dealt with in sub-para. (a), is that the error is due to the gross negligence of the mistaken party. In such a situation it would be unfair to the other party to allow the mistaken party to avoid the contract.

Sub-para. (b) contemplates the situation where the mistaken party either has assumed the risk of mistake or where this risk should in the circumstances be borne by it. An assumption of the risk of mistake is a frequent feature of speculative contracts. A party may conclude a contract in the hope that its assumption of the existence of certain facts will prove to be correct, but may nevertheless undertake to assume the risk of this not being so. In such circumstances it will not be entitled to avoid the contract for its mistake.

Illustration

> 2. A sells to B a picture "attributed" to the relatively unknown painter C at a fair price for such paintings. It is subsequently discovered that the work was painted by the famous artist D. A cannot avoid its contract with B on the ground of its mistake, since the fact that the picture was only "attributed" to C implied the risk that it might have been painted by a more famous artist.

Sometimes both parties assume a risk. However, speculative contracts involving conflicting expectations of future developments, e.g. those concerning prices and exchange rates, may not be avoided on the ground of mistake, since the mistake would not be one as to facts existing at the time of the conclusion of the contract.

ARTICLE 3.6

(Error in expression or transmission)

An error occurring in the expression or transmission of a declaration is considered to be a mistake of the person from whom the declaration emanated.

COMMENT

This article equates an error in the expression or transmission of a declaration with an ordinary mistake of the person making the declaration or sending it and thus the rules of Art. 3.5 and of Arts. 3.12 to 3.19 apply also to these kinds of error.

1. Relevant mistake

If an error in expression or transmission is of sufficient magnitude (especially if it has resulted in the misstatement of figures), the receiver will be, or ought to be, aware of the error. Since nothing in the Principles prevents the receiver/offeree from accepting the erroneously expressed or transmitted offer, it is for the sender/offeror to invoke the error and to avoid the contract provided that the conditions of Art. 3.5 are met, in particular that it was contrary to reasonable commercial standards of fair dealing for the receiver/offeree not to inform the sender/offeror of the error.

In some cases the risk of the error may have been assumed by, or may have to be imposed upon, the sender if it uses a method of transmission which it knows or ought to know to be unsafe either in general or in the special circumstances of the case.

Illustration

> A, a potential Italian client, asks B, an English law firm, for legal advice and by way of reply receives a telegram indicating that B's hourly rate is "£ 150", whereas the form handed by B to the English post office had read "£ 250". Since it is well known that numbers in telegrams are often wrongly transmitted, B is considered to have assumed that risk and is not entitled to invoke the error in the transmission, even if the other conditions of Art. 3.5 are met.

2. Mistakes on the part of the receiver

Transmission ends as soon as the message reaches the receiver. See Art. 1.9.

If the message is correctly transmitted, but the receiver misunderstands its content, the case falls outside the scope of the present article.

If the message is correctly transmitted to the receiver's machine which, however, due to a technical fault, prints out a mutilated text, the case is again outside the scope of this article. The same is true if, at the receiver's request, a message is given orally to the receiver's messenger who misunderstands it or transmits it wrongly.

In the two above-mentioned situations the receiver may however be entitled to invoke its own mistake in accordance with Art. 3.5, if it replies to the sender and bases its reply upon its own misunderstanding of the sender's message and if all the conditions of Art. 3.5 are met.

ARTICLE 3.7

(Remedies for non-performance)

A party is not entitled to avoid the contract on the ground of mistake if the circumstances on which that party relies afford, or could have afforded, a remedy for non-performance.

COMMENT

1. Remedies for non-performance preferred

This article is intended to resolve the conflict which may arise between the remedy of avoidance for mistake and the remedies for non-performance. In the event of such a conflict, preference is given to the remedies for non-performance since they seem to be better suited and are more flexible than the radical solution of avoidance.

2. Actual and potential conflicts

An actual conflict between the remedies for mistake and those for non-performance arises whenever the two sets of remedies are invoked in relation to what are essentially the same facts.

Illustration

> A, a farmer, who finds a rusty cup on the land sells it to B, an art dealer, for 100,000 Austrian schillings. The high price is based upon the assumption of both parties that the cup is made of silver (other silver objects had previously been found on the land). It subsequently turns out that the object in question is an ordinary iron cup worth only 1,000 schillings. B refuses to accept the cup and to pay for it on the ground that it lacks the assumed quality. B also avoids the contract on the ground of mistake as to the quality of the cup. B is entitled only to the remedies for non-performance.

It may be that the conflict between the two sets of remedies is only potential, since the mistaken party could have relied upon a remedy for non-performance, but is actually precluded from doing so by special circumstances, for example because a statutory limitation period has lapsed. Even in such a case the present article applies with the consequence that the remedy of avoidance for mistake is excluded.

ARTICLE 3.8

(Fraud)

A party may avoid the contract when it has been led to conclude the contract by the other party's fraudulent representation, including language or practices, or fraudulent non-disclosure of cir-

cumstances which, according to reasonable commercial standards of fair dealing, the latter party should have disclosed.

COMMENT

1. Fraud and mistake

Avoidance of a contract by a party on the ground of fraud bears some resemblance to avoidance for a certain type of mistake. Fraud may be regarded as a special case of mistake caused by the other party. Fraud, like mistake, may involve either representations, whether express or implied, of false facts or non-disclosure of true facts.

2. Notion of fraud

The decisive distinction between fraud and mistake lies in the nature and purpose of the defrauding party's representations or non-disclosure. What entitles the defrauded party to avoid the contract is the "fraudulent" representation or non-disclosure of relevant facts. Such conduct is fraudulent if it is intended to lead the other party into error and thereby to gain an advantage to the detriment of the other party. The reprehensible nature of fraud is such that it is a sufficient ground for avoidance without the need for the presence of the additional conditions laid down in Art. 3.5 for the mistake to become relevant.

A mere "puff" in advertising or negotiations does not suffice.

ARTICLE 3.9

(Threat)

A party may avoid the contract when it has been led to conclude the contract by the other party's unjustified threat which, having regard to the circumstances, is so imminent and serious as to leave the first party no reasonable alternative. In particular, a threat is unjustified if the act or omission with which a party has been threatened is wrongful in itself, or it is wrongful to use it as a means to obtain the conclusion of the contract.

COMMENT

This article permits the avoidance of a contract on the ground of threat.

1. Threat must be imminent and serious

Threat of itself is not sufficient. It must be of so imminent and serious a character that the threatened person has no reasonable alternative but to conclude the contract on the terms proposed by the other party. The imminence and seriousness of the threat must be evaluated by an objective standard, taking into account the circumstances of the individual case.

2. Unjustified threat

The threat must in addition be unjustified. The second sentence of the present article sets out, by way of illustration, two examples of an unjustified threat. The first envisages a case where the act or omission with which the contracting party has been threatened is wrongful in itself (e.g. a physical attack). The second refers to a situation where the threatened act or omission is in itself lawful, but the purpose to be achieved is wrongful (e.g. the bringing of a court action for the sole purpose of inducing the other party to conclude the contract on the terms proposed).

Illustration

1. A, who is in default with the repayment of a loan, is threatened by B, the lender, with proceedings for the recovery of the money. The only purpose of this threat is to obtain on particularly advantageous terms a lease of A's warehouse. A signs the lease, but is entitled to avoid the contract.

3. Threat affecting reputation or economic interests

For the purpose of the application of the present article, threat need not necessarily be made against a person or property, but may also affect reputation or purely economic interests.

Illustration

2. Faced with a threat by the players of a basketball team to go on strike unless they receive a much higher bonus than had already been agreed for winning the four remaining matches of the season, the owner of the team agrees to pay the requested bonus. The owner is entitled to avoid the new contract with the players, since

the strike would have led automatically to the team being relegated to a minor league and therefore represented a serious and imminent threat to both the reputation and the financial position of the club.

ARTICLE 3.10

(Gross disparity)

(1) A party may avoid the contract or an individual term of it if, at the time of the conclusion of the contract, the contract or term unjustifiably gave the other party an excessive advantage. Regard is to be had, among other factors, to

(a) the fact that the other party has taken unfair advantage of the first party's dependence, economic distress or urgent needs, or of its improvidence, ignorance, inexperience or lack of bargaining skill, and

(b) the nature and purpose of the contract.

(2) Upon the request of the party entitled to avoidance, a court may adapt the contract or term in order to make it accord with reasonable commercial standards of fair dealing.

(3) A court may also adapt the contract or term upon the request of the party receiving notice of avoidance, provided that that party informs the other party of its request promptly after receiving such notice and before the other party has acted in reliance on it. The provisions of Article 3.13(2) apply accordingly.

COMMENT

1. Excessive advantage

This provision permits a party to avoid a contract in cases where there is a gross disparity between the obligations of the parties, which gives one party an unjustifiably excessive advantage.

The excessive advantage must exist at the time of the conclusion of the contract. A contract which, although not grossly unfair when entered into, becomes so later may be adapted or terminated under the rules on hardship contained in Chapter 6, Section 2.

As the term "excessive" advantage denotes, even a considerable disparity in the value and the price or some other element which upsets the equilibrium of performance and counter-performance is not sufficient to permit the avoidance or the adaptation of the contract under this article. What is required is that the disequilibrium is in the circumstances so great as to shock the conscience of a reasonable person.

2. Unjustifiable advantage

Not only must the advantage be excessive, it must also be unjustifiable. Whether this requirement is met will depend upon an evaluation of all the relevant circumstances of the case. Para. (1) of the present article refers in particular to two factors which deserve special attention in this connection.

a. *Unequal bargaining position*

The first factor is that one party has taken unfair advantage of the other party's dependence, economic distress or urgent needs, or its improvidence, ignorance, inexperience, or lack of bargaining skill (sub-para. (a)). As to the dependence of one party vis-à-vis the other, superior bargaining power due to market conditions alone is not sufficient.

Illustration

> A, the owner of an automobile factory, sells an outdated assembly line to B, a governmental agency from a country eager to set up its own automobile industry. Although A makes no representations as to the efficiency of the assembly line, it succeeds in fixing a price which is manifestly excessive. B, after discovering that it has paid an amount which corresponds to that of a much more modern assembly line, may be entitled to avoid the contract.

b. *Nature and purpose of the contract*

The second factor to which special regard must be had is the nature and purpose of the contract (sub-para. (b)). There are situations where an excessive advantage is unjustifiable even if the party who will benefit from it has not abused the other party's weak bargaining position.

Whether this is the case will often depend upon the nature and purpose of the contract. Thus, a contract term providing for an extremely short period for giving notice of defects in goods or services to be supplied may or may not be excessively advantageous to the seller or supplier, depending on the character of the goods or services in question. Equally, an agent's fee expressed in terms of a fixed percentage of the price of the goods or services to be sold or rendered, although justified in the event of the agent's contribution to the conclusion of the transaction being substantial and/or the value of the goods or services concerned not being very high, may well turn out to confer an excessive advantage on the agent if the latter's contribution is almost negligible and/or the value of the goods or services are extraordinarily high.

c. *Other factors*

Other factors may need to be taken into consideration, for example the ethics prevailing in the business or trade.

3. Avoidance or adaptation

The avoidance of the contract or of any of its individual terms under this article is subject to the general rules laid down in Arts. 3.14 - 3.18.

However, according to para. (2) of the present article, at the request of the party who is entitled to avoidance, the court may adapt the contract in order to bring it into accord with reasonable commercial standards of fair dealing. Similarly, according to para. (3) the party receiving notice of avoidance may also request such adaptation provided it informs the avoiding party of its request promptly after receiving the notice of avoidance, and before the avoiding party has acted in reliance on that notice.

If the parties are in disagreement as to the procedure to be adopted, it will be for the court to decide whether the contract is to be avoided or adapted and, if adapted, on which terms.

If, in its notice or subsequently, a party entitled to avoidance requests adaptation only, its right to avoidance will be lost. See Art. 3.13(2).

ARTICLE 3.11

(Third persons)

(1) Where fraud, threat, gross disparity or a party's mistake is imputable to, or is known or ought to be known by, a third person for whose acts the other party is responsible, the contract may be avoided under the same conditions as if the behaviour or knowledge had been that of the party itself.

(2) Where fraud, threat or gross disparity is imputable to a third person for whose acts the other party is not responsible, the contract may be avoided if that party knew or ought to have known of the fraud, threat or disparity, or has not at the time of avoidance acted in reliance on the contract.

COMMENT

This article deals with situations, frequent in practice, in which a third person has been involved or has interfered in the negotiation process, and the ground for avoidance is in one way or another imputable to that person.

1. Third person for whom a party is responsible

Para. (1) is concerned with cases in which fraud, threat, gross disparity or a party's mistake is caused by a third person for whose acts the other party is responsible, or cases in which, without causing the mistake, the third person knew or ought to have known of it. A party is responsible for the acts of a third person in a variety of situations ranging from those in which that person is an agent of the party in question to those where the third person acts for the benefit of that party on its own initiative. In all such cases it seems justified to impute to that party the third person's acts or its knowledge, whether actual or constructive, of certain circumstances, and this irrespective of whether the party in question knew of the third person's acts.

2. Third person for whom a party is not responsible

Para. (2) deals with cases where a party is defrauded, threatened or otherwise unduly influenced by a third person for whom the other party is not responsible. Such acts may be imputed to the latter party only if it knew or ought to have known of them.

There is however one exception to this rule: the defrauded, threatened or otherwise unduly influenced party is entitled to avoid the contract, even if the other party did not know of the third person's acts, whenever the latter party has not acted in reliance on the contract before the time of avoidance. This exception is justified because in this situation the other party is not in need of protection.

ARTICLE 3.12

(Confirmation)

If the party entitled to avoid the contract expressly or impliedly confirms the contract after the period of time for giving notice of avoidance has begun to run, avoidance of the contract is excluded.

COMMENT

This article lays down the rule according to which the party entitled to avoid the contract may either expressly or impliedly confirm the contract.

For there to be an implied confirmation it is not sufficient, for example, for the party entitled to avoid the contract to bring a claim against the other party based on the latter's non-performance. A confirmation can only be assumed if the other party acknowledges the claim or if a court action has been successful.

There is also confirmation if the party entitled to avoidance continues to perform the contract without reserving its right to avoid the contract.

ARTICLE 3.13

(Loss of right to avoid)

(1) If a party is entitled to avoid the contract for mistake but the other party declares itself willing to perform or performs the contract as it was understood by the party entitled to

avoidance, the contract is considered to have been concluded as the latter party understood it. The other party must make such a declaration or render such performance promptly after having been informed of the manner in which the party entitled to avoidance had understood the contract and before that party has acted in reliance on a notice of avoidance.

(2) After such a declaration or performance the right to avoidance is lost and any earlier notice of avoidance is ineffective.

COMMENT

1. Performance of the contract as understood by the mistaken party

According to this article a mistaken party may be prevented from avoiding the contract if the other party declares itself willing to perform or actually performs the contract as it was understood by the mistaken party. The interest of the other party in so doing may lie in the benefit to be derived from the contract, even in its adapted form.

Such regard for the interests of the other party is only justified in the case of mistake and not in other cases of defective consent (threat and fraud) where it would be extremely difficult to expect the parties to keep the contract alive.

2. Decision to be made promptly

The other party has to declare its decision to perform or actually to perform the contract in its adapted form promptly after having been informed of the manner in which the mistaken party had understood the contract. How the other party is to receive the information about the erroneous understanding of the terms of the contract will depend on the circumstances of the case.

3. Loss of right to avoid

Para. (2) expressly states that after the other party's declaration or performance the right of the mistaken party to avoid the contract is lost and that any earlier notice of avoidance becomes ineffective.

Conversely, the other party is no longer entitled to adapt the contract if the mistaken party has not only given notice of avoidance but has also acted in reliance on that notice.

4. Damages

The adaptation of the contract by the other party does not preclude the mistaken party from claiming damages in accordance with Art. 3.18 if it has suffered loss which is not compensated by the adaptation of the contract.

ARTICLE **3.14**

(Notice of avoidance)

**The right of a party to avoid the contract
is exercised by notice to the other party.**

COMMENT

1. The requirement of notice

This article states the principle that the right of a party to avoid the contract is exercised by notice to the other party without the need for any intervention by a court.

2. Form and content of notice

No provision is made in this article for any specific requirement as to the form or content of the notice of avoidance. It follows that in accordance with the general rule laid down in Art. 1.9(1), the notice may be given by any means appropriate to the circumstances. As to the content of the notice, it is not necessary that the term "avoidance" actually be used, or that the reasons for avoiding the contract be stated expressly. However, for the sake of clarity a party would be well advised to give some reasons for the avoidance in its notice, although in cases of fraud or gross disparity the avoiding party may assume that those reasons are already known to the other party.

Illustration

A, B's employer, threatens B with dismissal if B does not sell A a Louis XVI chest of drawers. B ultimately agrees to the sale. Two days later A receives a letter from B announcing B's resignation and stating that B has sold the chest of drawers to C. B's letter is sufficient notice of avoidance of the contract of sale with A.

3. Notice must be received

The notice of avoidance becomes effective when it reaches the other party. See Art. 1.9(2).

ARTICLE 3.15

(Time limits)

(1) Notice of avoidance shall be given within a reasonable time, having regard to the circumstances, after the avoiding party knew or could not have been unaware of the relevant facts or became capable of acting freely.

(2) Where an individual term of the contract may be avoided by a party under Article 3.10, the period of time for giving notice of avoidance begins to run when that term is asserted by the other party.

COMMENT

According to para. (1) of this article notice of avoidance must be given within a reasonable time after the avoiding party became aware or could not have been unaware of the relevant facts or became capable of acting freely. More precisely, the mistaken or defrauded party must give notice of avoidance within a reasonable time after it became aware or could no longer be unaware of the mistake or fraud. The same applies in cases of gross disparity which result from an abuse of the innocent party's ignorance, improvidence or inexperience. In cases of threat or abuse of the innocent party's dependence, economic distress or urgent needs the period runs from the time the threatened or abused party becomes capable of acting freely.

In case of avoidance of an individual term of the contract in accordance with Art. 3.10, para. (2) of this article states that the period of time for giving notice begins to run when that term is asserted by the party.

ARTICLE 3.16

(Partial avoidance)

Where a ground of avoidance affects only individual terms of the contract, the effect of avoidance is limited to those terms unless, having regard to the circumstances, it is unreasonable to uphold the remaining contract.

COMMENT

This article deals with situations where the grounds of avoidance affect only individual terms of the contract. In such cases the effects of avoidance will be limited to the terms affected unless it would in the circumstances be unreasonable to uphold the remaining contract. This will generally depend upon whether or not a party would have entered into the contract had it envisaged that the terms in question would have been affected by grounds of avoidance.

Illustrations

1.   A, a contractor, agrees to build two houses on plots of land X and Y for B, one of which B intends to live in and the other to rent. B was mistaken in assuming that it had a licence to build on both plots, since in fact the licence covered only plot X. Unless the circumstances indicate otherwise, notwithstanding the avoidance of the contract concerning the building of the house on plot Y, it would be reasonable to uphold the remaining contract concerning the building of the house on plot X.

2.   The situation is the same as in Illustration 1, the difference being that a school was to be built on plot X and living quarters for the students on plot Y. Unless the circumstances indicate otherwise, after the avoidance of the contract concerning the building of the living quarters on plot Y it would not be reasonable to uphold the remaining contract for the building of the school on plot X.

ARTICLE 3.17

(Retroactive effect of avoidance)

(1) Avoidance takes effect retroactively.

(2) On avoidance either party may claim restitution of whatever it has supplied under the contract or the part of it avoided, provided that it concurrently makes restitution of whatever it has received under the contract or the part of it avoided or, if it cannot make restitution in kind, it makes an allowance for what it has received.

COMMENT

1. Avoidance generally of retroactive effect

Para. (1) of this article states the rule that avoidance takes effect retroactively. In other words, the contract is considered never to have existed. In the case of a partial avoidance under Art. 3.16 the rule applies only to the avoided part of the contract.

There are however individual terms of the contract which may survive even in cases of total avoidance. Arbitration, jurisdiction and choice-of-law clauses are considered to be different from the other terms of the contract which may be upheld notwithstanding the avoidance of the contract in whole or in part. Whether in fact such clauses remain operative is to be determined by the applicable domestic law.

2. Restitution

According to para. (2) of the present article either party may claim restitution of what it has supplied under the contract or the part of it avoided. The only condition for such restitution is that each party makes restitution of whatever it has received under the contract or the part of it avoided. If restitution in kind is not possible, as is typically the case with services, a party must make an allowance for what it has received, except where the performance received is of no value to it.

Illustration

A commissions B to decorate a restaurant. B begins the work. When A later discovers that B is not the famous decorator who had made similar decorations in a number of another restaurants, A avoids the contract. Since the decorations so far made cannot be returned and they have no value for A, B is not entitled to any allowance from A for the work done.

ARTICLE 3.18

(Damages)

Irrespective of whether or not the contract has been avoided, the party who knew or ought to have known of the ground for avoidance is liable for damages so as to put the other party in the same position in which it would have been if it had not concluded the contract.

COMMENT

1. Damages if ground for avoidance known to the other party

This article provides that a party which knew or ought to have known of a ground for avoidance is liable for damages to the other party. The right to damages arises irrespective of whether or not the contract has been avoided.

2. The measure of damages

Unlike the damages in case of non-performance under Chapter 7, Section 4, the damages contemplated by the present article are intended simply to put the other party in the same position in which it would have been if it had not concluded the contract.

Illustration

A sells software to B, and could not have been unaware of B's mistake as to its appropriateness for the use intended by B. Irrespective of whether or not B avoids the contract, A is liable to B for all the expenses incurred by B in training its personnel in the use of the software, but not for the loss suffered by B as a consequence of the impossibility to use the software for the intended purpose.

ARTICLE 3.19

(Mandatory character of the provisions)

The provisions of this Chapter are mandatory, except insofar as they relate to the binding force of mere agreement, initial impossibility or mistake.

COMMENT

This article declares the provisions of this Chapter relating to fraud, threat and gross disparity to be of a mandatory character. It would be contrary to good faith for the parties to exclude or modify these provisions when concluding their contract. However, nothing prevents the party entitled to avoidance to waive that right once it learns of the true facts or is able to act freely.

On the other hand, the provisions of this Chapter relating to the binding force of mere agreement, to initial impossibility or to mistake are not mandatory. Thus the parties may well reintroduce special requirements of domestic law, such as consideration or *cause*; they may likewise agree that their contract shall be invalid in case of initial impossibility, or that mistake by one of them is not a ground for avoidance.

ARTICLE 3.20

(Unilateral declarations)

The provisions of this Chapter apply with appropriate adaptations to any communication of intention addressed by one party to the other.

COMMENT

This article takes account of the fact that apart from the contract itself the parties, either before or after the conclusion of the contract, often exchange a number of communications of intention which may likewise be affected by invalidity.

In a commercial setting, the most important example of unilateral communications of intention which are external, but preparatory, to a contract are bids for investment, works, delivery of goods or provision of services. Communications of intention made after the conclusion of a contract take a variety of forms, such as notices, declarations, demands and requests. In particular, waivers and declarations by which a party assumes an obligation may be affected by a defect of consent.

CHAPTER 4

INTERPRETATION

ARTICLE 4.1
(Intention of the parties)

(1) A contract shall be interpreted according to the common intention of the parties.

(2) If such an intention cannot be established, the contract shall be interpreted according to the meaning that reasonable persons of the same kind as the parties would give to it in the same circumstances.

COMMENT

1. Common intention of the parties to prevail

Para. (1) of this article lays down the principle that in determining the meaning to be attached to the terms of a contract, preference is to be given to the intention common to the parties. In consequence, a contract term may be given a meaning which differs both from the literal sense of the language used and from the meaning which a reasonable person would attach to it, provided that such a different understanding was common to the parties at the time of the conclusion of the contract.

The practical importance of the principle should not be over-estimated, first because parties to commercial transactions are unlikely to use language in a sense entirely different from that usually attached to it, and secondly because even if this were to be the case it would be extremely difficult, once a dispute arises, to prove that a particular meaning which one of the parties claims to have been their common intention was in fact shared by the other party at the time of the conclusion of the contract.

2. Recourse to the understanding of reasonable persons

For those cases where the common intention of the parties cannot be established, para. (2) provides that the contract shall be interpreted in accordance with the meaning which reasonable persons of the same kind as the parties would give to it in the same circumstances. The test is not a general and abstract criterion of reasonableness, but rather the understanding which could reasonably be expected of persons with, for example, the same linguistic knowledge, technical skill, or business experience as the parties.

3. How to establish the common intention of the parties or to determine the understanding of reasonable persons

In order to establish whether the parties had a common intention and, if so, what that common intention was, regard is to be had to all the relevant circumstances of the case, the most important of which are listed in Art. 4.3. The same applies to the determination of the understanding of reasonable persons when no common intention of the parties can be established.

4. Interpretation of standard terms

Both the "subjective" test laid down in para. (1) and the "reasonableness" test in para. (2) may not always be appropriate in the context of standard terms. Indeed, given their special nature and purpose, standard terms should be interpreted primarily in accordance with the reasonable expectations of their average users irrespective of the actual understanding which either of the parties to the contract concerned, or reasonable persons of the same kind as the parties, might have had. For the definition of "standard terms", see Art. 2.19(2).

ARTICLE 4.2

(Interpretation of statements and other conduct)

(1) The statements and other conduct of a party shall be interpreted according to that party's intention if the other party knew or could not have been unaware of that intention.

(2) If the preceding paragraph is not applicable, such statements and other conduct shall be interpreted according to the meaning that a reasonable person of the same kind as the other party would give to it in the same circumstances.

COMMENT

1. Interpretation of unilateral acts

By analogy to the criteria laid down in Art. 4.1 with respect to the contract as a whole, this article states that in the interpretation of unilateral statements or conduct preference is to be given to the intention of the party concerned, provided that the other party knew (or could not have been unaware) of that intention, and that in all other cases such statements or conduct are to be interpreted according to the understanding that a reasonable person of the same kind as the other party would have had in the same circumstances.

In practice the principal field of application of this article, which corresponds almost literally to Art. 8(1) and (2) CISG, will be in the process of the formation of contracts where parties make statements and engage in conduct whose precise legal significance may have to be established in order to determine whether or not a contract is ultimately concluded. There are however also unilateral acts performed after the conclusion of the contract which may give rise to problems of interpretation: for example, a notification of defects in goods, notice of avoidance or of termination of the contract, etc.

2. How to establish the intention of the party performing the act or to determine the understanding of a reasonable person

In applying both the "subjective" test laid down in para. (1) and the "reasonableness" test in para. (2), regard is to be had to all the relevant circumstances, the most important of which are listed in Art. 4.3.

ARTICLE 4.3

(Relevant circumstances)

In applying Articles 4.1 and 4.2, regard shall be had to all the circumstances, including

(a) preliminary negotiations between the parties;

(b) practices which the parties have established between themselves;

(c) the conduct of the parties subsequent to the conclusion of the contract;

(d) the nature and purpose of the contract;

(e) the meaning commonly given to terms and expressions in the trade concerned;

(f) usages.

COMMENT

1. Circumstances relevant in the interpretation process

This article indicates circumstances which have to be taken into consideration when applying both the "subjective" test and the "reasonableness" test in Arts. 4.1 and 4.2. The list mentions only those circumstances which are the most important and is in no way intended to be exhaustive.

2. "Particular" and "general" circumstances compared

Of the circumstances listed in the present article some relate to the particular relationship which exists between the parties concerned, while others are of a more general character. Although in principle all the circumstances listed may be relevant in a given case, the first three are likely to have greater weight in the application of the "subjective" test.

Illustrations

1. A contract for the writing of a book between A and B, a publisher, indicates that the book should consist of "about 300 pages". During their negotiations B had assured A that an approximate indication of the number of pages was necessary for administrative reasons and that A was not bound to stick precisely to that number of pages, but could exceed it, substantially if need be. A submits a manuscript of 500 pages. In interpreting the

meaning of "about 300 pages" due consideration should be given to these preliminary negotiations. See Art. 4.3(a).

2.   A, a Canadian manufacturer, and B, a United States retailer, conclude a number of contracts for the delivery of optical lenses in which the price is always expressed in Canadian dollars. A makes B a new offer indicating the price in "dollars" without further specification, but intending to refer again to Canadian dollars. In the absence of any indication to the contrary, A's intention will prevail. See Art. 4.3(b).

The remaining circumstances listed in this article, i.e. the nature and purpose of the contract, the meaning commonly given to terms and expressions in a trade concerned and usages, are important primarily, although not exclusively, in the application of the "reasonableness" test.

The criteria in sub-paras. (e) and (f) may at first sight appear to overlap. There is however a difference between them: while the "usages" apply only if they meet the requirements laid down in Art. 1.8, the "meaning commonly given [...] in the trade concerned" can be relevant even if it is peculiar to a trade sector to which only one, or even neither, party belongs, provided that the expression or term concerned is one which is typical in that trade sector.

Illustrations

3.   A and B conclude a contract for the sale of a cargo of oil at US$ 20.5 per barrel. The parties subsequently disagree on the size of the barrel to which they had referred, A having intended a barrel of 42 standard gallons and B one of 36 Imperial gallons. In the absence of any indications to the contrary, A's understanding prevails, since in the international oil trade it is a usage to measure barrels in standard gallons. See Art. 4.3(f)

4.   A, a shipowner, concludes a charterparty agreement with B for the carriage of grain containing the standard term "whether in berth or not" with respect to the commencement of the lay-time of the ship after its reaching the port of destination. When it subsequently emerges that the parties attached different meanings to the term, preference should, in the absence of any indication to the contrary, be given to the meaning commonly attached to it in the shipping trade since the term is typical in the shipping trade. See Art. 4.3(e).

3. "Merger" clauses

Parties to international commercial transactions frequently include a provision indicating that the contract document completely embodies the terms on which they have agreed. For the effect of these so-called "merger" or "integration" clauses, in particular whether and to what extent they exclude the relevance of preliminary negotiations between the parties, albeit only for the purpose of the interpretation of the contract, see Art. 2.17.

ARTICLE 4.4

(Reference to contract or statement as a whole)

Terms and expressions shall be interpreted in the light of the whole contract or statement in which they appear.

COMMENT

1. Interpretation in the light of the whole contract or statement

Terms and expressions used by one or both parties are clearly not intended to operate in isolation but have to be seen as an integral part of their general context. In consequence they should be interpreted in the light of the whole contract or statement in which they appear.

Illustration

> A, a licensee, hears that, despite a provision in their contract granting A an exclusive licence, B, the licensor, has concluded a similar contract with C, one of A's competitors. A sends B a letter complaining of B's breach and ending with the words "your behaviour has clearly demonstrated that it was a mistake on our part to rely on your professional correctness. We hereby avoid the contract we have with you". Despite the use of the term "avoid", A's words interpreted in the light of the letter as a whole, must be understood as a notice of termination.

2. In principle no hierarchy among contract terms

In principle there is no hierarchy among contract terms, in the sense that their respective importance for the interpretation of the remaining part of the contract is the same regardless of the order in which they appear. There are, however, exceptions to this rule. First, declarations of intent made in the preamble may or may not be of relevance for the interpretation of the operative provisions of the contract. Secondly, it goes without saying that, in cases of conflict, provisions of a specific character prevail over provisions laying down more general rules. Finally, the parties may themselves expressly establish a hierarchy among the different provisions or parts of their contract. This is frequently the case with complex agreements consisting of different documents relating to the legal, economic and technical aspects of the transaction.

ARTICLE 4.5

(All terms to be given effect)

Contract terms shall be interpreted so as to give effect to all the terms rather than to deprive some of them of effect.

COMMENT

It is to be expected that when drafting their contract parties do not use words to no purpose. It is for this reason that this article lays down the rule that unclear contract terms should be interpreted so as to give effect to all the terms rather than to deprive some of them of effect. The rule however comes into play only if the terms in question remain unclear notwithstanding the application of the basic rules of interpretation laid down in Arts. 4.1 - 4.3.

Illustration

> A, a commercial television network, enters into an agreement with B, a film distributor, for the periodic supply of a certain number of films to be transmitted on A's network in the afternoon, when only those films that are admissible for all viewers may be transmitted. According to the contract the films submitted must "have passed the admission test" of the competent censorship commission. A dispute arises between A and B as to the meaning of this term. B maintains that it implies only that the films must have been released for circulation, even if they are X-rated, while A insists that they must have been classified as admissible for everybody. If it is not possible otherwise to establish the meaning to be attached to the term in question, A's understanding prevails since B's interpretation would deprive the provision of any effect.

ARTICLE 4.6

(Contra proferentem rule)

If contract terms supplied by one party are unclear, an interpretation against that party is preferred.

COMMENT

A party may be responsible for the formulation of a particular contract term, either because that party has drafted it or otherwise supplied it, for example, by using standard terms prepared by others. Such a party should bear the risk of possible lack of clarity of the formulation chosen. It is for this reason that the present article states that if contract terms supplied by one party are unclear, there is a preference for their interpretation against that party. The extent to which this rule applies will depend on the circumstances of the case; the less the contract term in question was the subject of further negotiations between the parties, the greater the justification for interpreting it against the party who included it in the contract.

Illustration

> A contract between A, a contractor, and B for the construction of an industrial plant contains a provision drafted by A and not discussed further stating that "[t]he Contractor shall be liable for and shall indemnify the Purchaser for all losses, expenses and claims in respect of any loss of or damage to physical property (other than the works), death or personal injury caused by negligence of the Contractor, its employees and agents". One of A's employees plays around with some of B's equipment after working hours and damages it. A denies liability, contending that the provision in question covers only cases where A's employees act within the scope of their employment. In the absence of any indication to the contrary, the provision will be interpreted in the manner which is less favourable to A, i.e. as also covering cases where his employees are not acting within the scope of their employment.

ARTICLE 4.7

(Linguistic discrepancies)

Where a contract is drawn up in two or more language versions which are equally authoritative there is, in case of discrepancy between the versions, a preference for the interpretation according to a version in which the contract was originally drawn up.

COMMENT

International commercial contracts are often drawn up in two or more language versions which may diverge on specific points. Sometimes the parties expressly indicate which version shall prevail. If all versions are equally authoritative the question arises of how possible discrepancies should be dealt with. The present article does not lay down a hard and fast rule, but merely indicates that preference should be given to the version in which the contract was originally drawn up or, should it have been drawn up in more than one original language version, to one of those versions.

Illustration

> 1. A and B, neither of them native English speakers, negotiate and draw up a contract in English before translating it into their respective languages. The parties agree that all three versions are equally authoritative. In case of divergencies between the texts, the English version will prevail unless circumstances indicate the contrary.

A situation where a different solution may be preferable could arise where the parties have contracted on the basis of internationally and widely known instruments such as INCOTERMS or the *Uniform Customs and Practices on Documentary Credits*. In case of divergencies between the different versions used by the parties it may be preferable to refer to yet another version if that version is much clearer than the ones used.

Illustration

> 2. A contract between a Mexican and a Swedish company drawn up in three equally authoritative versions, Spanish, Swedish and English, contains a reference to INCOTERMS 1990. If the French version of INCOTERMS is much clearer than the other three on a point in dispute, that version might be referred to.

ARTICLE **4.8**

(Supplying an omitted term)

(1) Where the parties to a contract have not agreed with respect to a term which is important for a determination of their rights and duties, a term which is appropriate in the circumstances shall be supplied.

(2) In determining what is an appropriate term regard shall be had, among other factors, to

(a) the intention of the parties;

(b) the nature and purpose of the contract;

(c) good faith and fair dealing;

(d) reasonableness.

COMMENT

1. Supplying of omitted terms and interpretation

Articles 4.1 - 4.7 deal with the interpretation of contracts in the strict sense, i.e. with the determination of the meaning which should be given to contract terms which are unclear. This article addresses a different though related issue, namely that of the supplying of omitted terms. Omitted terms or gaps occur when, after the conclusion of the contract, a question arises which the parties have not regulated in their contract at all, either because they preferred not to deal with it or simply because they did not foresee it.

2. When omitted terms are to be supplied

In many cases of omitted terms or gaps in the contract the Principles will themselves provide a solution to the issue. See, for example, Arts. 5.6, (Determination of quality of performance), 5.7 (Price determination), 6.1.1 (Time of performance), 6.1.4 (Order of performance), 6.1.6 (Place of performance) and 6.1.10 (Currency not expressed). See also, in general, Art. 5.2 on implied obligations. However, even when there are such suppletive, or "stop-gap", rules of a general character they may not be applicable in a given case because they would not provide a solution appropriate in the circumstances in view of the expectations of the parties or the special nature of the contract. This article then applies.

3. Criteria for the supplying of omitted terms

The terms supplied under the present article must be appropriate to the circumstances of the case. In order to determine what is appropriate, regard is first of all to be had to the intention of the parties as inferred from, among other factors, the terms expressly stated in the contract, prior negotiations or any conduct subsequent to the conclusion of the contract.

Illustration

> 1. The parties to a construction contract agree on a special interest rate to be paid by the purchaser in the event of delay in payment of the price. Before the beginning of the work, the parties decide to terminate the contract. When the constructor delays restitution of the advance payment the question arises of the applicable interest rate. In the absence of an express term in the contract dealing with this question, the circumstances may make it appropriate to apply the special interest rate agreed for delay in payment of the price by the purchaser also to delay in restitution by the constructor.

If the intention of the parties cannot be ascertained, the term to be supplied may be determined in accordance with the nature and purpose of the contract, and the principles of good faith and fair dealing and reasonableness.

Illustration

> 2. A distribution franchise agreement provides that the franchisee may not engage in any similar business for a year after the termination of the agreement. Although the agreement is silent on the territorial scope of this prohibition, it is, in view of the particular nature and purpose of a franchise agreement, appropriate that the prohibition be restricted to the territory where the franchisee had exploited the franchise.

CHAPTER 5

CONTENT

ARTICLE 5.1
(Express and implied obligations)

The contractual obligations of the parties may be express or implied.

COMMENT

This provision restates the widely accepted principle according to which the obligations of the parties are not necessarily limited to that which has been expressly stipulated in the contract. Other obligations may be implicit (see Art. 5.2, comments and illustrations).

Close links exist between this rule and some of the other provisions of the Principles. Thus Art. 5.1 is a direct corollary of the rule according to which "[e]ach party must act in accordance with good faith and fair dealing in international trade" (Art. 1.7). Insofar as the rules on interpretation (Chapter 4) provide criteria for filling lacunae (besides criteria for solving ambiguities), those rules may assist in determining the precise content of the contract and therefore in establishing the terms which must be considered as implied.

ARTICLE 5.2
(Implied obligations)

Implied obligations stem from
(a) the nature and purpose of the contract;
(b) practices established between the parties and usages;
(c) good faith and fair dealing;
(d) reasonableness.

COMMENT

Art. 5.2 describes the sources of implied obligations. Different reasons may account for the fact that they have not been expressly stated. The implied obligations may for example have been so obvious, given the nature or the purpose of the obligation, that the parties felt that the obligations "went without saying". Alternatively, they may already have been included in the practices established between the parties or prescribed by trade usages according to Art. 1.8. Yet again, they may be a consequence of the principles of good faith and fair dealing and reasonableness in contractual relations.

Illustrations

1. A rents a full computer network to B and installs it. The contract says nothing as to A's possible obligation to give B at least some basic information concerning the operation of the system. This may however be considered to be an implied obligation since it is obvious, and necessary for the accomplishment of the purpose of such a contract, that the provider of sophisticated goods should supply the other party with a minimum of information. See Art. 5.2(a).

2. A broker who has negotiated a charterparty claims the commission due. Although the brokerage contract is silent as to the time when the commission is due, the usages of the sector can provide an implied term according to which the commission is due, for example only when the hire is earned, or alternatively when the charterparty was signed, regardless of whether or not the hire will effectively be paid. See Art. 5.2(b).

3. A and B, who have entered into the negotiation of a co-operation agreement, conclude an agreement concerning a complex feasibility study, which will be most time-consuming for A. Long before the study is completed, B decides that it will not pursue the negotiation of the co-operation agreement. Even though nothing has been stipulated regarding such a situation, good faith requires B to notify A of its decision without delay. See Art. 5.2(c).

ARTICLE 5.3

(Co-operation between the parties)

Each party shall cooperate with the other party when such co-operation may reasonably be expected for the performance of that party's obligations.

COMMENT

A contract is not merely a meeting point for conflicting interests but must also, to a certain extent, be viewed as a common project in which each party must cooperate. This view is clearly related to the principle of good faith and fair dealing (Art. 1.7) which permeates the law of contract, as well as to the obligation to mitigate harm in the event of non-performance (Art. 7.4.8).

The duty of co-operation must of course be confined within certain limits (the provision refers to reasonable expectations), so as not to upset the allocation of duties in the performance of the contract. Although the principal concern of the provision is the duty not to hinder the other party's performance, there may also be circumstances which call for more active co-operation.

Illustrations

1. A, after contracting with B for the immediate delivery of a certain quantity of oil, buys all the available oil on the spot market from another source. Such conduct, which will hinder B in performing its obligation, is contrary to the duty of co-operation.

2. A, an art gallery in country X, buys a sixteenth century painting from B, a private collector in country Y. The painting may not be exported without a special authorisation and the contract requires B to apply for that permission. B, who has no experience of such formalities, encounters serious difficulties with the application whereas A is familiar with such procedures. In these circumstances, and notwithstanding the contractual provision, A can be expected to give at least some assistance to B.

ARTICLE 5.4

(Duty to achieve a specific result
Duty of best efforts)

(1) To the extent that an obligation of a party involves a duty to achieve a specific result, that party is bound to achieve that result.

(2) **To the extent that an obligation of a party involves a duty of best efforts in the performance of an activity, that party is bound to make such efforts as would be made by a reasonable person of the same kind in the same circumstances.**

COMMENT

1. Distinction between the duty to achieve a specific result and the duty of best efforts

The degree of diligence required of a party in the performance of an obligation varies considerably depending upon the nature of the obligation incurred. Sometimes a party is bound only by a duty of best efforts. That party must then exert the efforts that a reasonable person of the same kind would exert in the same circumstances, but does not guarantee the achievement of a specific result. In other cases, however, the obligation is more onerous and such a specific result is promised.

The distinction between a "duty to achieve a specific result" and a "duty of best efforts" corresponds to two frequent and typical degrees of severity in the assumption of a contractual obligation, although it does not encompass all possible situations.

Obligations of both types may coexist in the same contract. For instance, a firm that repairs a defective machine may be considered to be under a duty of best efforts concerning the quality of the repair work in general, and under a duty to achieve a specific result as regards the replacement of certain spare parts.

2. Distinction provides criteria for determining whether a party has performed its obligations

Taken together, the two paragraphs of this article provide judges and arbitrators with criteria by which correct performance can be evaluated. In the case of an obligation to achieve a specific result, a party is bound simply to achieve the promised result, failure to achieve which amounts in itself to non-performance, subject to the application of the force majeure provision (Art. 7.1.7). On the other hand, the assessment of non-performance of an obligation of best efforts calls for a less severe judgment, based on a comparison with the efforts a reasonable person of the same kind would have made in similar circumstances. This distinction signifies that more will be expected from a highly specialised firm selected for its expertise than from a less sophisticated partner.

Illustrations

1. A, a distributor, promises that it will reach a quota of 15,000 sales within a year in the contract zone. If at the end of the period A has sold only 13,000 items, it has clearly failed to perform its obligation. See Art. 5.4(1).

2. B, another distributor, promises "to use our best efforts to expand the sales of the product" in the contract zone, without any stipulation that it must reach a minimum quantity. This provision creates an obligation of best efforts; it obliges B to take all the steps that a reasonable person, placed in similar circumstances (nature of the product, characteristics of the market, importance and experience of the firm, presence of competitors, etc.) would take to promote the sales (advertising, visits to customers, proper service, etc.). B does not promise the specific result of selling a certain number of items per year, but does undertake to do all that can be expected of it when acting as a reasonable person. See Art. 5.4(2).

ARTICLE 5.5

(Determination of kind of duty involved)

In determining the extent to which an obligation of a party involves a duty of best efforts in the performance of an activity or a duty to achieve a specific result, regard shall be had, among other factors, to

(a) the way in which the obligation is expressed in the contract;

(b) the contractual price and other terms of the contract;

(c) the degree of risk normally involved in achieving the expected result;

(d) the ability of the other party to influence the performance of the obligation.

COMMENT

1. Criteria for determining the nature of the obligation

It is important to determine whether an obligation involves a duty to achieve a specific result or simply a duty of best efforts, as the obligation is more onerous in the former case. Such a determination may sometimes be difficult. This article therefore establishes criteria which may offer guidance to parties, judges and arbitrators, although the list is not exhaustive. The problems involved are frequently matters of interpretation.

2. Nature of the obligation as expressed by the contract

The way in which an obligation is expressed in the contract may often be of assistance in determining whether the parties intended to create a duty to achieve a specific result or a duty of best efforts.

Illustration

1.   A, a contractor, agrees to build storage facilities for B, who is most keen that the work be finished in an unusually short time. If A undertakes that "the work will be completed before 31 December", it assumes an obligation to achieve the specific result of meeting that deadline. If it merely undertakes "to try to complete the work before 31 December", its obligation involves a duty of best efforts to attempt to meet the deadline, but no guarantee that it will definitely be met. See Art. 5.5(a).

3. Price or other terms of the contract

The contractual price or other terms of the contract may also offer clues as to the nature of an obligation. An unusually high price or another particular non-monetary reciprocal obligation may indicate a duty to achieve a specific result in cases where a mere duty of best efforts would normally be assumed. Clauses linking payment of the price to the successful outcome of the operation, penalty clauses applicable if the result is not achieved and hardship clauses enabling a party to adapt the contract if circumstances make it too harsh to perform as initially agreed are other examples of contractual terms which may - in one way or another - assist in determining the nature of the obligation in question. See Art. 5.5(b).

4. Degree of risk in performance of an obligation

When a party's performance of an obligation normally involves a high degree of risk it is generally to be expected that that party does not intend to guarantee a result, and that the other party does not expect such a guarantee. The opposite conclusion will be drawn when the desired result can as a rule be achieved without any special difficulty. See Art. 5.5(c).

Illustrations

> 2. A space agency undertakes to put a telecommunication satellite into orbit, the rate of failure of past launchings having been 22%. The space agency cannot be expected to guarantee that the orbiting will be successful. The obligation is merely to observe the degree of diligence required for such launchings in view of the present state of technology.

> 3. A promises to deliver 20 tons of steel to B on 30 June. Such a relatively simple operation is subject to no special risk. A is committed to the specific result of delivering the required quantity of steel on the date specified and not merely to attempting to do so.

5. Influence of obligee over performance of an obligation

In some situations one party may have a degree of influence over the performance of the other party's obligations. This fact may transform into duties of best efforts obligations which might otherwise be characterised as duties to achieve specific results.

Illustration

> 4. A is prepared to provide B with the technical assistance necessary to apply a newly discovered chemical process, and it is agreed that B will send some of its engineers to attend training sessions organised by A. A cannot promise that the new process will be mastered by the other party, since that result depends in part on B's effectively sending its engineers to the training sessions, on those engineers' competence and on their attentiveness at the sessions. See Art. 5.5(d).

ARTICLE 5.6

(Determination of quality of performance)

Where the quality of performance is neither fixed by, nor determinable from, the contract a party is bound to render a performance of a quality that is reasonable and not less than average in the circumstances.

COMMENT

Standards have been set in Art. 5.4 concerning the exercise of "best efforts", but quality of performance is a wider problem addressed by Art. 5.6. If goods are to be supplied, or services rendered, it is not sufficient to supply those goods or to render those services; they must also be of a certain quality.

The contract will often be explicit as regards the quality due ("grade 1 oil"), or it will provide elements making that quality determinable. In other cases, the rule established by Art. 5.6 is that the quality must be "reasonable and not less than average in the circumstances". Two criteria are thus combined.

Illustration

> 1. A undertakes to build a hotel next to a busy railway station. The contract provides for "adequate sound isolation", the quality of which is not more precisely determined. It is, however, determinable from the contract that the sound isolation must meet the high standards needed in view of the hotel's proximity to a railway station.

1. Performance must be of average quality

The minimum requirement is that of providing goods of average quality. The supplier is not bound to provide goods or services of superior quality if that is not required by the contract, but neither may it deliver goods or services of inferior quality. This average quality is determined according to the circumstances, which normally means that which is available on the relevant market at the time of performance (there may for example have been a recent technological advance). Other factors may also be of relevance, such as the specific qualifications for which the performing party was chosen.

Illustration

> 2. A buys 500 kgs. of oranges from B. If the contract says nothing more precise, and no other circumstances call for a different solution, those oranges may not be of less than average quality. Average quality will however suffice unless it is unreasonably defective.

2. Performance must be reasonable

The additional reference to reasonableness is intended to prevent a party from claiming that it has performed adequately if it has rendered an "average" performance in a market where the average quality is most unsatisfactory and is intended to give the judge or arbitrator an opportunity to raise those insufficient standards.

Illustration

> 3. A company based in country X organises a banquet to celebrate its 50th anniversary. Since the cuisine in country X is mediocre, the company orders the meal from a renowned restaurant in Paris. In these circumstances the quality of the food provided must not be less than the average standards of the Parisian restaurant; it would clearly not be sufficient simply to meet the average standards of country X.

ARTICLE 5.7

(Price determination)

(1) Where a contract does not fix or make provision for determining the price, the parties are considered, in the absence of any indication to the contrary, to have made reference to the price generally charged at the time of the conclusion of the contract for such performance in comparable circumstances in the trade concerned or, if no such price is available, to a reasonable price.

(2) Where the price is to be determined by one party and that determination is manifestly unreasonable, a reasonable price shall be substituted notwithstanding any contract term to the contrary.

(3) Where the price is to be fixed by a third person, and that person cannot or will not do so, the price shall be a reasonable price.

(4) Where the price is to be fixed by reference to factors which do not exist or have ceased to exist or to be accessible, the nearest equivalent factor shall be treated as a substitute.

COMMENT

1. General rule governing price determination

A contract usually fixes the price to be paid, or makes provision for its determination. If however this is not the case, para. (1) of this article presumes that the parties have made reference to the price generally charged at the time of the conclusion of the contract for such performance in comparable circumstances in the trade concerned. All these qualifications are of course significant. The provision also permits the rebuttal of the presumption if there is any indication to the contrary.

This article is inspired by Art. 55 CISG. The rule has the necessary flexibility to meet the needs of international trade.

It is true that in some cases the price usually charged on the market may not satisfy the reasonableness test which prevails elsewhere in this article. Recourse would then have to be made to the general provision on good faith and fair dealing (Art. 1.7), or possibly to some of the provisions on mistake, fraud and gross disparity (Chapter 3).

Some international contracts relate to operations which are unique or at least very specific, in respect of which it is not possible to refer to the price charged for similar performance in comparable circumstances. According to para. (1) the parties are then deemed to have made reference to a reasonable price and the party in question will fix the price at a reasonable level, subject to the possible review by courts or arbitral tribunals.

Illustrations

1. A, a firm specialised in express mailing throughout the world, receives from B a parcel to be delivered as soon as possible from France to the United States. Nothing is said as to the price. A should bill B with the price usually charged in the sector for such a service.

2.   The next order which A receives from B is one to deliver another parcel as soon as possible to Antarctica where a team of explorers is in need of urgent supplies. Again, nothing is said as to price, but since no possible market comparison can be made A must act reasonably when fixing the price.

2. Determination of price by one party

In some cases the contract expressly provides that the price will be determined by one of the parties. This happens frequently in several sectors, for example the supply of services. The price cannot easily be determined in advance, and the performing party is in the best position to place a value on what it has done.

In those cases where the parties have made such a provision for determining the price, it will be enforced. To avoid possible abuses however, para. (2) enables judges or arbitrators to replace a manifestly unreasonable price by a reasonable one. This provision is mandatory.

3. Determination of price by third person

A provision that the price will be determined by a third person can give rise to serious difficulty if that third person is unable to accomplish the mission (not being the expert he or she was thought to be) or refuses to do so. Para. (3) provides that the price, possibly determined by judges or arbitrators, shall be reasonable. If the third person determines the price in circumstances that may involve fraud, gross disparity or threat, Art. 3.11(2) may apply.

4. Determination of price by reference to external factors

In some situations the price is to be fixed by reference to external factors, typically a published index, or quotations on a commodity exchange. In cases where the reference factor ceases to exist or to be accessible, para. (4) provides that the nearest equivalent factor shall be treated as a substitute.

Illustration

3.   The price of a construction contract is linked to several indexes, including the "official index of charges in the construction sector", regularly published by the local Government. Several instalments of the price still have to be calculated when that index ceases to be published. The Construction Federation, a private trade association, decides however to start publishing a similar index to replace the former one and in these circumstances the new index will serve as a substitute.

ARTICLE 5.8

(Contract for an indefinite period)

A contract for an indefinite period may be ended by either party by giving notice a reasonable time in advance.

COMMENT

The duration of a contract is often specified by an express provision, or it may be determined from the nature and purpose of the contract (e.g. technical expertise provided in order to assist in performing specialised work). However, there are cases when the duration is neither determined nor determinable. Parties can also stipulate that their contract is concluded for an indefinite period.

This article provides that in such cases either party may end the contractual relationship by giving notice a reasonable time in advance. What a reasonable time in advance will be will depend on circumstances such as the period of time the parties have been cooperating, the importance of their relative investments in the relationship, the time needed to find new partners, etc.

The rule can be understood as a gap-filling provision in cases where parties have failed to specify the duration of their contract. More generally, it also relates to the widely recognised principle that contracts may not bind the parties eternally and that they may always opt out of such contracts provided they give notice a reasonable time in advance.

This situation is to be distinguished from the case of hardship which is covered by Arts. 6.2.1 - 6.2.3. Hardship requires a fundamental change of the equilibrium of the contract, and gives rise, at least in the first instance, to renegotiations. The rule in Art. 5.8 requires no special condition to be met, except that the duration of the contract be indefinite and that it permit unilateral cancellation.

Illustration

A agrees to distribute B's products in country X. The contract is concluded for an indefinite period. Either party may cancel this arrangement unilaterally, provided that it gives the other party notice a reasonable time in advance.

CHAPTER 6

PERFORMANCE

SECTION 1: PERFORMANCE IN GENERAL

ARTICLE 6.1.1
(Time of performance)

A party must perform its obligations:

(a) if a time is fixed by or determinable from the contract, at that time;

(b) if a period of time is fixed by or determinable from the contract, at any time within that period unless circumstances indicate that the other party is to choose a time;

(c) in any other case, within a reasonable time after the conclusion of the contract.

COMMENT

With a view to determining when a contractual obligation is to be performed, this article, which is inspired by Art. 33 CISG, distinguishes three situations. The first is where the contract stipulates the precise time for performance or makes it determinable. If the contract does not specify a precise moment but a period of time for performing, any time during that period chosen by the performing party will be acceptable unless circumstances indicate that the other party is to choose the time. Finally, in all other cases, performance is due within a reasonable time.

Illustrations

1. A offers to advise B in the latter's plans to buy computer equipment and software, and it is agreed that A's experts will visit B "in May" It is in principle for A to announce when precisely in May that visit will take place. The circumstances may however

leave the option to B, as would be the case if the contract expressly left to B the choice of the precise dates, or where, for example, it was understood that some of B's staff who are often absent on business trips must be present when A's experts arrive. See Art. 6.1.1(b).

2.   A, a building contractor, encounters unusual difficulties when excavating a site, and needs special equipment to continue the work which it does not have. A immediately telephones B, another contractor, who has the necessary equipment and agrees to lend it to A. Nothing however is said as to when the equipment should be delivered to A. Performance is then to take place "within a reasonable time" in the circumstances. Since the work has been interrupted because of the above-mentioned difficulties, A urgently needs to receive the equipment and in such a case "within a reasonable time" probably means that performance is due almost immediately. See Art. 6.1.1(c).

ARTICLE 6.1.2

(Performance at one time or in instalments)

In cases under Article 6.1.1(b) or (c), a party must perform its obligations at one time if that performance can be rendered at one time and the circumstances do not indicate otherwise.

COMMENT

A party's performance is of necessity sometimes rendered at one time (e.g. delivery of a single object), or, alternatively, must take place over a period of time (e.g. construction). There are however also cases where it can be rendered either at one time or in instalments (e.g. delivery of quantities of goods). Art. 6.1.2 addresses the latter situation, in circumstances where there is no contractual provision as to how such performance should be rendered, or where it is not determinable from the contract. The principle stated is that performance is due at one time, unless the circumstances indicate otherwise.

Illustrations

1.   A promises to deliver 100 tons of coal to B "in March". It would be materially possible and perhaps convenient for A to deliver the 100 tons in instalments, for instance 25 tons each week

of the month. In principle however, according to Art. 6.1.2, A must deliver the 100 tons at one time.

2. The facts are the same as in Illustration 1, the difference being that B needs the coal gradually, to meet the needs of its operations. B also has limited storage facilities and could not cope adequately with a consignment of 100 tons at any one time. A knows of B's specific needs. Here the circumstances suggest that A should instead deliver in instalments during the month of March.

ARTICLE **6.1.3**

(Partial performance)

(1) The obligee may reject an offer to perform in part at the time performance is due, whether or not such offer is coupled with an assurance as to the balance of the performance, unless the obligee has no legitimate interest in so doing.

(2) Additional expenses caused to the obligee by partial performance are to be borne by the obligor without prejudice to any other remedy.

COMMENT

1. Partial performance distinguished from performance at one time or in instalments

The situation covered by Art. 6.1.3 should be distinguished from that of Art. 6.1.2.

The provision on "[p]erformance at one time or in instalments" attempts to solve a preliminary question which concerns only certain special cases. If a party's performance can be rendered at one time or in instalments and if the contract does not make it clear or determinable how that party is to perform, it must in principle perform at one time.

Art. 6.1.3 (Partial performance) has a more general scope. It provides that at the time performance is due the obligee may in principle reject an offer of partial performance. This applies at maturity, irrespective of whether what is due then is a global performance or an instalment of a wider obligation (which, in some cases, has been previously determined on the basis of Art. 6.1.2).

Illustration

> 1. A owes US$ 1,000,000 to a bank and it has been agreed that A will pay back US$ 100,000 on the first day of each month, starting in January. On 1 April A offers to reimburse only US$ 50,000, and the balance two weeks later. In principle, the bank is entitled to refuse A's proposal.

2. Obligee entitled in principle to reject partial performance

When performance is due at maturity (be it the whole performance or an instalment), that which is due must be performed completely. In principle, the obligee may reject an offer of partial performance, whether or not it is coupled with an assurance as to the balance of the performance, since it is entitled to receive the whole of what was stipulated. Subject to what will be said below, partial performance normally constitutes a breach of contract. A party who does not obtain full performance at maturity may resort to the available remedies. As a rule, the obligee has a legitimate interest in requiring full performance of what was promised at the time that performance is due.

The obligee may of course also refrain from rejecting the offer to perform in part, while reserving its rights as to the breach, or may accept it without any reservation, in which case partial performance can no longer be treated as a non-performance.

Illustration

> 2. A wishes to open a branch office in Brussels and rents the necessary office space in a building under construction, due to be finished in time for the move on 1 September. On that date, only four of the ten offices are made available for A, with an assurance that the remaining six will be ready in one month. In principle, A may refuse to move into those four offices.

3. Obligee's right to reject partial performance conditional on its legitimate interest in so doing

There may be situations where the obligee's legitimate interest in receiving full performance is not apparent and where temporary acceptance of partial performance will not cause any significant harm to the obligee. If the party tendering partial performance proves this to be the case, the obligee cannot then refuse such partial performance (subject to para. (2)), and there is no non-performance in such cases.

This may be seen as a consequence of the general principle of good faith and fair dealing enunciated in Art. 1.7.

Illustration

> 3. An airline promises to transport 10 automobiles from Italy to Brazil in one single consignment due to be delivered on a definite date. When performance is due, some circumstances make it difficult, although not impossible, for the airline to find sufficient space in a single aircraft. The airline suggests making two successive deliveries within a week. It is established that this will cause no inconvenience to the purchaser of the cars, which will not actually be used before the following month. In such a case the obligee has no legitimate interest in refusing partial performance.

4. Additional expenses entailed by partial performance to be borne by obligor

If partial performance is accepted, it may entail additional expenses for the obligee. In all cases, such expenses are to be borne by the other party. If partial performance amounts to a non-performance (as it usually does), these expenses will be part of the damages, without prejudice to any other available remedy. If partial performance does not amount to a non-performance (the obligee has been shown not to have any legitimate interest in rejecting the offer of partial performance, or has found the offer to be acceptable without reservation), it will only be entitled to those expenses.

Illustration

> 4. The facts are the same as in Illustration 3. If the purchaser has to meet additional expenses on account of having to make double arrangements for picking up the cars at the airport, those extra costs will be borne by the airline.

ARTICLE 6.1.4

(Order of performance)

(1) To the extent that the performances of the parties can be rendered simultaneously, the parties are bound to render them simultaneously unless the circumstances indicate otherwise.

(2) To the extent that the performance of only one party requires a period of time, that party is bound to render its performance first, unless the circumstances indicate otherwise.

COMMENT

In bilateral contracts, where both parties have obligations towards the other, the basic but complex question arises of which party is to perform first. If the parties have not made any specific arrangements, then in practice much will depend on usages and it must also be recalled that there are often several obligations on each side which may have to be performed at different times.

Art. 6.1.4 states two broad principles, while recognising that in both cases the circumstances may indicate otherwise. In effect, the main purpose of this article is to draw the parties' attention to the problem of order of performance, and to encourage them, where necessary, to draft appropriate contractual provisions.

A distinction is drawn between cases where the parties' performances can be rendered simultaneously and those where the performance of only one party requires a period of time.

1. Simultaneous performance to be made when possible

In the first situation, the rule is that the parties are bound to perform simultaneously (para. (1)). A seller is entitled to payment on delivery but circumstances may indicate otherwise, for example any exception originating from the terms of the contract or from usages which may allow a party to perform some time after the other.

Illustration

> 1. A and B agree to barter a certain quantity of oil against a certain quantity of cotton. Unless circumstances indicate otherwise, the commodities should be exchanged simultaneously.

2. Exception where performance requires a period of time

If the performance of only one party's obligation by its very nature requires a period of time, for example in construction and most service contracts, the rule established in para. (2) is that that party is bound to render its performance first. Circumstances may frequently however indicate the contrary. Thus, insurance premiums are normally paid in advance, as also are rent and freight charges. In construction contracts, payments are usually made in agreed instalments throughout the duration of the work.

Illustration

> 2. A promises to write a legal opinion to assist B in an arbitration. If no arrangement is made as to when A should be paid for the services, A must prepare the opinion before asking to be paid.

3. Relation of order of performance to withholding of performance

This article sets out the rules which will condition the application of Art. 7.1.3 concerning the withholding of performance.

ARTICLE 6.1.5

(Earlier performance)

(1) The obligee may reject an earlier performance unless it has no legitimate interest in so doing.

(2) Acceptance by a party of an earlier performance does not affect the time for the performance of its own obligations if that time has been fixed irrespective of the performance of the other party's obligations.

(3) Additional expenses caused to the obligee by earlier performance are to be borne by the obligor, without prejudice to any other remedy.

COMMENT

1. Obligee in principle entitled to reject earlier performance

When performance is due at a certain moment (to be determined in accordance with Art. 6.1.1), it must take place at that time and in principle the obligee may reject an earlier performance. Usually, the time set for performance is geared to the obligee's activities, and earlier performance may cause it inconvenience. The obligee has therefore a legitimate interest in refusing it. Earlier performance, in principle, constitutes non-performance of the contract.

The obligee may of course also abstain from rejecting an earlier performance while reserving its rights as to the non-performance. It may also accept such performance without reservation, in which case earlier performance can no longer be treated as non-performance.

Illustration

> 1.　A agrees to carry out the annual maintenance of all lifts in B's office building on 15 October. A's employees arrive on 14 October, a day on which important meetings, with many visitors, are taking place in the building. B is entitled to refuse such earlier performance which would cause it obvious inconvenience.

2. Obligee's right to reject earlier performance conditional on its legitimate interest in so doing

Situations may arise in which the obligee's legitimate interest in timely performance is not apparent and when its accepting earlier performance will not cause it any significant harm. If the party offering earlier performance proves this to be the case, the other party cannot reject earlier performance.

Illustration

> 2.　The facts are the same as in Illustration 1, the difference being that neither 14 nor 15 October has any special significance. A can probably prove that B has no legitimate interest in refusing the earlier performance.

3. Effect of acceptance by obligee on its own performance of earlier performance of the other party's obligations

If one party accepts earlier performance by the other, the question arises of whether this affects the time for performance of its own obligations. Para. (2) deals with cases where obligations are due at a certain time which is not linked to the performance of the other party's obligations; that time for performance remains unchanged.

This provision does not however deal with the converse case where the performances are linked in time. Several situations may then arise. This circumstance may in itself establish the obligee's legitimate interest in rejecting earlier performance. If earlier performance is thus rejected, the obligee's time of performance is unaffected. If earlier performance is accepted with all due reservations as to the non-performance involved, the obligee may also reserve its rights as to its time for performance. If earlier performance is acceptable to the obligee it may at the same time decide whether or not to accept the consequences as regards its own obligations.

Illustrations

> 3.   B undertakes to deliver goods to A on 15 May and A to pay the price on 30 June. B wishes to deliver the good. on 10 May and A has no legitimate interest in refusing such earlier performance. This will however have no effect on the time agreed for payment of the price, which was determined irrespective of the date of delivery.

> 4.   B undertakes to deliver goods to A on 15 May and A to pay the price "on delivery". If B tenders the goods on 10 May, A, depending on the circumstances, may reject such earlier performance, claiming that it is not in a position to pay at that date, take delivery of the goods subject to observing the original deadline for payment of the price, or decide to accept the goods and pay for them immediately.

4. Additional expenses entailed by earlier performance to be borne by the performing party

If earlier performance is accepted, it may entail additional expenses for the obligee. In all cases, such expenses are to be borne by the other party. If earlier performance amounts to non-performance (the normal case), those expenses will be part of the damages, without prejudice to any other remedy available. If earlier performance does not amount to non-performance (the obligee has been shown not to have any legitimate interest in rejecting the offer of earlier performance, or has found that offer to be acceptable without reservation), the obligee will only be entitled to those expenses.

Illustration

> 5.   A has no legitimate interest in refusing delivery of goods on 10 May instead of 15 May, but some additional storage fees are payable for those five extra days. Those costs will be borne by B.

ARTICLE **6.1.6**

(Place of performance)

(1) If the place of performance is neither fixed by, nor determinable from, the contract, a party is to perform:

(a) a monetary obligation, at the obligee's place of business;

(b) any other obligation, at its own place of business.

(2) A party must bear any increase in the expenses incidental to performance which is caused by a change in its place of business subsequent to the conclusion of the contract.

COMMENT

1. Place of performance fixed by, or determined from, the contract when possible

The place where an obligation is to be performed is often determined by an express term of the contract or is determinable from it. It is obvious, for instance, that an obligation to build must be performed on the construction site, and that an obligation to transport goods must be performed in accordance with the agreed route.

2. Need for suppletive rules

Rules are however needed to cover cases where the contract is silent on the matter and circumstances do not indicate where performance should take place. Art. 6.1.6(1) provides two solutions.

The general rule is that a party is to perform its obligations at its own place of business. The second rule is specific to monetary obligations where the converse solution applies, namely that the obligor is to perform its obligations at the obligee's place of business (subject to the application of Art. 6.1.8 concerning payments by funds transfers).

These solutions may not be the most satisfactory in all cases, but they do reflect the need for rules where the parties have not made any other arrangement or where the circumstances do not indicate otherwise.

Illustrations

1. A wishes some of its engineers to learn the language of country X, where they will be employed for some time. It agrees with B, a language school, for a series of intensive lessons. If nothing else is stipulated, the lessons are to take place at B's place of business. See Art. 6.1.6(1)(b)

2. The facts are the same as in Illustration 1. The language school sends its bill to A. The cost of the lessons must, in principle, be paid at B's place of business. See Art. 6.1.6(1)(a).

3. Consequences of change in a party's place of business subsequent to conclusion of contract

In view of the importance of the parties' respective places of business for the application of para. (1), it is necessary to cater for the situation where a party changes its location after the conclusion of the contract, a move which may involve additional expense for the performing party. The rule established in para. (2) is that each party must bear any such increase of expenses occasioned by a change in its place of business.

It is moreover possible that a party's move may entail other inconvenience for the other party. The obligation to act in good faith (Art. 1.7) and the duty to cooperate (Art. 5.3) will often impose on the moving party an obligation to inform the other party in due time so as to enable the latter to make such arrangements as may be necessary.

Illustrations

3.   A enters into a technical assistance agreement with B, under the terms of which A undertakes to train ten of B's engineers for a period of two months on A's premises. The engineers are to be accommodated at a local hotel which offers very reasonable rates on account of A's location in a rural area. After the agreement has been concluded, but before B's engineers arrive, A notifies B that it has moved to the capital city where hotel rates are much higher. Irrespective of whether the initial costs of accommodation were to be paid by A or by B, the additional costs will be borne by A.

4.   Each year on 3 May, A must pay royalties to B at B's place of business. B moves to another country, to which it takes some time (e.g. two months) for a payment to arrive. A formerly gave its bank the transfer order on or about 15 April, but from now on the order must be given towards the end of March at the latest if A wishes to avoid late payment. B is under a duty to inform A of its new place of business in sufficient time to permit A to make the necessary arrangements for payment and B will bear the additional costs.

ARTICLE 6.1.7

(Payment by cheque or other instrument)

(1) Payment may be made in any form used in the ordinary course of business at the place for payment.

(2) However, an obligee who accepts, either by virtue of paragraph (1) or voluntarily, a cheque, any other order to pay or a promise to pay, is presumed to do so only on condition that it will be honoured.

COMMENT

Discharge of monetary obligations is frequently made by cheques or similar instruments, or by transfers between financial institutions. The problems involved have however very seldom been the subject of codification, one notable exception being the *UNCITRAL Model Law on International Credit Transfers*. Without attempting to provide a detailed regulation, which would not be compatible with the very rapid evolution of techniques in this field, Arts. 6.1.7 and 6.1.8 establish some basic principles which should be of assistance in regard to international payments.

1. General rule regarding form of payment

Para. (1) allows for payment to be made in any form that is usual at the place for payment. Subject to the reservation contained in para. (2), the obligor may for instance pay in cash, by cheque, banker's draft, a bill of exchange, credit card, or in any other form such as the newly developing electronic means of payment, provided it chooses a mode that is usual at the place for payment, i.e. normally at the obligee's place of business. In principle, the obligee should be satisfied to receive payment in a form that is customary at its place of business.

Illustration

1.   A, an importer in Luxembourg, receives a bill for goods bought from B, a firm in Central America, and sends a eurocheque in payment. B may reject this mode of payment if the banks in its country are not familiar with eurocheques.

2. Presumption that payment will be honoured a condition for acceptance

Para. (2) states the generally recognised principle according to which the obligee's acceptance of an instrument that has to be honoured by a financial institution or another person (a third person or the obligor itself) is given only on condition that the instrument will actually be honoured.

The presumption can sometimes be overturned by usages. There are for instance countries where delivery of instruments such as certified cheques, banker's drafts and cashier's cheques is considered as being equivalent to payment by the obligor, with the consequence that the risk of the bank's insolvency is transferred to the obligee. In such countries, the rule in Art. 6.1.7(2) would apply only to so-called personal cheques.

Illustration

2.   A, a contractor, must pay B, a sub-contractor, for work completed by the latter on a building site. A is experiencing a cash-flow crisis as its client C is late in paying the first instalment due. C has however given A a set of promissory notes up to the amount of its debt. A offers to pay B by assigning a sufficient number of promissory notes. If B accepts them (in this case it probably does not have to do so as this is not a usual form of payment), the effectiveness of the payment by A to B is conditional on C's honouring the promissory notes at maturity.

ARTICLE 6.1.8

(Payment by funds transfer)

(1) Unless the obligee has indicated a particular account, payment may be made by a transfer to any of the financial institutions in which the obligee has made it known that it has an account.

(2) In case of payment by a transfer the obligation of the obligor is discharged when the transfer to the obligee's financial institution becomes effective.

COMMENT

1. Admissibility of funds transfers

Although the principle enunciated in Art. 6.1.6 that payment of a monetary obligation should be made at the obligee's place of business still stands, para. (1) of this article provides that it can also be made to one of the financial institutions in which the obligee has made it known that it keeps an account. If however the obligee has indicated a particular account, payment should then be made to that account. Naturally, the obligee can also make it known that it does not wish payment to be made by transfer.

Illustration

> 1. A, a shipyard established in Helsinki, repairs a ship belonging to B, a Swedish company, and the bill is sent on a letter-head that mentions a bank account in Finland and another in Sweden. Unless A states that payment has to be made to the Finnish account, or by a means other than a bank transfer, B is entitled to make payment to the Swedish account.

2. Time at which the obligor's obligation is discharged by a funds transfer

Para. (2) of this article deals with the difficult question of determining when a payment by funds transfer is to be considered as completed, i.e. when the obligor's obligation is discharged. This matter is of importance, for example when deciding whether a payment was made in time, or in the event of one of the banks not forwarding the funds it has received. The choice of a satisfactory solution has been the centre of considerable controversy in many countries and international fora. Various possible times have been suggested such as that of the debiting of the account of the transferor, the crediting to the account of the transferee bank, the notice of credit to that account, the decision of the transferee bank to accept a credit transfer, the entry of credit to the transferee's account, the notice of credit to the transferee, etc. The matter is further complicated by the changes in the procedures for the transfer of funds entailed by new electronic transfer mechanisms, while bank practices may also differ from one case to another.

This uncertainty makes it extremely difficult to establish a definite rule providing when payment by a transfer is completed. Para. (2) of this article nevertheless serves a useful purpose in that it states the basic principle which will permit the finding of a more precise rule in each case. Such a payment will be effective when the transfer to the obligee's financial institution becomes effective, a solution founded on the notion that the institution acts as the obligee's agent. This means that the payment will not be effective simply because an order has been given to the transferor's financial institution, and the transferor's account has been debited. However, payment is effective before the transferee is notified or credited with it by its financial institution although the precise moment at which payment to the obligee's financial institution can be considered as being effective will depend on banking practices in the case concerned.

Illustration

> 2.   A, a licensee, gives its bank, C, a transfer order for US$ 5,000, royalties due to B, a licensor, who has an account with Bank D. C debits A's account, but fails to forward the funds to D and becomes bankrupt. A has not effectively paid B.

ARTICLE **6.1.9**

(Currency of payment)

(1) If a monetary obligation is expressed in a currency other than that of the place for payment, it may be paid by the obligor in the currency of the place for payment unless

(a)   that currency is not freely convertible; or

(b) the parties have agreed that payment should be made only in the currency in which the monetary obligation is expressed.

(2) If it is impossible for the obligor to make payment in the currency in which the monetary obligation is expressed, the obligee may require payment in the currency of the place for payment, even in the case referred to in paragraph (1)(b).

(3) Payment in the currency of the place for payment is to be made according to the applicable rate of exchange prevailing there when payment is due.

(4) However, if the obligor has not paid at the time when payment is due, the obligee may require payment according to the applicable rate of exchange prevailing either when payment is due or at the time of actual payment.

COMMENT

Monetary obligations are usually expressed in a certain currency (currency of account), and payment must normally be made in the same currency. However, when the currency of the place for payment is different from the currency of account, paras. (1) and (2) of this article provide for those cases where the obligor may or must make payment in the former currency.

1. Monetary obligation expressed in currency different from that of place for payment

As a general rule, the obligor is given the alternative of paying in the currency of the place for payment, which may have definite practical advantages and, if that currency is freely convertible, this should cause no difficulty to the obligee.

If, however, the currency of the place for payment is not freely convertible, the rule does not apply. Parties may also exclude the application of the rule by agreeing that payment is to be made only in the currency in which the monetary obligation is expressed (*effectivo* clause). If it has an interest in the payment actually being made in the currency of account, the obligee should specify this in the contract.

Illustrations

1. A French firm receives an order for machinery from a Brazilian buyer, the price being expressed in United States dollars. According to Art. 6.1.6, payment of that monetary obligation must in principle be made at the obligee's place of business, i.e. France. If the Brazilian firm finds it more convenient, it may pay the price in French francs. See Art. 6.1.9(1).

2. The same French firm frequently needs to buy from United States sources certain parts to be included in the machines, and has stipulated that the Brazilian buyer should pay only in dollars. In this case, payment may only be made in dollars. See Art. 6.1.9(1)(b).

3. The same French firm has a plant in country X, where the machines will be assembled. The contract provides that the Brazilian buyer has to pay the price to the firm's subsidiary in country X. Since the currency of country X is not convertible, payment may only be made in dollars. See Art. 6.1.9(1)(a).

2. Impossibility for obligor to make payment in currency in which obligation is expressed

In some instances, the obligor may find it impossible to make payment in the currency in which the obligation was expressed. This may be the result of the application of exchange regulations or other mandatory rules, or due to any other cause preventing the obligor from obtaining that currency in sufficient quantity. Para. (2) gives the obligee the option of requiring payment in the currency of the place for payment, even if the contract contains an *effectivo* clause. This is an additional option open to the obligee who may find it acceptable or even advantageous in the circumstances. It does not preclude the exercise of any available remedy in the event of the obligor's inability to pay in the currency of account amounting to a non-performance of the contract (e.g. damages).

Illustration

4. A, a Swiss bank, lends US$ 1,000,000 to B, to be reimbursed in Lugano. At maturity, B is unable to find the necessary dollars. A, which knows that B has deposits in Swiss francs with another local bank, may require payment in Swiss francs, even though the loan agreement stipulated that reimbursement was to be made only in United States dollars. See Art. 6.1.9(2).

3. Determination of applicable rate of exchange

Paras. (3) and (4) deal with the problem of the determination of the rate of exchange to be chosen when payment is made in the currency of the place for payment rather than in a different currency stipulated in the contract. This may occur when the obligor avails itself of para. (1), or the obligee the provisions of para. (2).

Two widely accepted solutions are offered. In normal cases, the rate of exchange is that prevailing when payment is due. If, however, the obligor is in default, the obligee is given an option between the rate of exchange prevailing when payment was due or the rate at the time of actual payment.

The double reference to the "applicable" rate is justified by the fact that there may be different rates of exchange depending on the nature of the operation.

Illustration

> 5. The facts are the same as in Illustration 4. A chooses to be reimbursed in Swiss francs and payment, which was due on 10 April, actually takes place on 15 September. The rate of exchange on 10 April was Sfrs. 2 to US$ 1. By 15 September it has become Sfrs. 2,15 to US$ 1. A is entitled to apply the latter rate. If the dollar had depreciated rather than increased in value, A would have chosen the rate applicable on 10 April.

ARTICLE 6.1.10

(Currency not expressed)

Where a monetary obligation is not expressed in a particular currency, payment must be made in the currency of the place where payment is to be made.

COMMENT

Determining the currency of payment gives rise to a special problem if the contract does not state the currency in which a monetary obligation is due. Although such cases may be infrequent, they do exist; a contract may for example state that the price will be the "current price", or that it will be determined by a third person, or that some expenses or costs will be reimbursed by one party to the other, without specifying in which currency those sums are due. The rule laid down in Art. 6.1.10 is that in such situations payment must be made in the currency of the place where payment is to be made.

Article 6.1.10 is not concerned with the currency in which damages are to be assessed, a matter dealt with in Art. 7.4.12 in the context of non-performance.

Illustration

> A Dutch client, A, instructs its broker, B, to buy shares on the Frankfurt stock exchange. If B pays for them in German marks, should A be billed in marks or in Dutch guilders? If A is to pay B in Amsterdam, it will pay in guilders.

ARTICLE 6.1.11

(Costs of performance)

Each party shall bear the costs of performance of its obligations.

COMMENT

The performance of obligations often entails costs, which may be of different kinds: transportation costs in delivering goods, bank commission in making a monetary transfer, fees to be paid when applying for a permission, etc. In principle, such costs are to be borne by the performing party.

Other arrangements may of course be made by the parties and there is nothing to prevent the performing party from including those costs in advance in the price it quotes. The rule set out in Art. 6.1.11 applies in the absence of such arrangements.

The provision states who shall bear the costs, not who shall pay them. Usually, it will be the same party, but there may be different situations, for example where tax regulations place the burden of payment on a specific party; in such cases, if the person who has to pay is different from the person who must bear the costs under Art. 6.1.11, the latter must reimburse the former.

Illustration

> A, a consultant, agrees to send five experts to perform an audit of B's firm. Nothing is said concerning the experts' travel expenses, and A does not take those costs into account when determining its fees. A may not add the travel expenses to the bill.

ARTICLE 6.1.12

(Imputation of payments)

(1) An obligor owing several monetary obligations to the same obligee may specify at the time of payment the debt to which it intends the payment to be applied. However, the payment discharges first any expenses, then interest due and finally the principal.

(2) If the obligor makes no such specification, the obligee may, within a reasonable time after payment, declare to the obligor the obligation to which it imputes the payment, provided that the obligation is due and undisputed.

(3) In the absence of imputation under paragraphs (1) or (2), payment is imputed to that obligation which satisfies one of the following criteria in the order indicated:

(a) an obligation which is due or which is the first to fall due;

(b) the obligation for which the obligee has least security;

(c) the obligation which is the most burdensome for the obligor;

(d) the obligation which has arisen first.

If none of the preceding criteria applies, payment is imputed to all the obligations proportionally.

COMMENT

Arts. 6.1.12 and 6.1.13 deal with the classic problem of imputation of payments. If an obligor owes several monetary obligations at the same time to the same obligee and makes a payment the amount of which is not sufficient to discharge all those debts, the question arises of the debts to which that payment applies.

Art. 6.1.12, which is inspired by widely recognised principles, offers the obligor the possibility of imputing its payment to a particular debt, provided that any expenses and interest due are discharged before the principal. In the absence of any imputation by the obligor, this provision enables the obligee to impute the payment received, although not to a disputed debt. Para. (3) lays down criteria which will govern in the absence of any imputation by either party.

Illustration

A receives under separate contracts three loans, each of US$ 100,000, from bank B payment of which is due on 31 December. B receives US$ 100,000 from A on 2 January with the imprecise message: "Reimbursement of the loan". B pays little attention to the matter and at first does not react, but three months later sues A for payment of the remaining US$ 200,000 and the parties disagree as to which of the loans had been reimbursed by the January payment. B had similar security in each case, but the interest rates were not the same: 8% on the first loan, 8,50% on the second and 9% on the third. The January payment will be imputed to the third loan.

ARTICLE 6.1.13

(Imputation of non-monetary obligations)

Article 6.1.12 applies with appropriate adaptations to the imputation of performance of non-monetary obligations.

COMMENT

The problem of imputation of payments normally concerns monetary obligations, but similar difficulties may sometimes occur in relation to obligations of a different nature. Art. 6.1.13 provides that the rules governing monetary obligations will apply, with appropriate adaptations to these cases also.

Illustration

A is performing construction work on several sites in an African country and, through five separate and successive contracts with B, purchases different quantities of cement, all to be delivered in Antwerp on the same date and to be loaded on the same ship. The contracts are similar, except that the third and fifth contracts stipulate very high liquidated damages in the event of late delivery. On account of certain difficulties, B can only deliver part of what it was supposed to. Upon delivery B is entitled to specify that the quantities delivered are to be imputed to the third and fifth contracts.

ARTICLE 6.1.14

(Application for public permission)

Where the law of a State requires a public permission affecting the validity of the contract or its performance and neither that law nor the circumstances indicate otherwise

(a) if only one party has its place of business in that State, that party shall take the measures necessary to obtain the permission;

(b) in any other case the party whose performance requires permission shall take the necessary measures.

COMMENT

If the validity or the performance of a contract is subject to compliance with public permission requirements, several issues arise as to who has the burden of filing the application (Art. 6.1.14), the time for filing (Art. 6.1.15), the legal consequences of failure to obtain an administrative decision in due time (Art. 6.1.16) and the rejection of the application (Art. 6.1.17)

1. Scope of the permission requirement

The Principles do not deal with the relevance of public permission requirements. What kind of public permission is required, if any, is to be determined under the applicable law, including the rules of private international law.

National courts tend to give effect only to the public permission requirements of the *lex fori*, and sometimes to those prescribed by the *lex contractus*. Arbitral tribunals may enjoy wider discretion than national courts in deciding which public permissions are relevant to the contract.

Under Art. 7(2) of the 1980 Rome Convention and other conflict of laws rules, public permission requirements of the law of other jurisdictions connected with the contract may also come into play. Long-arm statutes in some jurisdictions may also impose public permission requirements on licensees or subsidiaries of companies located a road. This article assumes that the requirements prescribed by the applicable law are to be observed.

a. *Broad notion of "public permission"*

The term "public permission" is to be given a broad interpretation. It includes all permission requirements established pursuant to a concern of a public nature, such as health, safety, or particular trade policies. It is irrelevant whether a required licence or permit is to be granted by a governmental or by a non-governmental institution to which Governments have delegated public authority for a specific purpose. Thus, the authorisation of payments by a private bank pursuant to foreign exchange regulations is in the nature of a "public permission" for the purposes of this article.

b. *Timing of public permission*

The provisions on public permissions refer primarily to those required by the applicable law or by a regulation in force at the time of the conclusion of the contract. However, these provisions may also apply to public permissions that may be introduced after the conclusion of the contract.

c. *Public permission may affect the contract in whole or in part*

The provisions on public permissions apply both to those requirements affecting the contract as a whole and to those merely affecting individual terms of the contract. However, where the legal consequences of failing to obtain a public permission differ according to whether such permission affects the contract in whole or in part, different rules are established. See Arts. 6.1.16 (2) and 6.1.17.

d. *Public permission may affect the validity or performance of a contract*

The absence of the required permission may affect the validity of a contract or render its performance impossible. Notwithstanding differences in the legal consequences of failing to obtain a required public permission, the problems raised in connection with the application for, or the obtaining of, a public permission are the same. As to the further consequences, Art. 6.1.17(2) provides that the rules on non-performance apply to a situation where the refusal of a permission makes the performance of a contract impossible in whole or in part.

2. Duty to inform of the existence of a public permission requirement

There is as a rule no duty to provide information concerning the requirement to obtain a public permission. However, the existence of such a requirement must be disclosed by the party upon whom rests the burden of obtaining a public permission when such permission is required under rules which are not generally accessible. Thus, the overriding principle of good faith (Art. 1.7) may require the party whose place of business is located in the State requiring a public permission to inform the other party of the existence of that requirement. Failure to do so may lead a court to disregard the permission requirement altogether or to conclude that the party who failed to communicate the existence of the requirement implicitly guaranteed that it would be obtained.

3. Which party is bound to take measures to obtain a public permission

a. *Party with place of business in State requiring public permission*

The rule set out in sub-para. (a) of this article which places the burden to apply on the party who has its place of business in the State which requires the relevant public permission reflects current international trade practices. It is that party who is in the best position to apply promptly for a public permission, since it is probably more familiar with the application requirements and procedures.

If a party needs further information from the other to file an application (e.g. information relating to the final destination of the goods, or information as to the purpose or subject matter of the contract), the other party must furnish such information pursuant to the duty of co-operation (Art. 5.3). Should that party not furnish such information it may not rely on the obligation of the first party. This duty to cooperate with the other party applies even if the contract stipulates that one of the parties bears the burden of applying for a public permission. Thus, if the parties have incorporated in their contract the term "ex works", which imposes far-reaching obligations on the buyer, the seller is nevertheless bound to provide the buyer, "at the latter's request, risk and expense, every assistance in obtaining any export licence or other official authorisation necessary for the exportation of the goods" (INCOTERMS 1990, A 2, see also B 2).

b. *Party whose performance requires public permission*

Sub-para. (b) of this article contemplates those cases where none of the parties has a place of business in the State requiring the permission. It also envisions a contract which is truly international notwithstanding the fact that both parties have their places of business in that State. In either case, the party whose performance requires the public permission is bound to take the necessary measures to obtain such a permission.

Illustration

> 1.   A, a contractor whose place of business is located in country
> X, sells a plant on a turn-key basis to B, whose place of business is
> located in country Y. Acceptance is to take place after performance
> tests in country Y. On the one hand, A has to apply for all public
> permissions required in country X, as well as for permissions in
> third countries (transit, sub-deliveries). On the other, B has to
> apply for import licences, as well as for all other permissions
> relating to the site, the use of local services, and the technology
> imported into country Y. A is also bound to furnish the information
> and documentation needed by B to obtain import licences and other
> permissions related to B's performance. A is not responsible for
> applying for public permissions in country Y, unless this is agreed
> in the contract or is required, explicitly or implicitly, by the
> applicable law or the circumstances of the case (e.g. the applicable
> law may require certain technical permits in country Y to be
> applied for by the licensor).

c. *Suppletory nature of provisions on public permissions*

The purpose of this article is to determine the party who must apply
for a public permission in those cases where it is not clear who is to
bear that burden. It is a suppletory rule to be applied when neither the
contract, nor the law requiring the permission or the circumstances
specify which party is under an obligation to apply for the required
public permission.

Illustration

> 2.   The law of country X subordinates the granting of an export
> licence for computers to a sworn declaration indicating the country
> where the computers will ultimately be sent. However, neither the
> contract nor the law of country X indicates which party bears the
> burden of applying for a licence. Since it is reasonable to suppose
> that only the buyer knows what it plans to do with the computers,
> the policy behind the rule imposing the permission requirement
> leads to the conclusion that it is the buyer who has to file the
> application.

4. Nature of obligation to take the "necessary measures"

The party who has to apply for the permission must take the
"necessary measures" to obtain such permission, but is not responsible
for the outcome of the application. That party is bound to exhaust
available local remedies to obtain the permission, provided that they

have a good chance of success and that resorting to local remedies appears reasonable in view of the circumstances of the case (e.g. the value of the transaction, time constraints).

Which measures have to be taken depends on the relevant regulations and the procedural mechanisms available in the State where the permission is to be granted. The obligation is in the nature of an obligation of best efforts (see Art. 5.4(2)).

Illustration

3.   A, a principal whose place of business is in country X, enters into a contract with B, a self-employed agent, whose place of business is in country Y. B, who has no authority to conclude contracts, is to represent A in countries Y and Z. Among other duties, B must exhibit A's goods at a fair which is to take place in country Z. B must apply for all permissions which are required to undertake these professional activities in countries Y and Z. B's duty to take "necessary measures" includes that of applying for public permissions required to import A's goods temporarily into countries Y and Z, as well as any other public permission that would enable B to participate in the fair. However, unless otherwise agreed, B is not required to apply for public permissions required for goods imported through B by customers located in countries Y and Z.

ARTICLE 6.1.15

(Procedure in applying for permission)

(1) The party required to take the measures necessary to obtain the permission shall do so without undue delay and shall bear any expenses incurred.

(2) That party shall whenever appropriate give the other party notice of the grant or refusal of such permission without undue delay.

COMMENT

1. Time for filing an application

The party under an obligation to obtain a public permission must take action immediately after the conclusion of the contract and pursue this action as necessary under the circumstances.

2. Expenses

According to Art. 6.1.11, each party shall bear the costs of performance of its obligations. This rule has been restated in para. (1) of the present article for the sake of clarity.

3. Duty to give prompt notice of the grant or refusal of the permission

The parties to the contract need to know as soon as possible whether the permission can be obtained. Accordingly, para. (2) of this article provides that the party required to take the necessary measures must inform the other of the outcome of the application. This duty of information extends to other relevant facts, such as for example the timing and outcome of the application, whether a refusal is subject to appeal and whether an appeal is to be lodged.

4. Duty to give notice "whenever appropriate"

The "appropriateness" of giving notice of the grant or refusal refers to the need to give notice and the manner of providing it. The necessity of giving notice obviously exists where such notice is required by law, but may also be inferred from the mere fact that a permission requirement is referred to in the contract.

The "appropriateness" of the duty to give notice is also related to the relevance of the information to be provided. Accordingly, the applying party is not bound to inform the other party of the outcome of that application in cases where the latter party obtains the information from the granting authority, or where applications for permissions are regularly granted. The fact that the permission is, contrary to normal practice, refused in a given case makes the obligation to inform more compelling.

This article does not establish particular requirements concerning the formalities relating to the communication. See Art. 1.9.

5. Consequences of the failure to inform

Failure to provide information regarding the grant or refusal of the permission amounts to non-performance. Accordingly, the general consequences of non-performance, as set forth in Chapter 7, apply. The duty to give notice of the grant of the public permission is a contractual obligation arising at the time the contract comes into existence. The duty to give notice of the refusal of the permission is part of the duty to take the "necessary measures" to obtain the permission under Art. 6.1.14 (see comment 4).

Illustrations

1. A, whose place of business is in country X, and B, a contractor, enter into a contract for the construction of a plant in country X. The parties agree that B is not bound to begin the construction and A's advance payments are not due until the grant of a permission by the authorities of country X.

A applies for and obtains the permission but fails to inform B that the permission has been granted. Two months later, B learns through inquiries with the authorities of country X that the permission has been granted and begins work on the construction of the plant.

Although the parties had agreed that their performances were due as of the time of the granting of the permission, A's failure to inform B that the permission has been granted precludes A from relying on B's failure to perform as of that date (see Art. 7.1.2). Thus, the contractual period begins to run for B as from when it learns of the granting of the permission.

Moreover, B may also claim damages if it is able to establish, for example, damage resulting from failure to use its production capacity, additional costs arising from storing raw materials during that two-month period, etc. (see Art. 7.4.1 *et seq.*). A, who from the very beginning had notice of the grant of the permission, must observe the original date of its performance, as provided for in the contract. If A fails to make an advance payment due four weeks after the granting of the permission, A must pay interest as from that date.

2. The facts are the same as in Illustration 1, the difference being that the proper authority simultaneously informs A and B that the permission has been granted. B may not avail itself of A's failure to inform in order to postpone its performance, nor is it entitled to damages for A's failure to inform.

ARTICLE **6.1.16**

(Permission neither granted nor refused)

(1) If, notwithstanding the fact that the party responsible has taken all measures required, permission is neither granted nor refused within an agreed period or, where no period has been agreed, within a reasonable time from the conclusion of the contract, either party is entitled to terminate the contract.

(2) Where the permission affects some terms only, paragraph (1) does not apply if, having regard to the circumstances, it is reasonable to uphold the remaining contract even if the permission is refused.

COMMENT

Whereas Arts. 6.1.14 and 6.1.15 are concerned with the duties of the contracting parties, Arts. 6.1.16 and 6.1.17 deal with the legal consequences in cases respectively where there has been no decision on the application within a given period or where the public permission has been refused.

1. No decision taken as regards the permission

Para. (1) of the present article deals with the "nothing happens" situation, that is to say a situation where permission has neither been granted nor refused within the agreed period or, where no period has been agreed, within a reasonable time from the conclusion of the contract. The reasons for the absence of a pronouncement may vary, for example the slow pace of processing the application, a pending appeal, etc. In any event there is no longer any reason to keep the parties waiting and either party is entitled to terminate the contract.

2. Termination of the contract

Remedies other than termination may be appropriate depending on the legal role played by the permission in the creation of the contractual obligations. This is in particular the case where the granting of the public permission is a condition for the validity of the contract, since in the absence of the permission either party may simply disregard the contract. The reason why this article provides also in these cases for the termination of the contract is that the parties are, with a view to obtaining the permission, under a number of obligations which cannot be allowed to exist indefinitely.

The entitlement of the party responsible for obtaining the permission to terminate the contract under this article is conditional on that party's having taken "the necessary measures" to that effect.

Illustration

> 1.   A, situated in country X, sells rifles to B for resale by B in the hunting season starting in four months. The validity of the sale is subject to a public permission to be granted by the authorities of country X. No period is agreed for obtaining that permission. Notwithstanding the fact that A takes all the necessary measures to obtain the permission, after three months no decision has yet been taken on A's application. Either party may terminate the contract.

The termination envisaged under this article has no consequences for the expenses so far incurred by the parties for the purpose of obtaining the permission. The expenses will be borne by the party who has assumed the risk of not obtaining the permission.

3. Permission affecting individual terms only

Where the permission affects some terms only of the contract, para. (2) of this article excludes the right of termination in cases where, even if the permission had been refused, it would according to Art. 6.1.17(1) nevertheless be reasonable to uphold the contract.

Illustration

> 2.   A, situated in country X, enters into a contract with B, containing a penalty clause for delay, the validity of which is subject to a public permission to be granted by the authorities of country X. Notwithstanding the fact that A takes all the necessary measures to obtain the permission, time continues to pass without any decision being taken. It would be reasonable in the circumstances to uphold the contract. Even if the permission were to have been refused, neither party may terminate the contract.

ARTICLE **6.1.17**

(Permission refused)

(1) The refusal of a permission affecting the validity of the contract renders the contract void. If the refusal affects the validity of some terms only, only such terms are void if, having regard to the circumstances, it is reasonable to uphold the remaining contract.

(2) Where the refusal of a permission renders the performance of the contract impossible in whole or in part, the rules on non-performance apply.

COMMENT

1. Application for permission rejected

This article contemplates the situation where the application for a permission is expressly refused. The nature of the obligation imposed on the responsible party with respect to the application for the permission is such that a refusal under this article is one which is not subject to an appeal which has a reasonable prospect of success. See comment 4 on Art. 6.1.14. Moreover, means of recourse against the refusal need not be exhausted whenever a final decision on the permission would be taken only after the time at which the contract could meaningfully be performed.

2. Legal consequences of a refusal of permission

The consequences of a refusal to grant the permission vary depending on whether the permission affects the validity of the contract or its performance.

a. *Refusal of permission affecting validity of the contract*

Where the permission affects the validity of the whole contract, a refusal renders the whole contract void, i.e. the contract is considered as never having come into being.

Illustration

1.   A, situated in country X, enters into a contract with B, the validity of which is subject to a public permission to be granted by the authorities of country X. Notwithstanding the fact that A takes

all the necessary measures to obtain the permission, A's application is refused. The contract is considered never to have come into existence.

Where, on the other hand, a refusal affects the validity of some terms only of the contract, only such terms are void, while the remaining part of the contract may be upheld provided that such a result is reasonable in the circumstances.

Illustration

2. A, situated in country X, enters into a contract with B, containing a penalty clause for delay, the validity of which is subject to a public permission to be granted by the authorities of country X. Notwithstanding the fact that A takes all the necessary measures to obtain the permission, A's application is refused. If it is reasonable in the circumstances, the contract will be upheld without the penalty clause.

b. *Refusal rendering performance of the contract impossible*

If the refusal of the permission renders the performance impossible in whole or in part, para. (2) of this article refers to the rules on non-performance embodied in Chapter 7.

Illustration

3. Under a contract entered into with B, A owes B US$ 100,000. The transfer of the sum from country X, where A is situated, to B's bank account in country Y is subject to a permission by the Central Bank of country X. Notwithstanding the fact that A takes all the necessary measures to obtain the permission, A's application is refused. The refusal of the permission renders it impossible for A to pay B. The consequences of A's non-performance are determined in accordance with the provisions of Chapter 7.

The refusal of the permission may render impossible the performance of a party only in the State imposing the permission requirement, while it may be possible for that party to perform the same obligation elsewhere. In such cases the general principle of good faith (see Art. 1.7) will prevent that party from relying on the refusal of the permission as an excuse for non-performance.

Illustration

4. The facts are the same as in Illustration 3, the difference being that A has in country Z, where no such permission requirement exists, sufficient funds to pay B. A may not rely on the refusal of the permission by the authorities of country X as an excuse for not paying B.

SECTION 2: HARDSHIP

ARTICLE 6.2.1

(Contract to be observed)

Where the performance of a contract becomes more onerous for one of the parties, that party is nevertheless bound to perform its obligations subject to the following provisions on hardship.

COMMENT

1. Binding character of the contract the general rule

The purpose of this article is to make it clear that as a consequence of the general principle of the binding character of the contract (see Art. 1.3) performance must be rendered as long as it is possible and regardless of the burden it may impose on the performing party. In other words, even if a party experiences heavy losses instead of the expected profits or the performance has become meaningless for that party the terms of the contract must nevertheless be respected.

Illustration

> In January 1990 A, a forwarding agent, enters into a two-year shipping contract with B, a carrier. Under the contract B is bound to ship certain goods from Hamburg to New York at a fixed price, on a monthly basis throughout the two-year period. Alleging a substantial increase in the price of fuel in the aftermath of the 1990 Gulf crisis, B requests a five per cent increase in the rate for August 1990. B is not entitled to such an increase because B bears the risk of its performance becoming more onerous.

2. Change in circumstances relevant only in exceptional cases

The principle of the binding character of the contract is not however an absolute one. When supervening circumstances are such that they lead to a fundamental alteration of the equilibrium of the contract, they create an exceptional situation referred to in these Principles as "hardship" and dealt with in the following articles of this section.

The phenomenon of hardship has been acknowledged by various legal systems under the guise of other concepts such as frustration of purpose, *Wegfall der Geschäftsgrundlage, imprévision, eccessiva onerosità sopravvenuta*, etc. The term "hardship" was chosen because it is widely known in international trade practice as confirmed by the inclusion in many international contracts of so-called "hardship clauses".

ARTICLE 6.2.2

(Definition of hardship)

There is hardship where the occurrence of events fundamentally alters the equilibrium of the contract either because the cost of a party's performance has increased or because the value of the performance a party receives has diminished, and

(a) the events occur or become known to the disadvantaged party after the conclusion of the contract;

(b) the events could not reasonably have been taken into account by the disadvantaged party at the time of the conclusion of the contract;

(c) the events are beyond the control of the disadvantaged party; and

(d) the risk of the events was not assumed by the disadvantaged party.

COMMENT

1. Hardship defined

This article defines hardship as a situation where the occurrence of events fundamentally alters the equilibrium of the contract, provided that those events meet the requirements which are laid down in sub-paras. (a) to (d).

2. Fundamental alteration of equilibrium of the contract

Since the general principle is that a change in circumstances does not affect the obligation to perform (see Art. 6.2.1), it follows that hardship may not be invoked unless the alteration of the equilibrium of the contract is fundamental. Whether an alteration is "fundamental" in a given case will of course depend upon the circumstances. If, however, the performances are capable of precise measurement in monetary terms, an alteration amounting to 50% or more of the cost or the value of the performance is likely to amount to a "fundamental" alteration.

Illustration

1.   In September 1989 A, a dealer in electronic goods situated in the former German Democratic Republic, purchases stocks from B, situated in country X, also a former socialist country. The goods are to be delivered by B in December 1990. In November 1990, A informs B that the goods are no longer of any use to it, claiming that after the unification of the German Democratic Republic and the Federal Republic of Germany there is no longer any market for such goods imported from country X. Unless the circumstances indicate otherwise, A is entitled to invoke hardship.

a. *Increase in cost of performance*

In practice a fundamental alteration in the equilibrium of the contract may manifest itself in two different but related ways. The first is characterised by a substantial increase in the cost for one party of performing its obligation. This party will normally be the one who is to perform the non-monetary obligation. The substantial increase in the cost may, for instance, be due to a dramatic rise in the price of the raw materials necessary for the production of the goods or the rendering of the services, or to the introduction of new safety regulations requiring far more expensive production procedures.

b. *Decrease in value of the performance received by one party*

The second manifestation of hardship is characterised by a substantial decrease in the value of the performance received by one party, including cases where the performance no longer has any value at all for the receiving party. The performance may be that either of a monetary or of a non-monetary obligation. The substantial decrease in the value or the total loss of any value of the performance may be due either to drastic changes in market conditions (e.g. the effect of a dramatic increase in inflation on a contractually agreed price) or the frustration of the purpose for which the performance was required (e.g. the effect of a prohibition to build on a plot of land acquired for building purposes or the effect of an export embargo on goods acquired with a view to their subsequent export).

Naturally the decrease in value of the performance must be capable of objective measurement: a mere change in the personal opinion of the receiving party as to the value of the performance is of no relevance. As to the frustration of the purpose of the performance, this can only be taken into account when the purpose in question was known or at least ought to have been known to both parties.

3. Additional requirements for hardship to arise

a. *Events occur or become known after conclusion of the contract*

According to sub-para. (a) of this article, the events causing hardship must take place or become known to the disadvantaged party after the conclusion of the contract. If that party had known of those events when entering into the contract, it would have been able to take them into account at that time and may not subsequently rely on hardship.

b. *Events could not reasonably have been taken into account by disadvantaged party*

Even if the change in circumstances occurs after the conclusion of the contract, sub-para. (b) of this article makes it clear that such circumstances cannot cause hardship if they could reasonably have been taken into account by the disadvantaged party at the time the contract was concluded.

Illustration

> 2. A agrees to supply B with crude oil from country X at a fixed price for the next five years, notwithstanding the acute political tensions in the region. Two years after the conclusion of the contract, a war erupts between contending factions in neighbouring countries. The war results in a world energy crisis and oil prices increase drastically. A is not entitled to invoke hardship because such a rise in the price of crude oil was not unforeseeable.

Sometimes the change in circumstances is gradual, but the final result of those gradual changes may constitute a case of hardship. If the change began before the contract was concluded, hardship will not arise unless the pace of change increases dramatically during the life of the contract.

Illustration

> 3.   In a sales contract between A and B the price is expressed in the currency of country X, a currency whose value was already depreciating slowly against other major currencies before the conclusion of the contract. One month afterwards a political crisis in country X leads to a massive devaluation of the order of 80% of its currency. Unless the circumstances indicate otherwise, this constitutes a case of hardship, since such a dramatic acceleration of the loss of value of the currency of country X was not foreseeable.

c. *Events beyond the control of disadvantaged party*

Under sub-para. (c) of this article a case of hardship can only arise if the events causing the hardship are beyond the control of the disadvantaged party.

d. *Risks must not have been assumed by disadvantaged party*

Under sub-para. (d) there can be no hardship if the disadvantaged party had assumed the risk of the change in circumstances. The word "assumption" makes it clear that the risks need not have been taken over expressly, but that this may follow from the very nature of the contract. A party who enters into a speculative transaction is deemed to accept a certain degree of risk, even though it may not have been fully aware of that risk at the time it entered into the contract.

Illustration

> 4.   A, an insurance company specialised in the insurance of shipping risks, requests an additional premium from those of its customers who have contracts which include the risks of war and civil insurrection, so as to meet the substantially greater risk to which it is exposed following upon the simultaneous outbreak of war and civil insurrection in three countries in the same region. A is not entitled to such an adaptation of the contract, since by the war and civil insurrection clause insurance companies assume these risks even if three countries are affected at the same time.

4. Hardship relevant only to performance not yet rendered

By its very nature hardship can only become of relevance with respect to performances still to be rendered: once a party has performed, it is no longer entitled to invoke a substantial increase in the costs of its performance or a substantial decrease in the value of the performance it receives as a consequence of a change in circumstances which occurs after such performance.

If the fundamental alteration in the equilibrium of the contract occurs at a time when performance has been only partially rendered, hardship can be of relevance only to the parts of the performance still to be rendered.

Illustration

> 5. A enters into a contract with B, a waste disposal company in country X, for the purpose of arranging the storage of its waste. The contract provides for a four-year term and a fixed price per ton of waste. Two years after the conclusion of the contract, the environmental movement in country X gains ground and the Government of country X prescribes prices for storing waste which are ten times higher than before. B may successfully invoke hardship only with respect to the two remaining years of the life of the contract.

5. Hardship normally relevant to long-term contracts

Although this article does not expressly exclude the possibility of hardship being invoked in respect of other kinds of contracts, hardship will normally be of relevance to long-term contracts, i.e. those where the performance of at least one party extends over a certain period of time.

6. Hardship and force majeure

In view of the respective definitions of hardship and force majeure (see Art. 7.1.7) under these Principles there may be factual situations which can at the same time be considered as cases of hardship and of force majeure. If this is the case, it is for the party affected by these events to decide which remedy to pursue. If it invokes force majeure, it is with a view to its non-performance being excused. If, on the other hand, a party invokes hardship, this is in the first instance for the purpose of renegotiating the terms of the contract so as to allow the contract to be kept alive although on revised terms.

7. Hardship and contract practice

The definition of hardship in this article is necessarily of a rather general character. International commercial contracts often contain much more precise and elaborate provisions in this regard. The parties may therefore find it appropriate to adapt the content of this article so as to take account of the particular features of the specific transaction.

ARTICLE 6.2.3

(Effects of hardship)

(1) In case of hardship the disadvantaged party is entitled to request renegotiations. The request shall be made without undue delay and shall indicate the grounds on which it is based.

(2) The request for renegotiation does not in itself entitle the disadvantaged party to withhold performance.

(3) Upon failure to reach agreement within a reasonable time either party may resort to the court.

(4) If the court finds hardship it may, if reasonable,

(a) terminate the contract at a date and on terms to be fixed, or

(b) adapt the contract with a view to restoring its equilibrium.

COMMENT

1. Disadvantaged party entitled to request renegotiations

Since hardship consists in a fundamental alteration of the equilibrium of the contract, para. (1) of this article in the first instance entitles the disadvantaged party to request the other party to enter into renegotiation of the original terms of the contract with a view to adapting them to the changed circumstances.

Illustration

1.   A, a construction company situated in country X, enters into a lump sum contract with B, a governmental agency, for the erection of a plant in country Y. Most of the sophisticated machinery has to be imported from abroad. Due to an unexpected devaluation of the currency of country Y, which is the currency of payment, the cost of the machinery increases by more than 50%. A is entitled to request B to renegotiate the original contract price so as to adapt it to the changed circumstances.

A request for renegotiations is not admissible where the contract itself already incorporates a clause providing for the automatic adaptation of the contract (e.g. a clause providing for automatic indexation of the price if certain events occur).

Illustration

> 2. The facts are the same as in Illustration 1, the difference being that the contract contains a price indexation clause relating to variations in the cost of materials and labour. A is not entitled to request a renegotiation of the price.

However, even in such a case renegotiation on account of hardship would not be precluded if the adaptation clause incorporated in the contract did not contemplate the events giving rise to hardship.

Illustration

> 3. The facts are the same as in Illustration 2, the difference being that the substantial increase in A's costs is due to the adoption of new safety regulations in country Y. A is entitled to request B to renegotiate the original contract price so as to adapt it to the changed circumstances.

2. Request for renegotiations without undue delay

The request for renegotiations must be made as quickly as possible after the time at which hardship is alleged to have occurred (para. (1)). The precise time for requesting renegotiations will depend upon the circumstances of the case: it may, for instance, be longer when the change in circumstances takes place gradually (see comment 3(b) on Art. 6.2.2).

The disadvantaged party does not lose its right to request renegotiations simply because it fails to act without undue delay. The delay in making the request may however affect the finding as to whether hardship actually existed and, if so, its consequences for the contract.

3. Grounds for request for renegotiations

Para. (1) of this article also imposes on the disadvantaged party a duty to indicate the grounds on which the request for renegotiations is based so as to permit the other party better to assess whether or not the request for renegotiations is justified. An incomplete request is to be considered as not being raised in time, unless the grounds of the alleged hardship are so obvious that they need not be spelt out in the request.

Failure to set forth the grounds on which the request for renegotiations is based may have similar effects to those resulting from undue delay in making the request (see comment 2 on this article).

4. Request for renegotiations and withholding of performance

Para. (2) of this article provides that the request for renegotiations does not of itself entitle the disadvantaged party to withhold performance. The reason for this lies in the exceptional character of hardship and in the risk of possible abuses of the remedy. Withholding performance may be justified only in extraordinary circumstances.

Illustration

> 4.   A enters into a contract with B for the construction of a plant. The plant is to be built in country X, which adopts new safety regulations after the conclusion of the contract. The new regulations require additional apparatus and thereby fundamentally alter the equilibrium of the contract making A's performance substantially more onerous. A is entitled to request renegotiations and may withhold performance in view of the time it needs to implement the new safety regulations, but it may also withhold the delivery of the additional apparatus, for as long as the corresponding price adaptation is not agreed.

5. Renegotiations in good faith

Although nothing is said in this article to that effect, both the request for renegotiations by the disadvantaged party and the conduct of both parties during the renegotiation process are subject to the general principle of good faith (Art. 1.7) and to the duty of co-operation (Art. 5.3). Thus the disadvantaged party must honestly believe that a case of hardship actually exists and not request renegotiations as a purely tactical manoeuvre. Similarly, once the request has been made, both parties must conduct the renegotiations in a constructive manner, in particular by refraining from any form of obstruction and by providing all the necessary information.

6. Resort to the court upon failure to reach an agreement

If the parties fail to reach agreement on the adaptation of the contract to the changed circumstances within a reasonable time, para. (3) of the present article authorises either party to resort to the court. Such a situation may arise either because the non-disadvantaged party completely ignored the request for renegotiations or because the renegotiations, although conducted by both parties in good faith, did not achieve a positive outcome.

How long a party must wait before resorting to the court will depend on the complexity of the issues to be settled and the particular circumstances of the case.

7. Court measures in case of hardship

According to para. (4) of this article a court which finds that a hardship situation exists may react in a number of different ways.

A first possibility is for it to terminate the contract. However, since termination in this case does not depend on a non-performance by one of the parties, its effects on the performances already rendered might be different from those provided for by the rules governing termination in general (Arts. 7.3.1. *et seq.*). Accordingly, para. (4)(a) provides that termination shall take place "at a date and on terms to be fixed" by the court.

Another possibility would be for a court to adapt the contract with a view to restoring its equilibrium (para. (4)(b)). In so doing the court will seek to make a fair distribution of the losses between the parties. This may or may not, depending on the nature of the hardship, involve a price adaptation. However, if it does, the adaptation will not necessarily reflect in full the loss entailed by the change in circumstances, since the court will, for instance, have to consider the extent to which one of the parties has taken a risk and the extent to which the party entitled to receive a performance may still benefit from that performance.

Para. (4) of this article expressly states that the court may terminate or adapt the contract only when this is reasonable. The circumstances may even be such that neither termination nor adaptation is appropriate and in consequence the only reasonable solution will be for the court either to direct the parties to resume negotiations with a view to reaching agreement on the adaptation of the contract, or to confirm the terms of the contract as they stand.

Illustration

5.   A, an exporter, undertakes to supply B, an importer in country X, with beer for three years. Two years after the conclusion of the contract new legislation is introduced in country X prohibiting the sale and consumption of alcoholic drinks. B immediately invokes hardship and requests A to renegotiate the contract. A recognises that hardship has occurred, but refuses to accept the modifications of the contract proposed by B. After one month of fruitless discussions B resorts to the court.

If B has the possibility to sell the beer in a neighbouring country, although at a substantially lower price, the court may decide to uphold the contract but to reduce the agreed price.

If on the contrary B has no such possibility, it may be reasonable for the court to terminate the contract, at the same time however requiring B to pay A for the last consignment still en route.

CHAPTER 7

NON-PERFORMANCE

SECTION 1: NON-PERFORMANCE IN GENERAL

ARTICLE 7.1.1

(Non-performance defined)

Non-performance is failure by a party to perform any of its obligations under the contract, including defective performance or late performance.

COMMENT

This article defines "non-performance" for the purpose of the Principles. Particular attention should be drawn to two features of the definition.

The first is that "non-performance" is defined so as to include all forms of defective performance as well as complete failure to perform. So it is non-performance for a builder to erect a building which is partly in accordance with the contract and partly defective or to complete the building late.

The second feature is that for the purposes of the Principles the concept of "non-performance" includes both non-excused and excused non-performance.

Non-performance may be excused by reason of the conduct of the other party to the contract (see Arts. 7.1.2 (Interference by the other party) and 7.1.3 (Withholding performance) and comments) or because of unexpected external events (Art. 7.1.7 (Force majeure) and comment). A party is not entitled to claim damages or specific performance for an excused non-performance of the other party but a party who has not received performance will as a rule be entitled to terminate the contract whether or not the non-performance is excused. See Art. 7.3.1 *et seq.* and comment.

There is no general provision dealing with cumulation of remedies. The assumption underlying the Principles is that all remedies which are not logically inconsistent may be cumulated. So, in general, a party who successfully insists on performance will not be entitled to damages but there is no reason why a party may not terminate a contract for non-excused non-performance and simultaneously claim damages. See Arts. 7.2.5 (Change of remedy), 7.3.5 (Effects of termination in general) and 7.4.1 (Right to damages).

ARTICLE **7.1.2**

(Interference by the other party)

A party may not rely on the non-performance of the other party to the extent that such non-performance was caused by the first party's act or omission or by another event as to which the first party bears the risk.

COMMENT

1. Non-performance caused by act or omission of the party alleging non-performance

This article can be regarded as providing two excuses for non-performance. However conceptually, it goes further than this. When the article applies, the relevant conduct does not become excused non-performance but loses the quality of non-performance altogether. It follows, for instance, that the other party will not be able to terminate for non-performance.

Two distinct situations are contemplated. In the first, one party is unable to perform either wholly or in part because the other party has done something which makes performance in whole or in part impossible.

Illustration

1. A agrees to perform building work on B's land beginning on 1 February. If B locks the gate to the land and does not allow A entry, B cannot complain that A has failed to begin work. B's conduct will often amount to non-excused non-performance either

because of an express provision entitling A to access to the land or because B's conduct infringes the obligations of good faith and co-operation. This result does not however depend on B's non-performance being non-excused. The result will be the same where B's non-performance is excused, for instance because access to the land is barred by strikers.

The Principles contemplate the possibility of one party's interference acting only as a partial impediment to performance by the other party and in such cases it will be necessary to decide the extent to which non-performance was caused by the first party's interference and that to which it was caused by other factors.

2. Non-performance caused by event for which party alleging non-performance bears the risk

Another possibility is that non-performance may result from an event the risk of which is expressly or impliedly allocated by the contract to the party alleging non-performance.

Illustration

2. A, a builder, concludes a construction contract to be performed on the premises of B who already has many buildings on those premises which are the subject of an insurance policy covering any damage to the buildings. If the parties agree that the risk of accidental damage is to fall on B as the person insured, there would normally be no reason to reject the parties' allocation of risk since risks of this kind are normally covered by insurance. Even therefore if a fire were to be caused by A's negligence, the risk may be allocated to B although it would clearly need more explicit language to carry this result than would be the case if the fire which destroyed the building were the fault of neither party.

ARTICLE 7.1.3

(Withholding performance)

(1) Where the parties are to perform simultaneously, either party may withhold performance until the other party tenders its performance.

(2) Where the parties are to perform consecutively, the party that is to perform later may withhold its performance until the first party has performed.

COMMENT

This article must be read together with Art. 6.1.4 (Order of performance). The present article is concerned with remedies and corresponds in effect to the civil law concept of *exceptio non adimpleti contractus*.

Illustration

A agrees to sell to B a thousand tons of white wheat, cif Rotterdam, payment to be made by confirmed letter of credit opened in German marks on a German bank. A is not obliged to ship the goods unless and until B opens the letter of credit in conformity with its contractual obligations.

The text does not explicitly address the question which arises where one party performs in part but does not perform completely. In such a case the party entitled to receive performance may be entitled to withhold performance but only where in normal circumstances this is consonant with good faith (Art. 1.7).

ARTICLE 7.1.4

(Cure by non-performing party)

(1) The non-performing party may, at its own expense, cure any non-performance, provided that

(a) without undue delay, it gives notice indicating the proposed manner and timing of the cure;

(b) cure is appropriate in the circumstances;

(c) the aggrieved party has no legitimate interest in refusing cure; and

(d) cure is effected promptly.

(2) The right to cure is not precluded by notice of termination.

(3) Upon effective notice of cure, rights of the aggrieved party that are inconsistent with the non-performing party's performance are suspended until the time for cure has expired.

(4) The aggrieved party may withhold performance pending cure.

(5) Notwithstanding cure, the aggrieved party retains the right to claim damages for delay as well as for any harm caused or not prevented by the cure.

COMMENT

1. General principle

Para. (1) of this article provides that, if certain conditions are met, the non-performing party may cure by correcting the non-performance. In effect, by meeting these conditions, the non-performing party is able to extend the time for performance for a brief period beyond that stipulated in the contract, unless timely performance is required by the agreement or the circumstances. This article thus favours the preservation of the contract. It also reflects the policy of minimising economic waste, as incorporated in Art. 7.4.8 (Mitigation of harm), and the basic principle of good faith stated in Art. 1.7. This article is related to the cure provisions contained in Arts. 37 and 48 CISG and in some domestic laws governing contracts and sales. Even many of those legal systems that do not have a rule permitting cure would normally take a reasonable offer of cure into account in assessing damages.

2. Notice of cure

Cure may be effected only after the non-performing party gives notice of cure. The notice must be reasonable with regard to its timing and content as well as to the manner in which it is communicated. Notice of cure must be given without undue delay after the non-performing party learns of the non-performance. To the extent information is then available, the notice must indicate how cure is to be effected and when. Notice must also be communicated to the aggrieved party in a manner that is reasonable in the circumstances.

Notice of cure is considered to be "effective" when the requirements of para. (1)(a) - (c) have been met.

3. Appropriateness of cure

Whether cure is appropriate in the circumstances depends on whether it is reasonable, given the nature of the contract, to permit the non-performing party to make another attempt at performance. As indicated in para. (2), cure is not precluded merely because the failure to perform amounts to a fundamental non-performance. The factors to be considered in determining the appropriateness of cure include whether the proposed cure promises to be successful in resolving the problem and whether the necessary or probable delay in effecting cure would be unreasonable or would itself constitute a fundamental non-performance. However, the right to cure is not defeated by the fact that the aggrieved party subsequently changes its position. If the non-performing party gives effective notice of cure, the aggrieved party's right to change position is suspended. Nonetheless, the situation may be different if the aggrieved party has changed position before receiving notice of cure.

4. The aggrieved party's interest

The non-performing party may not cure if the aggrieved party can demonstrate a legitimate interest in refusing cure. However, if notice of cure is properly given and if cure is appropriate in the circumstances, it is presumed that the non-performing party should be permitted to cure. A legitimate interest may arise, for example, if it is likely that, when attempting cure, the non-performing party will cause damage to person or property. On the other hand, a legitimate interest is not present if, on the basis of the non-performance, the aggrieved party has simply decided that it does not wish to continue contractual relations.

Illustration

1. A agrees to construct a road on B's property. When the road is complete, B discovers that the road grade is steeper than the contract permits. B also discovers that, during construction, A's trucks caused damage to B's timber. A gives notice of cure to regrade the road. Even if cure would otherwise be appropriate in the circumstances, B's desire to prevent further damage to the timber may provide a legitimate interest for refusing cure.

5. Timing of cure

Cure must be effected promptly after notice of cure is given. Time is of the essence in the exercise of the right to cure. The non-performing party is not permitted to lock the aggrieved party into an extended waiting period. The lack of inconvenience on the part of the aggrieved party does not justify the non-performing party in delaying cure.

6. Proper forms of cure

Cure may include repair and replacement as well as any other activities that remedy the non-performance and give to the aggrieved party all that it is entitled to expect under the contract. Repairs constitute cure only when they leave no evidence of the prior non-performance and do not threaten the value or the quality of the product as a whole. It is left to the courts to determine the number of times the non-performing party may attempt a cure.

Illustration

> 2.   A agrees to install an assembly line for high temperature enamel painting in B's factory. The motors are installed with insufficient lubricant and as a result "lock up" after a few hours of operation. A replaces the motors in a timely fashion, but refuses to examine and test the rest of the equipment to ensure that other parts of the line have not been damaged. A has not effectively cured.

7. Suspension of other remedies

When the non-performing party has given effective notice of cure, the aggrieved party may, in accordance with para. (4), withhold its own performance but, pursuant to para. (3), may not exercise any remedies inconsistent with the non-performing party's right to cure until it becomes clear that a timely and proper cure has not been or will not be effected. Inconsistent remedies include giving notice of termination, entering into replacement transactions and seeking damages or restitution.

8. Effect of a notice of termination

If the aggrieved party has rightfully terminated the contract pursuant to Arts. 7.3.1(1) and 7.3.2(1), the effects of termination (Art. 7.3.5) are also suspended by an effective notice of cure. If the non-performance is cured, the notice of termination is inoperative. On the other hand, termination takes effect if the time for cure has expired and any fundamental non-performance has not been cured.

9. Right of aggrieved party to damages

Under para. (5) of this article, even a non-performing party who successfully cures is liable for any harm that, before cure, was occasioned by the non-performance, as well as for any additional harm caused by the cure itself or by the delay or for any harm which the cure does not prevent. The principle of full compensation for damage suffered, as provided in Art. 7.4.2, is fundamental to these Principles.

10. The aggrieved party's obligations

The decision to invoke this article rests on the non-performing party. Once the aggrieved party receives effective notice of cure, it must permit cure and, as provided in Art. 5.3, cooperate with the non-performing party. For example, the aggrieved party must permit any inspection that is reasonably necessary for the non-performing party to effect cure. If the aggrieved party refuses to permit cure when required to do so, any notice of termination is ineffective. Moreover, the aggrieved party may not seek remedies for any non-performance that could have been cured.

Illustration

3.   A agrees to construct a shed on B's property in order to protect B's machinery from the weather. The roof is constructed in a defective manner. During a storm, water leaks into the shed and B's machinery is damaged. B gives notice of termination. A gives timely notice of cure. B does not wish to deal further with A and refuses the cure. If cure is appropriate in the circumstances and the other conditions for cure are met, B cannot invoke remedies for the faulty construction but can recover for damage caused to the machinery before the cure was to be effected. If cure is inappropriate in the circumstances, or if the proposed cure could not have solved the problem, the contract is terminated by B's notice.

ARTICLE 7.1.5

(Additional period for performance)

(1) In a case of non-performance the aggrieved party may by notice to the other party allow an additional period of time for performance.

(2) During the additional period the aggrieved party may withhold performance of its own reciprocal obligations and may claim damages but may not resort to any other remedy. If it receives notice from the other party that the latter will not perform within that period, or if upon expiry of that period due performance has not been made, the aggrieved party may resort to any of the remedies that may be available under this Chapter.

(3) Where in a case of delay in performance which is not fundamental the aggrieved party has given notice allowing an additional period of time of reasonable length, it may terminate the contract at the end of that period. If the additional period allowed is not of reasonable length it shall be extended to a reasonable length. The aggrieved party may in its notice provide that if the other party fails to perform within the period allowed by the notice the contract shall automatically terminate.

(4) Paragraph (3) does not apply where the obligation which has not been performed is only a minor part of the contractual obligation of the non-performing party.

COMMENT

This article deals with the situation where one party performs late and the other party is willing to give extra time for performance. It is inspired by the German concept of *Nachfrist* although similar results are obtained by different conceptual means in other legal systems.

1. Special characteristics of late performance

The article recognises that late performance is significantly different from other forms of defective performance. Late performance can never be remedied since once the date for performance has passed it will not occur again, but nevertheless in many cases the party who is entitled to performance will much prefer even a late performance to no performance at all. Secondly, at the moment when a party fails to perform on time it is often unclear how late performance will in fact be. The commercial interest of the party receiving performance may often therefore be that a reasonably speedy completion, although late, will be perfectly acceptable but that a long delayed completion will not. The procedure enables that party to give the performing party a second chance without prejudicing its other remedies.

2. Effects of granting extension of time for performance

The party who grants the extension of time cannot terminate or seek specific performance during the extension time. The right to recover damages arising from late performance is not affected.

The position at the end of the period of extension depends on whether the late performance was already fundamental at the time when the extension was granted. In this situation, if the contract is not completely performed during the extension, the right to terminate for fundamental non-performance simply springs into life again as soon as the extension period expires. On the other hand, if the late performance was not yet fundamental, termination would only be possible at the end of the period of extension if the extension was reasonable in length.

Illustrations

1. A agrees to construct a special bullet-proof body for B's Rolls Royce. The contract provides that the body is to be finished by 1 February so that the car can be shipped to B's country of residence. On 31 January the car is needed but not yet quite finished. A assures B that it will be able to complete the work if given another week and B agrees to a week's extension of time. If the car is finished within the week B must accept it but may recover any damages, for example extra shipping charges. If the work is not finished within the week, B may refuse to accept delivery and terminate the contract.

2. A, a company in country X, concludes a contract with B, a company in country Y, to build 100 km. of motorway in the latter country. The contract provides that the motorway will be finished within two years from the start of the work. After two years, A has in fact built 85 km. and it is clear that it will take at least three more months to finish the motorway. B gives A notice to complete within a further month. B is not entitled to terminate at the end of the month because the additional period of time is not reasonable; it shall be extended to the reasonable period of three months.

ARTICLE 7.1.6

(Exemption clauses)

A clause which limits or excludes one party's liability for non-performance or which permits one party to render performance substantially different from what the other party reasonably expected may not be invoked if it would be grossly unfair to do so, having regard to the purpose of the contract.

COMMENT

1. The need for a special rule on exemption clauses

The Principles contain no general rule permitting a court to strike down abusive or unconscionable contract terms. Apart from the principle of good faith and fair dealing (Art. 1.7) which may exceptionally be invoked in this respect, there is only one provision permitting the avoidance at any time of the contract as a whole as well as of any of its individual terms when they unjustifiably give one party an excessive advantage (Art. 3.10).

The reason for the inclusion of a specific provision on exemption clauses is that they are particularly common in international contract practice and tend to give rise to much controversy between the parties.

Ultimately, the present article has opted in favour of a rule which gives the court a broad discretionary power based on the principle of fairness. Terms regulating the consequences of non-performance are in principle valid but the court may ignore clauses which are grossly unfair.

2. "Exemption clauses" defined

For the purpose of this article exemption clauses are in the first instance those terms which directly limit or exclude the non-performing party's liability in the event of non-performance. Such clauses may be expressed in different ways (e.g. fixed sum, ceiling, percentage of the performance in question, deposit retained).

Exemption clauses are further considered to be those which permit a party to render a performance substantially different from what the other party reasonably expected. In practice clauses of this kind are in particular those whose purpose or effect is to allow the performing party unilaterally to alter the character of the performance promised in such a way as to transform the contract. Such clauses are to be distinguished from those which are limited to defining the performance undertaken by the party in question.

Illustration

    1.   A tour operator offers at a high price a tour providing for accommodation in specifically designated luxury hotels. A term of the contract provides that the operator may alter the accommodation if the circumstances so require. If the operator puts up its clients in second class hotels, it will be liable to them notwithstanding the contractual term since the clients expected to be accommodated in hotels of a category similar to that which had been promised.

    2.   A hotelkeeper exhibits a notice to the effect that the hotel is responsible for cars left in the garage but not for objects contained in the cars. This term is not an exemption clause for the purpose of this article since its purpose is merely that of defining the scope of the hotelkeeper's obligation.

3. Exemption clauses to be distinguished from forfeiture clauses

Exemption clauses are to be distinguished from forfeiture clauses which permit a party to withdraw from a contract on payment of an indemnity. In practice, however, there may be forfeiture clauses which are in reality intended by the parties to operate as disguised exemption clauses.

4. Exemption clauses and agreed payment for non-performance

A contract term providing that a party who does not perform is to pay a specified sum to the aggrieved party for such non-performance (see Art. 7.4.13) may also have the effect of limiting the compensation due to the aggrieved party. In such cases the non-performing party may not be entitled to rely on the term in question if the conditions laid down in the present article are satisfied.

Illustration

    3.   A enters into a contract with B for the building of a factory. The contract contains a penalty clause providing for payment of 10,000 Australian dollars for each week of delay. The work is not completed within the agreed period because A deliberately suspends the work for another project which was more lucrative for it and in respect of which the penalty for delay was higher. The actual harm suffered by B as a result of the delay amounts to 20,000 Australian dollars per week. A is not entitled to rely on the penalty clause and

B may recover full compensation of the actual harm sustained, as the enforcement of that clause would in the circumstances be grossly unfair in view of A's deliberate non-performance.

5. Cases where exemption clauses may not be relied upon

Following the approach adopted in most national legal systems this article starts out from the assumption that in application of the doctrine of freedom of contract (Art. 1.1) exemption clauses are in principle valid. A party may not however invoke such a clause if it would be grossly unfair to do so.

This will above all be the case where the term is inherently unfair and its application would lead to an evident imbalance between the performances of the parties. Moreover, there may be circumstances in which even a term that is not in itself manifestly unfair may not be relied upon: for instance, where the non-performance is the result of grossly negligent conduct or where the aggrieved party could not have obviated the consequences of the limitation or exclusion of liability by taking out appropriate insurance.

In all cases regard must be had to the purpose of the contract and in particular to what a party could legitimately have expected from the performance of the contract.

Illustrations

4. A, an accountant, undertakes to prepare B's accounts. The contract contains a term excluding any liability of A for the consequences arising from any inaccuracy whatsoever in A's performance of the contract. As a result of a serious mistake by A, B pays 100% more taxes than were due. A may not rely on the exemption clause which is inherently unfair.

5. A, a warehouse operator, enters into a contract with B for the surveillance of its premises. The contract contains a term limiting B's liability. Thefts occur in the terminal resulting in loss exceeding the amount of the limitation. Although the term, agreed upon by two professional parties, is not inherently unfair, it may not be relied upon by B if the thefts are committed by B's servants in the course of their employment.

6. Consequence of inability to rely on exemption clauses

If a party is not entitled to rely on an exemption clause, its liability is unaffected and the aggrieved party may obtain full compensation for the non-performance. Contrary to the rule laid down with respect to agreed payment for non-performance in Art. 7.4.13, the court has no power to modify the exemption clause.

ARTICLE 7.1.7

(Force majeure)

(1) Non-performance by a party is excused if that party proves that the non-performance was due to an impediment beyond its control and that it could not reasonably be expected to have taken the impediment into account at the time of the conclusion of the contract or to have avoided or overcome it or its consequences.

(2) When the impediment is only temporary, the excuse shall have effect for such period as is reasonable having regard to the effect of the impediment on the performance of the contract.

(3) The party who fails to perform must give notice to the other party of the impediment and its effect on its ability to perform. If the notice is not received by the other party within a reasonable time after the party who fails to perform knew or ought to have known of the impediment, it is liable for damages resulting from such non-receipt.

(4) Nothing in this article prevents a party from exercising a right to terminate the contract or to withhold performance or request interest on money due.

COMMENT

1. The notion of force majeure

This article covers the ground covered in common law systems by the doctrines of frustration and impossibility of performance and in civil law systems by doctrines such as force majeure, *Unmöglichkeit,* etc. but it is identical with none of these doctrines. The term "force majeure" was chosen because it is widely known in international trade practice, as confirmed by the inclusion in many international contracts of so-called "force majeure" clauses.

Illustration

    1.   A, a manufacturer in country X, sells a nuclear power station to B, a utility company in country Y. Under the terms of the contract A undertakes to supply all the power station's requirements of uranium for ten years at a price fixed for that period, expressed in United States dollars and payable in New York. The following separate events occur:

    (1) After five years the currency of country Y collapses to 1% of its value against the dollar at the time of the contract. B is not discharged from liability as the parties have allocated this risk by the payment provisions.

    (2) After five years the government of country Y imposes foreign exchange controls which prevent B paying in any currency other than that of country Y. B is excused from paying in United States dollars. A is entitled to terminate the contract to supply uranium.

    (3) After five years the world uranium market is cornered by a group of Texan speculators. The price of uranium on the world market rises to ten times the contract figure. A is not excused from delivering uranium as this is a risk which was foreseeable at the time of making the contract.

2. Effects of force majeure on the rights and duties of the parties

The article does not restrict the rights of the party who has not received performance to terminate if the non-performance is fundamental. What it does do, where it applies, is to excuse the non-performing party from liability in damages.

In some cases the impediment will prevent any performance at all but in many others it will simply delay performance and the effect of the article will be to give extra time for performance. It should be noted that in this event the extra time may be greater (or less) than the length of the interruption because the crucial question will be what is the effect of the interruption on the progress of the contract.

Illustration

    2.   A contracts to lay a natural gas pipeline across country X. Climatic conditions are such that it is normally impossible to work between 1 November and 31 March. The contract is timed to finish on 31 October but the start of work is delayed for a month by a civil war in a neighbouring country which makes it impossible to bring in all the piping on time. If the consequence is reasonably to prevent the completion of the work until its resumption in the

following spring, A may be entitled to an extension of five months even though the delay was itself of one month only.

3. Force majeure and hardship

The article must be read together with Chapter 6, section 2 of the Principles dealing with hardship. See comment 6 on Art. 6.2.2.

4. Force majeure and contract practice

The definition of force majeure in para. (1) of this article is necessarily of a rather general character. International commercial contracts often contain much more precise and elaborate provisions in this regard. The parties may therefore find it appropriate to adapt the content of this article so as to take account of the particular features of the specific transaction.

SECTION 2 : RIGHT TO PERFORMANCE

ARTICLE 7.2.1

(Performance of monetary obligation)

Where a party who is obliged to pay money does not do so, the other party may require payment.

COMMENT

This article reflects the generally accepted principle that payment of money which is due under a contractual obligation can always be demanded and, if the demand is not met, enforced by legal action before a court. The term "require" is used in this article to cover both the demand addressed to the other party and the enforcement, whenever necessary, of such a demand by a court.

The article applies irrespective of the currency in which payment is due or may be made. In other words, the right of the obligee to require payment extends also to cases of payment in a foreign currency. For the determination of the currency in which a monetary obligation is due or payment may be made, see Arts. 6.1.9, 6.1.10 and 7.4.12.

Exceptionally, the right to require payment of the price of the goods or services to be delivered or rendered may be excluded. This is in particular the case where a usage requires a seller to resell goods which are neither accepted nor paid for by the buyer. For the applicability of usages, see Art. 1.8.

ARTICLE 7.2.2

(Performance of non-monetary obligation)

Where a party who owes an obligation other than one to pay money does not perform, the other party may require performance, unless
(a) performance is impossible in law or in fact;

(b) performance or, where relevant, enforcement is unreasonably burdensome or expensive;

(c) the party entitled to performance may reasonably obtain performance from another source;

(d) performance is of an exclusively personal character; or

(e) the party entitled to performance does not require performance within a reasonable time after it has, or ought to have, become aware of the non-performance.

COMMENT

1. Right to require performance of non-monetary obligations

In accordance with the general principle of the binding character of the contract (see Art. 1.3), each party should as a rule be entitled to require performance by the other party not only of monetary, but also of non-monetary obligations, assumed by that party. While this is not controversial in civil law countries, common law systems allow enforcement of non-monetary obligations only in special circumstances.

Following the basic approach of CISG (Art. 46) this article adopts the principle of specific performance, subject to certain qualifications.

The principle is particularly important with respect to contracts other than sales contracts. Unlike the obligation to deliver something, contractual obligations to do something or to abstain from doing something can often be performed only by the other contracting party itself. In such cases the only way of obtaining performance from a party who is unwilling to perform is by enforcement.

2. Remedy not discretionary

While CISG provides that "a court is not bound to enter a judgement for specific performance unless the court would do so under its own law in respect of similar contracts of sale not governed by [the] Convention" (Art. 28), under the Principles specific performance is not a discretionary remedy, i.e. a court must order performance, unless one of the exceptions laid down in the present article applies.

3. Exceptions to the right to require performance

a. *Impossibility*

A performance which is impossible in law or in fact, cannot be required (sub-para. (a)). However, impossibility does not nullify a contract: other remedies may be available to the aggrieved party. See Arts. 3.3 and 7.1.7(4).

The refusal of a public permission which is required under the applicable domestic law and which affects the validity of the contract renders the contract void (see Art. 6.1.17(1)), with the consequence that the problem of enforceability of the performance cannot arise. When however the refusal merely renders the performance impossible without affecting the validity of the contract (see Art. 6.1.17(2)), sub-para. (a) of this article applies and performance cannot be required.

b. *Unreasonable burden*

In exceptional cases, particularly when there has been a drastic change of circumstances after the conclusion of a contract, performance, although still possible, may have become so onerous that it would run counter to the general principle of good faith and fair dealing (Art. 1.7) to require it.

Illustration

> 1. An oil tanker has sunk in coastal waters in a heavy storm. Although it would be possible to lift the ship from the bottom of the sea, the shipper may not require performance of the contract of carriage if this would involve the shipowner in expense vastly exceeding the value of the oil. See Art. 7.2.2(b).

The words "where relevant, enforcement" take account of the fact that in common law systems it is the courts and not the obligees who supervise the execution of orders for specific performance. As a consequence, in certain cases, especially those involving performances extended in time, courts in those countries refuse specific performance if supervision would impose undue burdens upon courts.

As to other possible consequences arising from drastic changes of circumstances amounting to a case of hardship, see Arts. 6.2.1 *et seq.*

c. *Replacement transaction*

Many goods and services are of a standard kind, i.e. the same goods or services are offered by many suppliers. If a contract for such staple goods or standard services is not performed, most customers will not wish to waste time and effort extracting the contractual performance from the other party. Instead, they will go into the market, obtain substitute goods or services and claim damages for non-performance.

In view of this economic reality sub-para. (c) excludes specific performance whenever the party entitled to performance may reasonably obtain performance from another source. That party may terminate the contract and conclude a replacement transaction. See Art. 7.4.5.

The word "reasonably" indicates that the mere fact that the same performance can be obtained from another source is not in itself sufficient, since the aggrieved party could not in certain circumstances reasonably be expected to have recourse to an alternative supplier.

Illustration

2.   A, situated in a developing country where foreign exchange is scarce, buys a machine of a standard type from B in Tokyo. In compliance with the contract, A pays the price of US$ 100,000 before delivery. B does not deliver. Although A could obtain the machine from another source in Japan, it would be unreasonable, in view of the scarcity and high price of foreign exchange in its home country, to require A to take this course. A is therefore entitled to require delivery of the machine from B.

d. *Performance of an exclusively personal character*

Where a performance has an exclusively personal character, enforcement would interfere with the personal freedom of the obligor. Moreover, enforcement of a performance often impairs its quality. The supervision of a very personal performance may also give rise to insuperable practical difficulties, as is shown by the experience of countries which have saddled their courts with this kind of responsibility. For all these reasons, sub-para. (d) excludes enforcement of performance of an exclusively personal character.

The precise scope of this exception depends essentially upon the meaning of the phrase "exclusively personal character". The modern tendency is to confine this concept to performances of a unique character. The exception does not apply to obligations undertaken by a company. Nor are ordinary activities of a lawyer, a surgeon or an engineer covered by the phrase for they can be performed by other persons with the same training and experience. A performance is of an exclusively personal character if it is not delegable and requires individual skills of an artistic or scientific nature or if it involves a confidential and personal relationship.

Illustrations

> 3. An undertaking by a firm of architects to design a row of 10 private homes can be specifically enforced as the firm can delegate the task to one of the partners or employ an outside architect to perform it.

> 4. By contrast, an undertaking by a world-famous architect to design a new city hall embodying the idea of a city of the 21st century cannot be enforced because it is highly unique and calls for the exercise of very special skills.

The performance of obligations to abstain from doing something does not fall under sub-para. (d).

e. *Request within reasonable time*

Performance of a contract often requires special preparation and efforts by the obligor. If the time for performance has passed but the obligee has failed to demand performance within a reasonable time, the obligor may be entitled to assume that the obligee will not insist upon performance. If the obligee were to be allowed to leave the obligor in a state of uncertainty as to whether performance will be required, the risk might arise of the obligee's speculating unfairly, to the detriment of the obligor, upon a favourable development of the market.

For these reasons sub-para. (e) excludes the right to performance if it is not required within a reasonable time after the obligee has become, or ought to have become, aware of the non-performance.

For a similar rule concerning the loss of the right to terminate the contract, see Art. 7.3.2(2).

ARTICLE 7.2.3

(Repair and replacement of defective performance)

The right to performance includes in appropriate cases the right to require repair, replacement, or other cure of defective performance. The provisions of Articles 7.2.1 and 7.2.2 apply accordingly.

COMMENT

1. Right to performance in case of defective performance

This article applies the general principles of Arts. 7.2.1 and 7.2.2 to a special, yet very frequent, case of non-performance, i.e. defective performance. For the sake of clarity the article specifies that the right to require performance includes the right of the party who has received a defective performance to require cure of the defect.

2. Cure of defective performance

Under the Principles cure denotes the right both of the non-performing party to correct its performance (Art. 7.1.4) and of the aggrieved party to require such correction by the non-performing party. The present article deals with the latter right.

The article expressly mentions two specific examples of cure, namely repair and replacement. Repairing defective goods (or making good an insufficient service) is the most common case and replacement of a defective performance is also frequent. The right to require repair or replacement may also exist with respect to the payment of money, for instance in case of an insufficient payment or of a payment in the wrong currency or to an account different from that agreed upon by the parties.

Apart from repair and replacement there are other forms of cure, such as the removal of the rights of third persons over goods or the obtaining of a necessary public permission.

3. Restrictions

The right to require cure of a defective performance is subject to the same limitations as the right to performance in general.

Most of the exceptions to the right to require performance that are set out in Art. 7.2.2 are easily applicable to the various forms of cure of a defective performance. Only the application of sub-para. (b) calls for specific comment. In many cases involving small, insignificant defects, both replacement and repair may involve "unreasonable effort or expense" and are therefore excluded.

Illustration

> A new car is sold which has a small painting defect which decreases the value of the car by 0,01 % of the purchase price. Repainting would cost 0,5% of the purchase price. A claim for repair is excluded but the buyer is entitled to require a reduction in the purchase price.

ARTICLE 7.2.4

(Judicial penalty)

(1) Where the court orders a party to perform, it may also direct that this party pay a penalty if it does not comply with the order.

(2) The penalty shall be paid to the aggrieved party unless mandatory provisions of the law of the forum provide otherwise. Payment of the penalty to the aggrieved party does not exclude any claim for damages.

COMMENT

1. Judicially imposed penalty

Experience in some legal systems has shown that the threat of a judicially imposed penalty for disobedience is a most effective means of ensuring compliance with judgments ordering the performance of contractual obligations. Other systems, on the contrary, do not provide for such sanctions because they are considered to constitute an inadmissible encroachment upon personal freedom.

The present article takes a middle course by providing for monetary but not for other forms of penalties, applicable to all kinds of orders for performance including those for payment of money.

2. Imposition of penalty at discretion of the court

The use of the word "may" in para. (1) of this article makes it clear that the imposition of a penalty is a matter of discretion for the court. Its exercise depends upon the kind of obligation to be performed. In the case of money judgments, a penalty should be imposed only in exceptional situations, especially where speedy payment is essential for the aggrieved party. The same is true for obligations to deliver goods. Obligations to pay money or to deliver goods can normally be easily enforced by ordinary means of execution. By contrast, in the case of obligations to do or to abstain from doing something, which moreover cannot easily be performed by a third person, enforcement by means of judicial penalties is often the most appropriate solution.

3. Beneficiary

Legal systems differ as to the question of whether judicial penalties should be paid to the aggrieved party, to the State, or to both. Some systems regard payment to the aggrieved party as constituting an unjustified windfall benefit which is contrary to public policy.

While rejecting this latter view and indicating the aggrieved party as the beneficiary of the penalty, the first sentence of para. (2) of this article expressly mentions the possibility of mandatory provisions of the law of the forum not permitting such a solution and indicating other possible beneficiaries of judicial penalties.

4. Judicial penalties distinguished from damages and from agreed payment for non-performance

The second sentence of para. (2) makes it clear that a judicial penalty paid to the aggrieved party does not affect its claim for damages. Payment of the penalty is regarded as compensating the aggrieved party for those disadvantages which cannot be taken into account under the ordinary rules for the recovery of damages. Moreover, since payment of damages will usually occur substantially later than payment of a judicial penalty, courts may to some degree be able, in measuring the damages, to take the payment of the penalty into account.

Judicial penalties are moreover to be distinguished from agreed payments for non-performance which are dealt with in Art. 7.4.13, although the latter fulfil a function similar to that of the former. If the court considers that the contractual stipulation of the payment of a sum in case of non-performance already provides a sufficient incentive for performance, it may refuse to impose a judicial penalty.

5. Form and procedure

A judicial penalty may be imposed in the form of a lump sum payment or of a payment by instalments.

The procedure relating to the imposition of a judicial penalty is governed by the *lex fori*.

6. Penalties imposed by arbitrators

Since according to Art. 1.10 "court" includes an arbitral tribunal, the question arises of whether arbitrators might also be allowed to impose a penalty.

While a majority of legal systems seems to deny such a power to arbitrators, some modern legislation and recent court practice have recognised it. This solution, which is in keeping with the increasingly important role of arbitration as an alternative means of dispute resolution, especially in international commerce, is endorsed by the Principles. Since the execution of a penalty imposed by arbitrators can only be effected by, or with the assistance of, a court, appropriate supervision is available to prevent any possible abuse of the arbitrators' power.

7. Recognition and enforcement of decisions imposing penalties

Attention must be drawn to the problems of recognition and enforcement, in countries other than the forum State, of judicial decisions and of arbitral awards imposing penalties. Special rules on this matter are sometimes to be found in national law and to some extent in international treaties.

ARTICLE 7.2.5

(Change of remedy)

(1) An aggrieved party who has required performance of a non-monetary obligation and who has not received performance within a period fixed or otherwise within a reasonable period of time may invoke any other remedy.

(2) Where the decision of a court for performance of a non-monetary obligation cannot be enforced, the aggrieved party may invoke any other remedy.

COMMENT

1. Aggrieved party entitled to change of remedy

This article addresses a problem which is peculiar to the right to require performance. The aggrieved party may abandon the remedy of requiring performance of a non-monetary obligation and opt instead for another remedy or remedies.

This choice is permitted on account of the difficulties usually involved in the enforcement of non-monetary obligations. Even if the aggrieved party first decides to invoke its right to require performance, it would not be fair to confine that party to this single option. The non-performing party may subsequently become unable to perform, or its inability may only become evident during the proceedings.

2. Voluntary change of remedy

Two situations must be addressed.

In the first case, the aggrieved party has required performance but changes its mind before execution of a judgment in its favour, perhaps because it has discovered the non-performing party's inability to perform. The aggrieved party now wishes to invoke one or more other remedies. Such a voluntary change of remedy can only be admitted if the interests of the non-performing party are duly protected. It may have prepared for performance, invested effort and incurred expense. For this reason para. (1) of this article makes it clear that the aggrieved party is entitled to invoke another remedy only if it has not received performance within a fixed period or otherwise within a reasonable period of time.

How much additional time must be made available to the non-performing party for performance depends upon the difficulty which the performance involves. The non-performing party has the right to perform provided it does so before the expiry of the additional period.

For similar conditions which restrict the right of termination in case of delay in performance, see Art. 7.3.2(2).

3. Unenforceable decision

Para. (2) addresses the second and less difficult case in which the aggrieved party has attempted without success to enforce a judicial decision or arbitral award directing the non-performing party to perform. In this situation it is obvious that the aggrieved party may immediately pursue other remedies.

4. Time limits

In the event of a subsequent change of remedy the time limit provided for a notice of termination under Art. 7.3.2(2) must, of course, be extended accordingly. The reasonable time for giving notice begins to run, in the case of a voluntary change of remedy, after the aggrieved party has or ought to have become aware of the non-performance at the expiry of the additional period of time available to the non-performing party to perform; and in the case of para. (2) of this article, it will begin to run after the aggrieved party has or ought to have become aware of the unenforceability of the decision or award requiring performance.

SECTION 3: TERMINATION

ARTICLE 7.3.1

(Right to terminate the contract)

(1) A party may terminate the contract where the failure of the other party to perform an obligation under the contract amounts to a fundamental non-performance.

(2) In determining whether a failure to perform an obligation amounts to a fundamental non-performance regard shall be had, in particular, to whether

(a) the non-performance substantially deprives the aggrieved party of what it was entitled to expect under the contract unless the other party did not foresee and could not reasonably have foreseen such result;

(b) strict compliance with the obligation which has not been performed is of essence under the contract;

(c) the non-performance is intentional or reckless;

(d) the non-performance gives the aggrieved party reason to believe that it cannot rely on the other party's future performance;

(e) the non-performing party will suffer disproportionate loss as a result of the preparation or performance if the contract is terminated.

(3) In the case of delay the aggrieved party may also terminate the contract if the other party fails to perform before the time allowed it under Article 7.1.5 has expired.

COMMENT

1. Termination even if non-performance is excused

The rules set out in this Chapter are intended to apply both to cases where the non-performing party is liable for the non-performance and to those where the non-performance is excused so that the aggrieved party can claim neither specific performance nor damages for non-performance.

Illustration

>1. A, a company located in country X, buys wine from B in country Y. The Government of country X subsequently imposes an embargo upon the import of agricultural products from country Y. Although the impediment cannot be attributed to A, B may terminate the contract.

2. Right to terminate the contract dependent on fundamental non-performance

Whether in a case of non-performance by one party the other party should have the right to terminate the contract depends upon the weighing of a number of considerations. On the one hand, performance may be so late or so defective that the aggrieved party cannot use it for its intended purpose, or the behaviour of the non-performing party may in other respects be such that the aggrieved party should be permitted to terminate the contract.

On the other hand, termination will often cause serious detriment to the non-performing party whose expenses in preparing and tendering performance may not be recovered.

For these reasons para. (1) of this article provides that an aggrieved party may terminate the contract only if the non-performance of the other party is "fundamental", i.e. material and not merely of minor importance. See also Arts. 7.3.3. and 7.3.4.

3. Circumstances of significance in determining whether non-performance is fundamental

Para. (2) of this article lists a number of circumstances which are relevant to the determination of whether, in a given case, failure to perform an obligation amounts to fundamental non-performance.

a. *Non-performance substantially depriving the other party of its expectations*

The first factor referred to in para. 2(a) is that the non-performance is so fundamental that the aggrieved party is substantially deprived of what it was entitled to expect at the time of the conclusion of the contract.

Illustration

> 2. On 1 May A contracts to deliver standard software before 15 May to B who has requested speedy delivery. If A tenders delivery on 15 June, B may refuse delivery and terminate the contract.

The aggrieved party cannot terminate the contract if the non-performing party can show that it did not foresee, and could not reasonably have foreseen, that the non-performance was fundamental for the other party.

Illustration

> 3. A undertakes to remove waste from B's site during 1992. B fails to inform A that B has hired excavators at high cost to begin work on the site on 2 January 1993. B cannot terminate its contract with A on the ground that A had not cleared the site on 2 January.

b. *Strict performance of contract of essence*

Para. (2)(b) looks not at the actual gravity of the non-performance but at the nature of the contractual obligation for which strict performance might be of essence. Such obligations of strict performance are not uncommon in commercial contracts. For example, in contracts for the sale of commodities the time of delivery is normally considered to be of the essence, and in a documentary credit transaction the documents tendered must conform strictly to the terms of the credit.

c. *Intentional non-performance*

Para. (2)(c) deals with the situation where the non-performance is intentional or reckless. It may, however, be contrary to good faith (Art. 1.7) to terminate a contract if the non-performance, even though committed intentionally, is insignificant.

d. *No reliance on future performance*

Under para. (2)(d) the fact that non-performance gives the aggrieved party reason to believe that it cannot rely on the other party's future performance is of significance. If a party is to make its performance in instalments, and it is clear that a defect found in one of the earlier performances will be repeated in all performances, the aggrieved party may terminate the contract even if the defects in the early instalment would not of themselves justify termination.

Sometimes an intentional breach may show that a party cannot be trusted.

Illustration

4. A, the agent of B, who is entitled to reimbursement for expenses, submits false vouchers to B. Although the amounts claimed are insignificant, B may treat A's behaviour as a fundamental non-performance and terminate the agency contract.

e. *Disproportionate loss*

Para. (2)(e) deals with situations where a party who fails to perform has relied on the contract and has prepared or tendered performance. In these cases regard is to be had to the extent to which that party suffers disproportionate loss if the non-performance is treated as fundamental. Non-performance is less likely to be treated as fundamental if it occurs late, after the preparation of performance, than if it occurs early before such preparation. Whether a performance tendered or rendered can be of any benefit to the non-performing party if it is refused or has to be returned to that party is also of relevance.

Illustration

5. On 1 May A undertakes to deliver software which is to be produced specifically for B. It is agreed that delivery shall be made before 31 December. A tenders delivery on 31 January, at which time B still needs the software, which A cannot sell to other users. B may claim damages from A, but cannot terminate the contract.

4. Termination after *Nachfrist*

Para. (3) makes reference to Art. 7.1.5, para. (3) of which provides that the aggrieved party may use the *Nachfrist* procedure to terminate a contract which may not otherwise be terminated in case of delay. See comment 2 on Art. 7.1.5.

ARTICLE 7.3.2

(Notice of termination)

(1) The right of a party to terminate the contract is exercised by notice to the other party.

(2) If performance has been offered late or otherwise does not conform to the contract the aggrieved party will lose its right to terminate the contract unless it gives notice to the other party within a reasonable time after it has or ought to have become aware of the offer or of the non-conforming performance.

COMMENT

1. The requirement of notice

Para. (1) of this article reaffirms the principle that the right of a party to terminate the contract is exercised by notice to the other party. The notice requirement will permit the non-performing party to avoid any loss due to uncertainty as to whether the aggrieved party will accept the performance. At the same time it prevents the aggrieved party from speculating on a rise or fall in the value of the performance to the detriment of the non-performing party.

2. Performance overdue

When performance is due but has not been made, the aggrieved party's course of action will depend upon its wishes and knowledge.

It may be the case that the aggrieved party does not know whether the other party intends to perform, and either it no longer wants the performance or is undecided. In this case the aggrieved party may wait and see whether performance is ultimately tendered and make up its mind if and when this happens (see para. (2)). Alternatively, it may still want the other party to perform, in which case it must seek performance within a reasonable time after it has or ought to have become aware of the non-performance. See Art. 7.2.2(e).

This article does not deal with the situation where the non-performing party asks the aggrieved party whether it will accept late performance. Nor does it deal with the situation where the aggrieved party learns from another source that the non-performing party intends nevertheless to perform the contract. In such cases good faith (Art. 1.7) may require that the aggrieved party inform the other party if it does not wish to accept the late performance. If it does not do so, it may be held liable in damages.

3. "Reasonable time"

An aggrieved party who intends to terminate the contract must give notice to the other party within a reasonable time after it becomes or ought to have become aware of the non-performance (para. (2)).

What is "reasonable" depends upon the circumstances. In situations where the aggrieved party may easily obtain a substitute performance and may thus speculate on a rise or fall in the price, notice must be given without delay. When it must make enquiries as to whether it can obtain substitute performance from other sources the reasonable period of time will be longer.

4. Notice must be received

The notice to be given by the aggrieved party becomes effective when the non-performing party receives it. See Art. 1.9.

ARTICLE 7.3.3

(Anticipatory non-performance)

Where prior to the date for performance by one of the parties it is clear that there will be a fundamental non-performance by that party, the other party may terminate the contract.

COMMENT

This article establishes the principle that a non-performance which is to be expected is to be equated with a non-performance which occurred at the time when performance fell due. It is a requirement that it be clear that there will be non-performance; a suspicion, even a well-founded one, is not sufficient. Furthermore, it is necessary that the non-performance be fundamental and that the party who is to receive performance give notice of termination.

An example of anticipatory non-performance is the case where one party declares that it will not perform the contract; however, the circumstances also may indicate that there will be a fundamental non-performance.

Illustration

A promises to deliver oil to B by M/S Paul in Montreal on 3 February. On 25 January M/S Paul is still 2000 kilometres from Montreal. At the speed it is making it will not arrive in Montreal on 3 February, but at the earliest on 8 February. As time is of the essence, a substantial delay is to be expected, and B may terminate the contract before 3 February.

ARTICLE 7.3.4

(Adequate assurance of due performance)

A party who reasonably believes that there will be a fundamental non-performance by the other party may demand adequate assurance of due performance and may meanwhile withhold its own performance. Where this assurance is not provided within a reasonable time the party demanding it may terminate the contract.

COMMENT

1. Reasonable expectation of fundamental non-performance

This article protects the interest of a party who has reason to believe that the other will be unable or unwilling to perform the contract at the due date but who cannot invoke Art. 7.3.3 since there is still a possibility that the other party will or can perform. In the absence of the rule laid down in the present article the former party would often be in a dilemma. If it were to wait until the due date of performance, and this did not take place, it might incur loss. If, on the other hand, it were to terminate the contract, and it then became apparent that the contract would have been performed by the other party, its action will amount to non-performance of the contract, and it will be liable in damages.

2. Right to withhold performance pending adequate assurance of performance

Consequently this article enables a party who reasonably believes that there will be a fundamental non-performance by the other party to demand an assurance of performance from the other party and in the meantime to withhold its own performance. What constitutes an adequate assurance will depend upon the circumstances. In some cases the other party's declaration that it will perform will suffice, while in others a request for security or for a guarantee from a third person may be justified.

Illustration

A, a boatbuilder with only one berth, promises to build a yacht for B to be delivered on 1 May, and no later. Soon afterwards, B learns from C that A has promised to build a yacht for C during the same period. B is entitled to ask A for an adequate assurance that the yacht will be delivered on time and A will then have to give B a satisfactory explanation of how it intends to perform its contract with B.

3. Termination of the contract

If adequate assurance of due performance is not given the other party may terminate the contract.

ARTICLE 7.3.5

(Effects of termination in general)

(1) Termination of the contract releases both parties from their obligation to effect and to receive future performance.

(2) Termination does not preclude a claim for damages for non-performance.

(3) Termination does not affect any provision in the contract for the settlement of disputes or any other term of the contract which is to operate even after termination.

COMMENT

1. Termination extinguishes future obligations

Para. (1) of this article states the general rule that termination has effects for the future in that it releases both parties from their duty to effect and to receive future performance.

2. Claim for damages not affected

The fact that, by virtue of termination, the contract is brought to an end, does not deprive the aggrieved party of its right to claim damages for non-performance in accordance with the rules laid down in section 4 of this Chapter (Arts. 7.4.1. *et seq.*).

Illustration

1. A sells B specified production machinery. After B has begun to operate the machinery serious defects in it lead to a shutdown of B's assembly plant. B declares the contract terminated but may still claim damages (Art. 7.3.5(2)).

3. Contract provisions not affected by termination

Notwithstanding the general rule laid down in para. (1), there may be provisions in the contract which survive its termination. This is the case in particular with provisions relating to dispute settlement but there may be others which by their very nature are intended to operate even after termination.

Illustration

> 2.   The facts are the same as in Illustration 1, the difference being that A discloses to B confidential information which is necessary for the production and which B agrees not to divulge for as long as it does not become public knowledge. The contract further contains a clause referring disputes to the courts of A's country. Even after termination of the contract by B, B remains under a duty not to divulge the confidential information, and any dispute relating to the contract and its effects are to be settled by the courts of A's country (Art. 7.3.5(3)).

ARTICLE 7.3.6

(Restitution)

(1) On termination of the contract either party may claim restitution of whatever it has supplied, provided that such party concurrently makes restitution of whatever it has received. If restitution in kind is not possible or appropriate allowance should be made in money whenever reasonable.

(2) However, if performance of the contract has extended over a period of time and the contract is divisible, such restitution can only be claimed for the period after termination has taken effect.

COMMENT

1. Entitlement of parties to restitution on termination

Para. (1) of this article provides for a right for each party to claim the return of whatever it has supplied under the contract provided that it concurrently makes restitution of whatever it has received.

Illustration

> 1. A sells a Renoir painting to B for US$ 2,000,000. B does not pay for the picture when it is delivered. A can claim back the picture.

If the non-performing party cannot make restitution it must make allowance in money for the value it has received. Thus, in the case described in Illustration 1, B has to make allowance for the value of the picture if B has sold and delivered it to a purchaser from whom it cannot be reclaimed.

The rule also applies when the aggrieved party has made a bad bargain. If in the case mentioned in Illustration 1 the true value of the picture is US$ 3,000,000, A may still require the return of the picture and, if it cannot be returned, claim the true value of US$ 3,000,000.

The present article also applies to the situation where the aggrieved party has supplied money in exchange for property, services etc. which it has not received or which are defective.

Illustration

> 2. The "Renoir" painting for which B has paid US$ 2,000,000 was not a Renoir but a copy. B can claim back the money and must return the copy to A.

Money returned for services or work which have not been performed or for property which has been rejected should be repaid to the party who paid for it and the same principle applies to custody of goods and to rent and leases of property.

2. Restitution not possible or appropriate

There are instances where instead of restitution in kind, allowance in money should be made. This is the case first of all where restitution in kind is not possible.

Illustration

> 3. A, who has contracted to excavate B's site, leaves it after only half the work has been performed. B, who then terminates the contract, will have to pay A a reasonable sum for the work done, measured by the value that work has for B.

Allowance in money is further envisaged by para. (1) of this article whenever restitution in kind would not be "appropriate". This is so in particular when the aggrieved party has received part of the performance and wants to retain that part.

The purpose of specifying that allowance should be made in money "whenever reasonable" is to make it clear that allowance should only be made if, and to the extent that, the performance received has conferred a benefit on the party claiming restitution.

Illustration

4. A, who has undertaken to decorate a bedroom suite for B, a furniture maker, abandons the work after having completed about half of the decorations. B can claim back the advance payments, but as the decorations made have no value for B, B does not have to pay for the work which has been done.

3. Contracts to be performed over a period of time

If the performance has extended over a period of time, restitution can, in accordance with para. (2) of this article, only be claimed in respect of the period after termination.

Illustration

5. A contracts to service B's computer hardware and software for a period of five years. After three years of regular service A is obliged by illness to discontinue the services and the contract is terminated. B, who has paid A for the fourth year, can claim return of the advance payment for that year but not the money paid for the three years of regular service.

This rule only applies if the contract is divisible.

Illustration

6. A undertakes to paint ten pictures depicting a historical event for B's festival hall. After delivering and having been paid for five paintings, A abandons the work. B can claim return of the advances paid to A and must return the five paintings to A.

4. Other rules applicable to restitution

Both the rule in Art. 7.1.3 on the right to withhold performance and Art. 7.2.2 on specific performance of non-monetary obligations apply with appropriate adaptations to a claim for the restitution of property. Thus the aggrieved party cannot claim the return of goods when this has become impossible or would put the non-performing party to unreasonable effort or expense (see Art. 7.2.2 (a) and (b)). In such cases the non-performing party must make allowance for the value of the property. See Art. 7.3.6(1).

5. Rights of third persons not affected

In common with other articles of the Principles, Art. 7.3.6 deals with the relationship between the parties and not with any rights which third persons may have acquired on the goods concerned. Whether, for instance, an obligee of the buyer, the buyer's receivers in bankruptcy, or a purchaser in good faith may oppose the restitution of goods sold is to be determined by the applicable national law.

SECTION 4: DAMAGES

ARTICLE 7.4.1
(Right to damages)

Any non-performance gives the aggrieved party a right to damages either exclusively or in conjunction with any other remedies except where the non-performance is excused under these Principles.

COMMENT

1. Right to damages in general

This article establishes the principle of a general right to damages in the event of non-performance, except where the non-performance is excused under the Principles, as in the case of force majeure (Art. 7.1.7) or of an exemption clause (Art. 7.1.6). Hardship (Art. 6.2.1 *et seq.*) does not in principle give rise to a right to damages.

The article recalls that the right to damages, like other remedies, arises from the sole fact of non-performance. It is enough for the aggrieved party simply to prove the non-performance, i.e. that it has not received what it was promised. It is in particular not necessary to prove in addition that the non-performance was due to the fault of the non-performing party. The degree of difficulty in proving the non-performance will depend upon the content of the obligation and in particular on whether the obligation is one of best efforts or one to achieve a specific result. See Art. 5.4.

The right to damages exists in the event of failure to perform any of the obligations which arise from the contract. Thus it is not necessary to draw a distinction between principal and accessory obligations.

2. Damages may be combined with other remedies

This article also states that the aggrieved party may request damages either as an exclusive remedy (for example damages for delay in the case of late performance or for defective performance accepted by the aggrieved party; damages in the event of impossibility of performance for which the non-performing party is liable), or in conjunction with other remedies. Thus, in the case of termination of the contract, damages may be requested to compensate the loss arising from such termination, or again, in the case of specific performance, to compensate for the delay with which the aggrieved party receives performance and for any expenses which might have been incurred. Damages may also be accompanied by other remedies (cure, publication in newspapers of, for example, an admission of error, etc.).

3. Damages and pre-contractual liability

The right to damages may arise not only in the context of non-performance of the contract, but also during the pre-contractual period. See, for instance, Art. 2.15 in case of negotiations in bad faith, Art. 2.16 in the event of breach of the duty of confidentiality, or Art. 3.18 in the case of mistake, fraud, threat or gross disparity. The rules governing damages for non-performance as laid down in this Section may be applied by analogy to those situations.

ARTICLE 7.4.2

(Full compensation)

(1) The aggrieved party is entitled to full compensation for harm sustained as a result of the non-performance. Such harm includes both any loss which it suffered and any gain of which it was deprived, taking into account any gain to the aggrieved party resulting from its avoidance of cost or harm.

(2) Such harm may be non-pecuniary and includes, for instance, physical suffering or emotional distress.

COMMENT

1. Aggrieved party entitled to full compensation

Para. (1) of this article establishes the principle of the aggrieved party's entitlement to full compensation for the harm it has sustained as a result of the non-performance of the contract. It further affirms the need for a causal link between the non-performance and the harm.

See also comment 3 on Art. 7.4.3. Non-performance must be a source neither of gain nor of loss for the aggrieved party.

The solution to be found in some legal systems which allows the court to reduce the amount of damages having regard to the circumstances has not been followed, since in international situations it could risk creating a considerable degree of uncertainty and its application might moreover vary from one court to another.

2. Damages cover loss suffered, including loss of profit

In specifying the harm for which damages are recoverable, para. (1) of this article, following the rule laid down in Art. 74 CISG, states that the aggrieved party is entitled to compensation in respect not only of loss which it has suffered, but also of any gain of which it has been deprived as a consequence of the non-performance.

The notion of loss suffered must be understood in a wide sense. It may cover a reduction in the aggrieved party's assets or an increase in its liabilities which occurs when an obligee, not having been paid by its obligor, must borrow money to meet its commitments. The loss of profit or, as it is sometimes called, consequential loss, is the benefit which would normally have accrued to the aggrieved party if the contract had been properly performed. The benefit will often be uncertain so that it will frequently take the form of the loss of a chance. See Art. 7.4.3(2).

Illustrations

> 1. The *Bibliothèque de France* sends a rare manuscript by special courier to New York for an exhibition. The manuscript is irreparably damaged during transport. Its loss in value is estimated at 50,000 French francs and it is this sum which is due by the courier.

> 2. A, who has not been paid by B under the terms of their contract, must borrow money from its bank at a high rate of interest. B must compensate A for the interest due by the latter to its bank.

> 3. A, a construction company, hires a crane from company B. The boom of the crane, which has been poorly maintained, breaks and in falling crushes the architect's car and results in an interruption of work on the site for eight days, for which A must pay a penalty for delay of 70,000 French francs to the owner. B must reimburse A for the expenses incurred as a consequence of the interruption of the work, the amount of the penalty and the cost of repairing the architect's car which A has had to pay.

4.   A, a singer, cancels an engagement with B, an impresario. A must pay damages to B in respect not only of the expenses incurred by B in preparing the concert, but also of the loss of profit resulting from the cancellation of the concert.

3. Damages must not enrich the aggrieved party

However, the aggrieved party must not be enriched by damages for non-performance. It is for this reason that para. (1) also provides that account must be taken of any gain resulting to the aggrieved party from the non-performance, whether that be in the form of expenses which it has not incurred (e.g. it does not have to pay the cost of a hotel room for an artist who fails to appear), or of a loss which it has avoided (e.g. in the event of non-performance of what would have been a losing bargain for it).

Illustration

5.   A hires out excavating machinery to B for two years at a monthly rental of 50,000 French francs. The contract is terminated after six months for non-payment of the rentals. Six months later, A succeeds in renting out the same machinery at a monthly charge of 55,000 French francs. The gain of 60,000 French francs realised by A as a result of the reletting of the machinery for the remainder of the initial contract, that is to say one year, should be deducted from the damages due by B to A.

4. Damages in case of changes in the harm

In application of the principle of full compensation regard is to be had to any changes in the harm, including its expression in monetary terms, which may occur between the time of the non-performance and that of the judgment. The rule however is not without exceptions: for example, if the aggrieved party has itself already made good the harm at its own expense, the damages awarded will correspond to the amount of the sums disbursed.

5. Compensation of non-material harm

Para. (2) of this article expressly provides for compensation also of non-pecuniary harm. This may be pain and suffering, loss of certain amenities of life, aesthetic prejudice, etc. as well as harm resulting from attacks on honour or reputation.

The rule might find application, in international commerce, in regard to contracts concluded by artists, outstanding sportsmen or women and consultants engaged by a company or by an organisation.

In these cases also, the requirement of the certainty of harm must be satisfied (see Art. 7.4.3), together with the other conditions for entitlement to damages.

Illustration

> 6.   A, a young architect who is beginning to build up a certain reputation, signs a contract for the modernisation of a municipal fine arts museum. The appointment receives wide press coverage. The municipal authorities subsequently decide to engage the services of a more experienced architect and terminate the contract with A. A may obtain compensation not only for the material loss suffered but also for the harm to A's reputation and the loss of the chance of becoming better known which the commission would have provided.

The compensation of non-material harm may assume different forms and it is for the court to decide which of them, whether taken alone or together, best assures full compensation. The court may not only award damages but also order other forms of redress such as the publication of a notice in newspapers designated by it (e.g. in case of breach of a clause prohibiting competition or the reopening of a business, defamation etc.).

ARTICLE 7.4.3

(Certainty of harm)

(1) **Compensation is due only for harm, including future harm, that is established with a reasonable degree of certainty.**

(2) **Compensation may be due for the loss of a chance in proportion to the probability of its occurrence.**

(3) **Where the amount of damages cannot be established with a sufficient degree of certainty, the assessment is at the discretion of the court.**

COMMENT

1. Occurrence of harm must be reasonably certain

This article reaffirms the well-known requirement of certainty of harm, since it is not possible to require the non-performing party to compensate harm which may not have occurred or which may never occur.

Para. (1) permits the compensation also of future harm, i.e. harm which has not yet occurred, provided that it is sufficiently certain. Para. (2) in addition covers loss of a chance, obviously only in proportion to the probability of its occurrence: thus, the owner of a horse which arrives too late to run in a race as a result of delay in transport cannot recover the whole of the prize money, even though the horse was the favourite.

2. Determination of extent of harm

Certainty relates not only to the existence of the harm but also to its extent. There may be harm whose existence cannot be disputed but which it is difficult to quantify. This will often be the case in respect of loss of a chance (there are not always "odds" as there are for a horse, for example a student preparing for a public examination) or of compensation for non-material harm (detriment to someone's reputation, pain and suffering, etc.).

Illustration

> A entrusts a file to B, an express delivery company, in response to an invitation to submit tenders for the construction of an airport. B undertakes to deliver the file before the closing date for tenders but delivers it after that date and A's application is refused. The amount of compensation will depend upon the degree of probability of A's tender having been accepted and calls for a comparison of it with the applications which were admitted for consideration. The compensation will therefore be calculated as a proportion of the profit which A might have made.

According to para. (3), where the amount of damages cannot be established with a sufficient degree of certainty then, rather than refuse any compensation or award nominal damages, the court is empowered to make an equitable quantification of the harm sustained.

3. Harm must be a direct consequence of non-performance as well as certain

There is a clear connection between the certainty and the direct nature of the harm. Although the latter requirement is not expressly dealt with by the Principles, it is implicit in Art. 7.4.2(1) which refers to the harm sustained "as a result of the non-performance" and which therefore presupposes a sufficient causal link between the non-performance and the harm. Harm which is too indirect will usually also be uncertain as well as unforeseeable.

ARTICLE 7.4.4

(Foreseeability of harm)

The non-performing party is liable only for harm which it foresaw or could reasonably have foreseen at the time of the conclusion of the contract as being likely to result from its non-performance.

COMMENT

The principle of limitation of recoverable harm to that which is foreseeable corresponds to the solution adopted in Art. 74 CISG. This limitation is related to the very nature of the contract: not all the benefits of which the aggrieved party is deprived fall within the scope of the contract and the non-performing party must not be saddled with compensation for harm which it could never have foreseen at the time of the conclusion of the contract and against the risk of which it could not have taken out insurance.

The requirement of foreseeability must be seen in conjunction with that of certainty of harm set out in Art. 7.4.3.

The concept of foreseeability must be clarified since the solution contained in the Principles does not correspond to certain national systems which allow compensation even for harm which is unforeseeable when the non-performance is due to wilful misconduct or gross negligence. Since the present rule does not provide for such an exception, a narrow interpretation of the concept of foreseeability is called for. Foreseeability relates to the nature or type of the harm but not to its extent unless the extent is such as to transform the harm into one of a different kind. In any event, foreseeability is a flexible concept which leaves a wide measure of discretion to the judge.

What was foreseeable is to be determined by reference to the time of the conclusion of the contract and to the non-performing party itself (including its servants or agents), and the test is what a normally diligent person could reasonably have foreseen as the consequences of non-performance in the ordinary course of things and the particular circumstances of the contract, such as the information supplied by the parties or their previous transactions.

Illustrations

1. A cleaning company orders a machine which is delivered five months late. The manufacturer is obliged to compensate the company for lost profit caused by the delay in delivery as it could have foreseen that the machine was intended for immediate use. On the other hand the harm does not include the loss of a valuable government contract that could have been concluded if the machine had been delivered on time since that kind of harm was not foreseeable.

2. A, a bank, usually employs the services of a security firm for the conveyance of bags containing coins to its branches. Without informing the security firm, A sends a consignment of bags containing new coins for collectors worth fifty times the value of previous consignments. The bags are stolen in a hold-up. A can only recover compensation corresponding to the value of the normal consignments as this was the only kind of harm that could have been foreseen and the value of the items lost was such as to transform the harm into one of another kind..

Unlike certain international conventions, particularly in the field of transport, the Principles follow CISG in not making provision for full compensation of harm, albeit unforeseeable, in the event of intentional non-performance.

ARTICLE 7.4.5

(Proof of harm in case of replacement transaction)

Where the aggrieved party has terminated the contract and has made a replacement transaction within a reasonable time and in a reasonable manner it may recover the difference between the contract price and the price of the replacement transaction as well as damages for any further harm.

COMMENT

1. Amount of harm presumed in case of replacement transaction

It seems advisable to establish, alongside the general rules applicable to the proof of the existence and of the amount of the harm, presumptions which may facilitate the task of the aggrieved party.

The first of these presumptions is provided by this article which corresponds in substance to Art. 75 CISG. It concerns the situation where the aggrieved party has made a replacement transaction, for instance because so required by the duty to mitigate harm or in conformity with usages. In such cases, the harm is considered to be the difference between the contract price and the price of the replacement transaction.

The presumption comes into play only if there is a replacement transaction and not where the aggrieved party has itself performed the obligation which lay upon the non-performing party (for example when a shipowner itself carries out the repairs to its vessel following the failure to do so of the shipyard which had been entrusted with the work).

Nor is there replacement, and the general rules will apply, when a company, after the termination of a contract, uses its equipment for the performance of another contract which it could have performed at the same time as the first ("lost volume").

The replacement transaction must be performed within a reasonable time and in a reasonable manner so as to avoid the non-performing party being prejudiced by hasty or malicious conduct.

2. Further damages recoverable for additional harm

The rule that the aggrieved party may recover the difference between the two contract prices establishes a minimum right of recovery. The aggrieved party may also obtain damages for additional harm which it may have sustained.

Illustration

A, a shipyard, undertakes to accommodate a ship belonging to B, a shipowner, in dry dock for repairs costing US$ 500,000 as from 1 July. B learns on 1 June that the dry dock will only be available as from 1 August. B terminates the contract and after lengthy and costly negotiations concludes with C, another shipyard, an identical contract at a price of US$ 700,000. B is entitled to recover from A not only the difference in the price of US$ 200,000 but also the expenses it has incurred and compensation for the longer period of unavailability of the ship.

ARTICLE 7.4.6

(Proof of harm by current price)

(1) Where the aggrieved party has terminated the contract and has not made a replacement transaction but there is a current price for the performance contracted for, it may recover the difference between the contract price and the price current at the time the contract is terminated as well as damages for any further harm.

(2) Current price is the price generally charged for goods delivered or services rendered in comparable circumstances at the place where the contract should have been performed or, if there is no current price at that place, the current price at such other place that appears reasonable to take as a reference.

COMMENT

1. Amount of harm presumed when no replacement transaction

The purpose of this article, which corresponds in substance to Art. 76 CISG, is to facilitate proof of harm where no replacement transaction has been made, but there exists a current price for the performance contracted for. In such cases the harm is presumed to be equal to the difference between the contract price and the price current at the time the contract was terminated.

2. Determination of "current price"

According to para. (2) "current price" is the price generally charged for the goods or services in question. The price will be determined in comparison with that which is charged for the same or similar goods or services. This will often, but not necessarily, be the price on an organised market. Evidence of the current price may be obtained from professional organisations, chambers of commerce etc.

For the purpose of this article the place relevant for determining the current price is that where the contract should have been performed or, if there is no current price at that place, the place that appears reasonable to take as a reference.

3. Further damages recoverable for additional harm

The rule that the aggrieved party may recover the difference between the contract price and the current price at the time of termination establishes only a minimum right of recovery. The aggrieved party may also obtain damages for additional harm which it may have sustained as a consequence of termination.

ARTICLE 7.4.7

(Harm due in part to aggrieved party)

Where the harm is due in part to an act or omission of the aggrieved party or to another event as to which that party bears the risk, the amount of damages shall be reduced to the extent that these factors have contributed to the harm, having regard to the conduct of each of the parties.

COMMENT

1. Contribution of the aggrieved party to the harm

In application of the general principle established by Art. 7.1.2 which restricts the exercise of remedies where non-performance is in part due to the conduct of the aggrieved party, the present article limits the right to damages to the extent that the aggrieved party has in part contributed to the harm. It would indeed be unjust for such a party to obtain full compensation for harm for which it has itself been partly responsible.

2. Ways of contributing to the harm

The contribution of the aggrieved party to the harm may consist either in its own conduct or in an event as to which it bears the risk. The conduct may take the form of an act (e.g. it gave a carrier a mistaken address) or an omission (e.g. it failed to give all the necessary instructions to the constructor of the defective machinery). Most frequently such acts or omissions will result in the aggrieved party failing to perform one or another of its own contractual obligations; they may however equally consist in tortious conduct or non-performance of another contract. The external events for which the aggrieved party bears the risk may, among others, be acts or omissions of persons for whom it is responsible such as its servants or agents.

Illustrations

1.   A, a franchisee bound by an "exclusivity" clause contained in the contract with B, acquires stock from C because B has required immediate payment despite the fact that the franchise agreement provides for payment at 90 days. B claims payment of the penalty stipulated for breach of the exclusivity clause. B will obtain only part of the sum due thereunder as it was B who provoked A's non-performance.

2.   A, a passenger on a liner effecting a luxury cruise, is injured when a lift fails to stop at the floor requested. B, the shipowner, is held liable for the consequences of A's injury and seeks recourse against C, the company which had checked the lifts before the liner's departure. It is proved that the accident would have been avoided if the floor had been better lit. Since this was B's responsibility, B will not obtain full recovery from C.

3. Apportionment of contribution to the harm

The conduct of the aggrieved party or the external events as to which it bears the risk may have made it absolutely impossible for the non-performing party to perform. If the requirements of Art. 7.1.7 (Force majeure) are satisfied, the non-performing party is totally exonerated from liability.

Otherwise, the exoneration will be partial, depending on the extent to which the aggrieved party contributed to the harm. The determination of each party's contribution to the harm may well prove to be difficult and will to a large degree depend upon the exercise of judicial discretion. In order to give some guidance to the court this article provides that the court shall have regard to the respective behaviour of the parties. The more serious a party's failing, the greater will be its contribution to the harm.

Illustrations

3.   The facts are the same as in Illustration 1. Since it was B who was the first not to observe the terms of the contract, B is deemed to have caused A's failure to respect the exclusivity clause. B may only recover 25% of the amount stipulated in the penalty clause.

4. The facts are the same as in Illustration 2. Since the failings of B and C seem to be equivalent, B can only recover from C 50% of the compensation it had to pay A.

4. Contribution to harm and mitigation of harm

- This article must be read in conjunction with the following article on mitigation of harm (Art. 7.4.8). While the present article is concerned with the conduct of the aggrieved party in regard to the cause of the initial harm, Art. 7.4.8 relates to that party's conduct subsequent thereto.

ARTICLE 7.4.8

(Mitigation of harm)

(1) The non-performing party is not liable for harm suffered by the aggrieved party to the extent that the harm could have been reduced by the latter party's taking reasonable steps.

(2) The aggrieved party is entitled to recover any expenses reasonably incurred in attempting to reduce the harm.

COMMENT

1. Duty of aggrieved party to mitigate harm

The purpose of this article is to avoid the aggrieved party passively sitting back and waiting to be compensated for harm which it could have avoided or reduced. Any harm which the aggrieved party could have avoided by taking reasonable steps will not be compensated.

Evidently, a party who has already suffered the consequences of non-performance of the contract cannot be required in addition to take time-consuming and costly measures. On the other hand, it would be unreasonable from the economic standpoint to permit an increase in harm which could have been reduced by the taking of reasonable steps.

The steps to be taken by the aggrieved party may be directed either to limiting the extent of the harm, above all when there is a risk of it lasting for a long time if such steps are not taken (often they will consist in a replacement transaction: see Art. 7.4.5), or to avoiding any increase in the initial harm.

Illustrations

1.   On 2 May, A requests B, a travel agency, to reserve a hotel room in Paris for 1 June, at a cost of 500 French francs. On 15 May, A learns that B has not made the reservation. A waits however until 25 May before making a new reservation and can only find a room costing 700 francs, whereas accommodation could have been secured for 600 francs if A had already taken action on 15 May. A can recover only 100 francs from B.

2.   A, a company which has been entrusted by B with the building of a factory, suddenly stops work when the project is nearing completion. B looks for another company to finish the building of the factory but takes no steps to protect the buildings on the site whose condition deteriorates as a result of bad weather. B cannot recover compensation for such deterioration as it is attributable to its failure to take interim protective measures.

2. Reimbursement of expenses

The reduction in damages to the extent that the aggrieved party has failed to take the necessary steps to mitigate the harm must not however cause loss to that party. The aggrieved party may therefore recover from the non-performing party the expenses incurred by it in mitigating the harm, provided that those expenses were reasonable in the circumstances (para. (2)).

Illustrations

3.   The facts are the same as in Illustration 2, the difference being that B has the necessary work carried out to ensure the interim protection of the buildings. The cost of such work will be added to the damages due by A for non-performance of the contract on condition that those costs were reasonable. If they were not, they will be reduced.

4.   The facts are the same as in Illustration 1, the difference being that A takes a room costing 2,000 French francs in a luxury hotel. A may only recover the hundred franc difference in respect of the room which A could have obtained for 600 francs.

ARTICLE 7.4.9

(Interest for failure to pay money)

(1) If a party does not pay a sum of money when it falls due the aggrieved party is entitled to interest upon that sum from the time when payment is due to the time of payment whether or not the non-payment is excused.

(2) The rate of interest shall be the average bank short-term lending rate to prime borrowers prevailing for the currency of payment at the place for payment, or where no such rate exists at that place, then the same rate in the State of the currency of payment. In the absence of such a rate at either place the rate of interest shall be the appropriate rate fixed by the law of the State of the currency of payment.

(3) The aggrieved party is entitled to additional damages if the non-payment caused it a greater harm.

COMMENT

1. Lump sum compensation for failure to pay a sum of money

This article reaffirms the widely accepted rule according to which the harm resulting from delay in the payment of a sum of money is subject to a special regime and is calculated by a lump sum corresponding to the interest accruing between the time when payment of the money was due and the time of actual payment.

Interest is payable whenever the delay in payment is attributable to the non-performing party, and this as from the time when payment was due, without any need for the aggrieved party to give notice of the default.

If the delay is the consequence of force majeure (e.g. the non-performing party is prevented from obtaining the sum due by reason of the introduction of new exchange control regulations), interest will still be due not as damages but as compensation for the enrichment of the debtor as a result of the non-payment as the debtor continues to receive interest on the sum which it is prevented from paying.

The harm is calculated as a lump sum. In other words, subject to para. (3) of this article, the aggrieved party may not prove that it could have invested the sum due at a higher rate of interest or the non-performing party that the aggrieved party would have obtained interest at a rate lower than the average lending rate referred to in para. (2).

The parties may of course agree in advance on a different rate of interest (which would in effect subject it to Art. 7.4.13).

2. Rate of interest

Para. (2) of this article fixes in the first instance as the rate of interest the average bank short-term lending rate to prime borrowers. This solution seems to be that best suited to the needs of international trade and most appropriate to ensure an adequate compensation of the harm sustained. The rate in question is the rate at which the aggrieved party will normally borrow the money which it has not received from the non-performing party. That normal rate is the average bank short-term lending rate to prime borrowers prevailing at the place for payment for the currency of payment.

No such rate may however exist for the currency of payment at the place for payment. In such cases, reference is made in the first instance to the average prime rate in the State of the currency of payment. For instance, if a loan is made in pounds sterling payable at Tunis and there is no rate for loans in pounds on the Tunis financial market, reference will be made to the rate in the United Kingdom.

In the absence of such a rate at either place, the rate of interest will be the "appropriate" rate fixed by the law of the State of the currency of payment. In most cases this will be the legal rate of interest and, as there may be more than one, that most appropriate for international transactions. If there is no legal rate of interest, the rate will be the most appropriate bank rate.

3. Additional damages recoverable

Interest is intended to compensate the harm normally sustained as a consequence of delay in payment of a sum of money. Such delay may however cause additional harm to the aggrieved party for which it may recover damages, always provided that it can prove the existence of such harm and that it meets the requirements of certainty and foreseeability (para. (3)).

Illustration

A concludes a contract with B, a specialised finance company, for a loan which will permit the renovation of its factory in Singapore. The loan specifically mentions the use of the funds. The money lent is transferred three months later than agreed. During that period the cost of the renovation has increased by ten percent. A is entitled to recover this additional sum from B.

ARTICLE 7.4.10

(Interest on damages)

Unless otherwise agreed, interest on damages for non-performance of non-monetary obligations accrues as from the time of non-performance.

COMMENT

This article determines the time from which interest on damages accrues in cases of non-performance of obligations other than monetary obligations. In such cases, at the time of non-performance the amount of damages will usually not yet have been assessed in monetary terms. The assessment will only be made after the occurrence of the harm, either by agreement between the parties or by the court.

The present article fixes as the starting point for the accrual of interest the date of the occurrence of the harm. This solution is that best suited to international trade where it is not the practice for businesspersons to leave their money idle. In effect, the aggrieved party's assets are diminished as from the occurrence of the harm whereas the non-performing party, for as long as the damages are not paid, continues to enjoy the benefit of the interest on the sum which it will have to pay. It is only natural that this gain passes to the aggrieved party.

However, when making the final assessment of the harm, regard is to be had to the fact that damages are awarded as from the date of the harm, so as to avoid double compensation, for instance when a currency depreciates in value.

The present article takes no stand on the question of compound interest, which in some national laws is subject to rules of public policy limiting compound interest with a view to protecting the non-performing party.

ARTICLE 7.4.11

(Manner of monetary redress)

(1) Damages are to be paid in a lump sum. However, they may be payable in instalments where the nature of the harm makes this appropriate.

(2) Damages to be paid in instalments may be indexed.

COMMENT

1. Lump sum or instalments

Although this article does not impose a fixed rule as to the manner in which damages are to be paid, the payment of damages as a lump sum is in general considered to be the mode of payment best suited to international trade. There are however situations in which payment by instalments will be more appropriate, having regard to the nature of the harm, for instance when the harm is on-going.

Illustrations

    1.   A, a consultant, is retained by B for the purpose of checking the safety of its factories. A is killed when travelling by helicopter to one of B's factories, for which accident B is held responsible. A leaves two children aged twelve and eight. So as to compensate for the loss of the maintenance of the family, a monthly allowance will be payable to the children until they reach the age of majority.

    2.   A, a consultant in safety matters, is recruited by B for a three year period. The remuneration is fixed at 0.5% of the production. A is wrongfully dismissed after six months. It may be appropriate that B be ordered to pay A monthly a sum corresponding to the agreed salary until A has found new employment or, at the most, for thirty months.

2. Indexation

Para. (2) of this article contemplates the possibility of indexation of damages to be paid in instalments so as to avoid the complex mechanism of a review of the original judgment in order to take account of inflation. Indexation may however be prohibited by the law of the forum.

Illustration

3.   The facts are the same as in Illustration 1. The monthly allowance may be adjusted in accordance with the cost of living index applicable where the children live.

ARTICLE 7.4.12

(Currency in which to assess damages)

Damages are to be assessed either in the currency in which the monetary obligation was expressed or in the currency in which the harm was suffered, whichever is more appropriate.

COMMENT

The harm resulting from the non-performance of an international contract may occur in different places and the question therefore arises of the currency in which it is to be assessed. This question is dealt with by the present article and should be kept distinct from that of the currency of payment of the damages addressed in Art. 6.1.9.

The article offers a choice between the currency in which the monetary obligation was expressed and that in which the harm was suffered, whichever is more appropriate in the circumstances.

While the first alternative calls for no particular comment, the second takes account of the fact that the aggrieved party may have incurred expenses in a particular currency to repair damage which it has sustained. In such a case it should be entitled to claim damages in that currency even if it is not the currency of the contract. Another currency which may be considered the most appropriate is that in which the profit would have been made.

The choice is left to the aggrieved party, provided that the principle of full compensation is respected.

Finally, it may be noted that in the absence of any indication to the contrary, a party is entitled to interest and to liquidated damages and penalties in the same currency as that in which the main obligation is expressed.

ARTICLE **7.4.13**

(Agreed payment for non-performance)

(1) Where the contract provides that a party who does not perform is to pay a specified sum to the aggrieved party for such non-performance, the aggrieved party is entitled to that sum irrespective of its actual harm.

(2) However, notwithstanding any agreement to the contrary the specified sum may be reduced to a reasonable amount where it is grossly excessive in relation to the harm resulting from the non-performance and to the other circumstances.

COMMENT

1. Agreed payment for non-performance defined

This article gives an intentionally broad definition of agreements to pay a specified sum in case of non-performance, whether such agreements be intended to facilitate the recovery of damages (liquidated damages according to the common law) or to operate as a deterrent against non-performance (penalty clauses proper), or both.

2. Agreed payment for non-performance in principle valid

National laws vary considerably with respect to the validity of the type of clauses in question, ranging from their acceptance in the civil law countries, with or without the possibility of judicial review of particularly onerous clauses, to the outright rejection in common law systems of clauses intended specifically to operate as a deterrent against non-performance, i.e. penalty clauses.

In view of their frequency in international contract practice, para. (1) of this article in principle acknowledges the validity of any clauses providing that a party who does not perform is to pay a specified sum to the aggrieved party for such non-performance, with the consequence that the latter is entitled to the agreed sum irrespective of the harm actually suffered by it. The non-performing party may not allege that the aggrieved party sustained less harm or none at all.

Illustration

> 1.   A, a former Brazilian international player, is recruited for three years to train the players of B, an Australian football team, at a monthly salary of 10,000 Australian dollars. Provision is made for a severance allowance of 200,000 Australian dollars in the event of unjustified dismissal. A is dismissed without any justification after six months. A is entitled to the agreed sum, even though A was immediately recruited by another team at double the salary received from B.

Normally, the non-performance must be one for which the non-performing party is liable, since it is difficult to conceive a clause providing for the payment of an agreed sum in case of non-performance operating in a force majeure situation. Exceptionally, however, such a clause may be intended by the parties also to cover non-performance for which the non-performing party is not liable.

In the case of partial non-performance, the amount may, unless otherwise agreed by the parties, be reduced in proportion.

3. Agreed sum may be reduced

In order to prevent the possibility of abuse to which such clauses may give rise, para. (2) of this article permits the reduction of the agreed sum if it is grossly excessive "in relation to the harm resulting from the non-performance and to the other circumstances". The same paragraph makes it clear that the parties may under no circumstances exclude such a possibility of reduction.

The agreed sum may only be reduced, but not entirely disregarded as would be the case were the judge, notwithstanding the agreement of the parties, to award damages corresponding to the exact amount of the harm. It may not be increased, at least under this article, where the agreed sum is lower than the harm actually sustained (see however comment 4 on Art. 7.1.6). It is moreover necessary that the amount agreed be "grossly excessive", i.e. that it would clearly appear to be so to any reasonable person. Regard should in particular be had to the relationship between the sum agreed and the harm actually sustained.

Illustration

> 2.   A enters into a contract with B for the purchase of machinery which provides for 48 monthly payments of 30,000 French francs. The contract contains a clause allowing immediate termination in the event of non-payment by A of one instalment, and authorises B to keep the sums already paid and to recover future instalments as

damages. A fails to pay the eleventh instalment. B keeps the 300,000 francs already paid and claims, in addition to the return of the machinery, the 1,140,000 francs representing the 38 outstanding instalments. The court will reduce the amount since A's non-performance would result in a grossly excessive benefit for B.

4. Agreed payment for non-performance to be distinguished from forfeiture and other similar clauses

The type of clauses dealt with in the present article must be distinguished from forfeiture and other similar clauses which permit a party to withdraw from a contract either by paying a certain sum or by losing a deposit already made. On the other hand a clause according to which the aggrieved party may retain sums already paid as part of the price falls within the scope of this article.

Illustrations

3. A undertakes to sell real estate to B for 900,000,000 Italian lire. B must exercise the option to purchase within three months and must pay a deposit of 50,000,000 lire, which A is entitled to retain if B does not exercise the option. Since this is not an agreed payment for non-performance it does not fall under the present article and the sum cannot be reduced thereunder even if grossly excessive in the circumstances.

4. A enters into a contract with B for the lease of a machine. The contract provides that in the event of A's failure to pay one single rental the contract will be terminated and that the sums already paid will be retained by B as damages. The clause falls under the present article and the agreed amount may be subject to reduction.

INDEX(*)

(*) Entries are keyed to the comments which follow each article, the number in square brackets indicating the number of the comment, where applicable.

UNIDROIT Principles

UNCITRAL Model Law, Preamble[4]
See UNIDROIT Principles

Assurances

partial performance, 6.1.3[2]
right to demand, 7.3.4[1]
    and termination, 7.3.4[3]
    and withholding performance,
      7.3.4[2]
security or guarantee from third
    person, 7.3.4[2]

Avoidance

confirmation of contract excludes,
    3.12
damages, 3.18[1]
    damages for non-performance
      distinguished, 3.18[2]
effects on third persons not dealt with,
    1.3[3]
ground for imputable to third person,
    3.11
    for whom a party is not
      responsible, 3.11[2]
        prior to reliance on contract,
          3.11[2]
    for whom a party is responsible,
      3.11[1]
individual terms, 3.10[3], 3.15, 3.16
notice of, 3.14[1]
    court intervention unnecessary,
      3.14[1]
    effective upon receipt, 3.14[3]
    form and content, no specific
      requirement as to, 3.14[2]
    interpretation of, 4.2[1], 4.4[1]
    time period for, 3.15
retroactive effect of, 3.17[1]
    restitution may be claimed,
      3.17[2]
    survival of certain terms, 3.17[1]
See Adaptation, Fraud, Gross
    disparity, Mistake, Threat

Battle of forms

See Standard terms

Best efforts

See Obligations

Breach of contract

See Non-performance

Cause

no need for, 3.2[2], 3.3
    parties free to reintroduce, 3.19
See Contract, Modification of
    contract, Termination

Choice-of-law

clauses may survive contract, 3.17[1]
See UNIDROIT Principles

Conclusion of contract

See Formation

Consideration

no need for, 3.2[1]
    parties free to reintroduce, 3.19
See Contract, Modification of
    contract, Termination

Contra proferentem rule

See Interpretation of contract

Contract

binding character of, 1.3[1], 6.2.1[1]
    exceptions, 1.3[2]
    vis-à-vis third persons, 1.3[3]
divisible, 7.3.6[3]
form, no requirements as to, 1.2[1]
    exceptions under applicable law,
      1.2[2]
    parties may agree to stipulate,
      1.2[3]
freedom of, 1.1[1]
    basic principle of international
      trade, 1.1[1]
      applied to negotiations,
        2.15[1]
      applied to usages, 1.8[3]
    exemption clauses and, 7.1.6[5]
    limitations on, 1.1[2], 1.1[3]
pacta sunt servanda, 1.3[1], 1.3[2]

Index

Index

Index

impossible, 6.1.14[1], 7.2.2[3]
rules for non-performance
apply, 6.1.17[2], 7.2.3[2]
See UNIDROIT Principles, Private
international law

Receipt principle

See Notice

Reliance

See Adaptation, Avoidance, Damages,
Offer, Writings in confirmation

Remedies

change of, 7.2.5[1], 7.2.5[2]
notice of, 7.2.5[4]
time limits, 7.2.5[4]
unenforceable decision, 7.2.5[3]
contribution to harm restricts exercise
of, 7.4.7[1]
cumulation of, 7.1.1, 7.4.1[2]
for breach of duty of confidentiality,
2.16[3]
for early performance, 6.1.5[4]
for failure to obtain public permission,
6.1.16[2]
for inability to pay in currency of
account, 6.1.9[2]
for non-performance, 3.4[2], 3.7[1],
3.7[2]
distinguished from remedies for
mistake, 3.4[2]
preferred to remedies for mistake,
3.7[1], 3.7[2]
for partial performance, 6.1.3[2],
6.1.3[4]
in case of impossibility, 7.2.2[3]
in case of notice of cure, 7.1.4[7]
withholding performance, 7.1.3,
7.1.4[7], 7.1.5
See Adaptation, Additional period for
performance, Avoidance, Cure by
non-performing party, Damages,
Repair and replacement,
Replacement transaction,
Restitution, Right to performance,
Termination

Repair and replacement

form of, 7.1.4[6]
of defective performance, 7.2.3[2]
unreasonable effort or expense,
7.2.3[3]

Replacement transaction

availability of precluding specific
performance, 7.2.2[3]
damages based on, 7.2.2[3], 7.4.5[1]
includes cost of negotiations,
7.4.5[2]
required by duty to mitigate, 7.4.5[1],
7.4.8[1]
required by usages, 7.2.1, 7.4.5[1]

Restitution

inconsistent with right to cure,
7.1.4[7]
on avoidance, 3.17[2]
allowance made in money,
3.17[2]
on termination, 7.3.6[1]
allowance made in money,
7.3.6[2], 7.3.6[4]
divisible contract, 7.3.6[3]
exception to right to restitution,
7.3.6[4]
rights of third persons unaffected,
7.3.6[5]

Right to performance

defective performance, 7.2.3[1]
repair and replacement, 7.2.3[2]
restrictions, 7.2.3[3]
non-performance of monetary
obligation, 7.2.1
exceptions, 7.2.1
non-performance of non-monetary
obligation, 7.2.2[1]
damages may be combined with,
7.4.1[2]
exceptions to right to
performance, 7.1.1, 7.2.2[3]
additional period for
performance granted,
7.1.5[2]
impossibility, 7.2.2[3]

ANNEX (*)

PREAMBLE
(Purpose of the Principles)

These Principles set forth general rules for international commercial contracts.

They shall be applied when the parties have agreed that their contract be governed by them.

They may be applied when the parties have agreed that their contract be governed by general principles of law, the *lex mercatoria* or the like.

They may provide a solution to an issue raised when it proves impossible to establish the relevant rule of the applicable law.

They may be used to interpret or supplement international uniform law instruments.

They may serve as a model for national and international legislators.

CHAPTER 1 — GENERAL PROVISIONS
ARTICLE 1.1
(Freedom of contract)

The parties are free to enter into a contract and to determine its content.

ARTICLE 1.2
(No form required)

Nothing in these Principles requires a contract to be concluded in or evidenced by writing. It may be proved by any means, including witnesses.

ARTICLE 1.3
(Binding character of contract)

A contract validly entered into is binding upon the parties. It can only be modified or terminated in accordance with its terms or by agreement or as otherwise provided in these Principles.

ARTICLE 1.4
(Mandatory rules)

Nothing in these Principles shall restrict the application of mandatory rules, whether of national, international or supranational origin, which are applicable in accordance with the relevant rules of private international law.

ARTICLE 1.5
(Exclusion or modification by the parties)

The parties may exclude the application of these Principles or derogate from or vary the effect of any of their provisions, except as otherwise provided in the Principles.

ARTICLE 1.6
(Interpretation and supplementation of the Principles)

(1) In the interpretation of these Principles, regard is to be had to their international character and to their purposes including the need to promote uniformity in their application.

(2) Issues within the scope of these Principles but not expressly settled by them are as far as possible to be settled in accordance with their underlying general principles.

ARTICLE 1.7
(Good faith and fair dealing)

(1)   Each party must act in accordance with good faith and fair dealing in international trade.

(2)   The parties may not exclude or limit this duty.

ARTICLE 1.8
(Usages and practices)

(1)   The parties are bound by any usage to which they have agreed and by any practices which they have established between themselves.

(2)   The parties are bound by a usage that is widely known to and regularly observed in international trade by parties in the particular trade concerned except where the application of such a usage would be unreasonable.

ARTICLE 1.9
(Notice)

(1)   Where notice is required it may be given by any means appropriate to the circumstances.

(2)   A notice is effective when it reaches the person to whom it is given.

(3)   For the purpose of paragraph (2) a notice "reaches" a person when given to that person orally or delivered at that person's place of business or mailing address.

(4)   For the purpose of this article "notice" includes a declaration, demand, request or any other communication of intention.

ARTICLE 1.10
(Definitions)

In these Principles
-   "court" includes an arbitral tribunal;
-   where a party has more than one place of business the relevant "place of business" is that which has the closest relationship to the contract and its performance, having regard to the circumstances known to or contemplated by the parties at any time before or at the conclusion of the contract;
-   "obligor" refers to the party who is to perform an obligation and "obligee" refers to the party who is entitled to performance of that obligation.
-   "writing" means any mode of communication that preserves a record of the information contained therein and is capable of being reproduced in tangible form.

CHAPTER 2 — FORMATION

ARTICLE 2.1
(Manner of formation)

A contract may be concluded either by the acceptance of an offer or by conduct of the parties that is sufficient to show agreement.

ARTICLE 2.2
(Definition of offer)

A proposal for concluding a contract constitutes an offer if it is sufficiently definite and indicates the intention of the offeror to be bound in case of acceptance.

Annex

ARTICLE 2.3
(Withdrawal of offer)

(1)   An offer becomes effective when it reaches the offeree.

(2)   An offer, even if it is irrevocable, may be withdrawn if the withdrawal reaches the offeree before or at the same time as the offer.

ARTICLE 2.4
(Revocation of offer)

(1)   Until a contract is concluded an offer may be revoked if the revocation reaches the offeree before it has dispatched an acceptance.

(2)   However, an offer cannot be revoked

(a)   if it indicates, whether by stating a fixed time for acceptance or otherwise, that it is irrevocable; or

(b)   if it was reasonable for the offeree to rely on the offer as being irrevocable and the offeree has acted in reliance on the offer.

ARTICLE 2.5
(Rejection of offer)

An offer is terminated when a rejection reaches the offeror.

ARTICLE 2.6
(Mode of acceptance)

(1)   A statement made by or other conduct of the offeree indicating assent to an offer is an acceptance. Silence or inactivity does not in itself amount to acceptance.

(2)   An acceptance of an offer becomes effective when the indication of assent reaches the offeror.

(3)   However, if, by virtue of the offer or as a result of practices which the parties have established between themselves or of usage, the offeree may indicate assent by performing an act without notice to the offeror, the acceptance is effective when the act is performed.

ARTICLE 2.7
(Time of acceptance)

An offer must be accepted within the time the offeror has fixed or, if no time is fixed, within a reasonable time having regard to the circumstances, including the rapidity of the means of communication employed by the offeror. An oral offer must be accepted immediately unless the circumstances indicate otherwise.

ARTICLE 2.8
(Acceptance within a fixed period of time)

(1)   A period of time for acceptance fixed by the offeror in a telegram or a letter begins to run from the moment the telegram is handed in for dispatch or from the date shown on the letter or, if no such date is shown, from the date shown on the envelope. A period of time for acceptance fixed by the offeror by means of instantaneous communication begins to run from the moment that the offer reaches the offeree.

(2)   Official holidays or non-business days occurring during the period for acceptance are included in calculating the period. However, if a notice of acceptance cannot be delivered at the address of the offeror on the last day of the period because

that day falls on an official holiday or a non-business day at the place of business of the offeror, the period is extended until the first business day which follows.

ARTICLE 2.9
(Late acceptance. Delay in transmission)

(1)   A late acceptance is nevertheless effective as an acceptance if without undue delay the offeror so informs the offeree or gives notice to that effect.

(2)   If a letter or other writing containing a late acceptance shows that it has been sent in such circumstances that if its transmission had been normal it would have reached the offeror in due time, the late acceptance is effective as an acceptance unless, without undue delay, the offeror informs the offeree that it considers the offer as having lapsed.

ARTICLE 2.10
(Withdrawal of acceptance)

An acceptance may be withdrawn if the withdrawal reaches the offeror before or at the same time as the acceptance would have become effective.

ARTICLE 2.11
(Modified acceptance)

(1)   A reply to an offer which purports to be an acceptance but contains additions, limitations or other modifications is a rejection of the offer and constitutes a counter-offer.

(2)   However, a reply to an offer which purports to be an acceptance but contains additional or different terms which do not materially alter the terms of the offer constitutes an acceptance, unless the offeror, without undue delay, objects to the discrepancy. If the offeror does not object, the terms of the contract are the terms of the offer with the modifications contained in the acceptance.

ARTICLE 2.12
(Writings in confirmation)

If a writing which is sent within a reasonable time after the conclusion of the contract and which purports to be a confirmation of the contract contains additional or different terms, such terms become part of the contract, unless they materially alter the contract or the recipient, without undue delay, objects to the discrepancy.

ARTICLE 2.13
(Conclusion of contract dependent on agreement on specific matters or in a specific form)

Where in the course of negotiations one of the parties insists that the contract is not concluded until there is agreement on specific matters or in a specific form, no contract is concluded before agreement is reached on those matters or in that form.

ARTICLE 2.14
(Contract with terms deliberately left open)

(1)   If the parties intend to conclude a contract, the fact that they intentionally leave a term to be agreed upon in further negotiations or to be determined by a third person does not prevent a contract from coming into existence.

(2)   The existence of the contract is not affected by the fact that subsequently
   (a)   the parties reach no agreement on the term; or

Annex

    (b)   the third person does not determine the term,

provided that there is an alternative means of rendering the term definite that is reasonable in the circumstances, having regard to the intention of the parties.

ARTICLE 2.15
(Negotiations in bad faith)

    (1)   A party is free to negotiate and is not liable for failure to reach an agreement.

    (2)   However, a party who negotiates or breaks off negotiations in bad faith is liable for the losses caused to the other party.

    (3)   It is bad faith, in particular, for a party to enter into or continue negotiations when intending not to reach an agreement with the other party.

ARTICLE 2.16
(Duty of confidentiality)

Where information is given as confidential by one party in the course of negotiations, the other party is under a duty not to disclose that information or to use it improperly for its own purposes, whether or not a contract is subsequently concluded. Where appropriate, the remedy for breach of that duty may include compensation based on the benefit received by the other party.

ARTICLE 2.17
(Merger clauses)

A contract in writing which contains a clause indicating that the writing completely embodies the terms on which the parties have agreed cannot be contradicted or supplemented by evidence of prior statements or agreements. However, such statements or agreements may be used to interpret the writing.

ARTICLE 2.18
(Written modification clauses)

A contract in writing which contains a clause requiring any modification or termination by agreement to be in writing may not be otherwise modified or terminated. However, a party may be precluded by its conduct from asserting such a clause to the extent that the other party has acted in reliance on that conduct.

ARTICLE 2.19
(Contracting under standard terms)

    (1)   Where one party or both parties use standard terms in concluding a contract, the general rules on formation apply, subject to Articles 2.20 - 2.22.

    (2)   Standard terms are provisions which are prepared in advance for general and repeated use by one party and which are actually used without negotiation with the other party.

ARTICLE 2.20
(Surprising terms)

    (1)   No term contained in standard terms which is of such a character that the other party could not reasonably have expected it, is effective unless it has been expressly accepted by that party.

    (2)   In determining whether a term is of such a character regard is to be had to its content, language and presentation.

ARTICLE 2.21
(Conflict between standard terms and non-standard terms)

In case of conflict between a standard term and a term which is not a standard term the latter prevails.

ARTICLE 2.22
(Battle of forms)

Where both parties use standard terms and reach agreement except on those terms, a contract is concluded on the basis of the agreed terms and of any standard terms which are common in substance unless one party clearly indicates in advance, or later and without undue delay informs the other party, that it does not intend to be bound by such a contract.

CHAPTER 3 — VALIDITY

ARTICLE 3.1
(Matters not covered)

These Principles do not deal with invalidity arising from
    (a)   lack of capacity;
    (b)   lack of authority;
    (c)   immorality or illegality.

ARTICLE 3.2
(Validity of mere agreement)

A contract is concluded, modified or terminated by the mere agreement of the parties, without any further requirement.

ARTICLE 3.3
(Initial impossibility)

(1)   The mere fact that at the time of the conclusion of the contract the performance of the obligation assumed was impossible does not affect the validity of the contract.

(2)   The mere fact that at the time of the conclusion of the contract a party was not entitled to dispose of the assets to which the contract relates does not affect the validity of the contract.

ARTICLE 3.4
(Definition of mistake)

Mistake is an erroneous assumption relating to facts or to law existing when the contract was concluded.

ARTICLE 3.5
(Relevant mistake)

(1)   A party may only avoid the contract for mistake if, when the contract was concluded, the mistake was of such importance that a reasonable person in the same situation as the party in error would only have concluded the contract on materially different terms or would not have concluded it at all if the true state of affairs had been known, and

(a) the other party made the same mistake, or caused the mistake, or knew or ought to have known of the mistake and it was contrary to reasonable commercial standards of fair dealing to leave the mistaken party in error; or

(b) the other party had not at the time of avoidance acted in reliance on the contract.

(2) However, a party may not avoid the contract if

(a) it was grossly negligent in committing the mistake; or

(b) the mistake relates to a matter in regard to which the risk of mistake was assumed or, having regard to the circumstances, should be borne by the mistaken party.

ARTICLE 3.6
(Error in expression or transmission)

An error occurring in the expression or transmission of a declaration is considered to be a mistake of the person from whom the declaration emanated.

ARTICLE 3.7
(Remedies for non-performance)

A party is not entitled to avoid the contract on the ground of mistake if the circumstances on which that party relies afford, or could have afforded, a remedy for non-performance.

ARTICLE 3.8
(Fraud)

A party may avoid the contract when it has been led to conclude the contract by the other party's fraudulent representation, including language or practices, or fraudulent non-disclosure of circumstances which, according to reasonable commercial standards of fair dealing, the latter party should have disclosed.

ARTICLE 3.9
(Threat)

A party may avoid the contract when it has been led to conclude the contract by the other party's unjustified threat which, having regard to the circumstances, is so imminent and serious as to leave the first party no reasonable alternative. In particular, a threat is unjustified if the act or omission with which a party has been threatened is wrongful in itself, or it is wrongful to use it as a means to obtain the conclusion of the contract.

ARTICLE 3.10
(Gross disparity)

(1) A party may avoid the contract or an individual term of it if, at the time of the conclusion of the contract, the contract or term unjustifiably gave the other party an excessive advantage. Regard is to be had, among other factors, to

(a) the fact that the other party has taken unfair advantage of the first party's dependence, economic distress or urgent needs, or of its improvidence, ignorance, inexperience or lack of bargaining skill; and

(b) the nature and purpose of the contract.

(2) Upon the request of the party entitled to avoidance, a court may adapt the contract or term in order to make it accord with reasonable commercial standards of fair dealing.

(3)   A court may also adapt the contract or term upon the request of the party receiving notice of avoidance, provided that that party informs the other party of its request promptly after receiving such notice and before the other party has acted in reliance on it. The provisions of Article 3.13(2) apply accordingly.

ARTICLE 3.11
(Third persons)

(1)   Where fraud, threat, gross disparity or a party's mistake is imputable to, or is known or ought to be known by, a third person for whose acts the other party is responsible, the contract may be avoided under the same conditions as if the behaviour or knowledge had been that of the party itself.

(2)   Where fraud, threat or gross disparity is imputable to a third person for whose acts the other party is not responsible, the contract may be avoided if that party knew or ought to have known of the fraud, threat or disparity, or has not at the time of avoidance acted in reliance on the contract.

ARTICLE 3.12
(Confirmation)

If the party entitled to avoid the contract expressly or impliedly confirms the contract after the period of time for giving notice of avoidance has begun to run, avoidance of the contract is excluded.

ARTICLE 3.13
(Loss of right to avoid)

(1)   If a party is entitled to avoid the contract for mistake but the other party declares itself willing to perform or performs the contract as it was understood by the party entitled to avoidance, the contract is considered to have been concluded as the latter party understood it. The other party must make such a declaration or render such performance promptly after having been informed of the manner in which the party entitled to avoidance had understood the contract and before that party has acted in reliance on a notice of avoidance.

(2)   After such a declaration or performance the right to avoidance is lost and any earlier notice of avoidance is ineffective.

ARTICLE 3.14
(Notice of avoidance)

The right of a party to avoid the contract is exercised by notice to the other party

ARTICLE 3.15
(Time limits)

(1)   Notice of avoidance shall be given within a reasonable time, having regard to the circumstances, after the avoiding party knew or could not have been unaware of the relevant facts or became capable of acting freely.

(2)   Where an individual term of the contract may be avoided by a party under Article 3.10, the period of time for giving notice of avoidance begins to run when that term is asserted by the other party.

Annex

ARTICLE 3.16
(Partial avoidance)

Where a ground of avoidance affects only individual terms of the contract, the effect of avoidance is limited to those terms unless, having regard to the circumstances, it is unreasonable to uphold the remaining contract.

ARTICLE 3.17
(Retroactive effect of avoidance)

(1)   Avoidance takes effect retroactively.

(2)   On avoidance either party may claim restitution of whatever it has supplied under the contract or the part of it avoided, provided that it concurrently makes restitution of whatever it has received under the contract or the part of it avoided or, if it cannot make restitution in kind, it makes an allowance for what it has received.

ARTICLE 3.18
(Damages)

Irrespective of whether or not the contract has been avoided, the party who knew or ought to have known of the ground for avoidance is liable for damages so as to put the other party in the same position in which it would have been if it had not concluded the contract.

ARTICLE 3.19
(Mandatory character of the provisions)

The provisions of this Chapter are mandatory, except insofar as they relate to the binding force of mere agreement, initial impossibility or mistake.

ARTICLE 3.20
(Unilateral declarations)

The provisions of this Chapter apply with appropriate adaptations to any communication of intention addressed by one party to the other.

CHAPTER 4 — INTERPRETATION

ARTICLE 4.1
(Intention of the parties)

(1)   A contract shall be interpreted according to the common intention of the parties.

(2)   If such an intention cannot be established, the contract shall be interpreted according to the meaning that reasonable persons of the same kind as the parties would give to it in the same circumstances.

ARTICLE 4.2
(Interpretation of statements and other conduct)

(1)   The statements and other conduct of a party shall be interpreted according to that party's intention if the other party knew or could not have been unaware of that intention.

(2)   If the preceding paragraph is not applicable, such statements and other conduct shall be interpreted according to the meaning that a reasonable person of the same kind as the other party would give to it in the same circumstances.

UNIDROIT Principles

ARTICLE 4.3
(Relevant circumstances)

In applying Articles 4.1 and 4.2, regard shall be had to all the circumstances, including

   (a)   preliminary negotiations between the parties;
   (b)   practices which the parties have established between themselves;
   (c)   the conduct of the parties subsequent to the conclusion of the contract;
   (d)   the nature and purpose of the contract;
   (e)   the meaning commonly given to terms and expressions in the trade concerned;
   (f)   usages.

ARTICLE 4.4
(Reference to contract or statement as a whole)

Terms and expressions shall be interpreted in the light of the whole contract or statement in which they appear.

ARTICLE 4.5
(All terms to be given effect)

Contract terms shall be interpreted so as to give effect to all the terms rather than to deprive some of them of effect.

ARTICLE 4.6
(Contra proferentem rule)

If contract terms supplied by one party are unclear, an interpretation against that party is preferred.

ARTICLE 4.7
(Linguistic discrepancies)

Where a contract is drawn up in two or more language versions which are equally authoritative there is, in case of discrepancy between the versions, a preference for the interpretation according to a version in which the contract was originally drawn up.

ARTICLE 4.8
(Supplying an omitted term)

   (1)   Where the parties to a contract have not agreed with respect to a term which is important for a determination of their rights and duties, a term which is appropriate in the circumstances shall be supplied.
   (2)   In determining what is an appropriate term regard shall be had, among other factors, to

   (a)   the intention of the parties;
   (b)   the nature and purpose of the contract;
   (c)   good faith and fair dealing;
   (d)   reasonableness.

Annex

CHAPTER 5 — CONTENT

ARTICLE 5.1
(Express and implied obligations)

The contractual obligations of the parties may be express or implied.

ARTICLE 5.2
(Implied obligations)

Implied obligations stem from
- (a) the nature and purpose of the contract;
- (b) practices established between the parties and usages;
- (c) good faith and fair dealing;
- (d) reasonableness.

ARTICLE 5.3
(Co-operation between the parties)

Each party shall co-operate with the other party when such co-operation may reasonably be expected for the performance of that party's obligations.

ARTICLE 5.4
(Duty to achieve a specific result
Duty of best efforts)

(1) To the extent that an obligation of a party involves a duty to achieve a specific result, that party is bound to achieve that result.

(2) To the extent that an obligation of a party involves a duty of best efforts in the performance of an activity, that party is bound to make such efforts as would be made by a reasonable person of the same kind in the same circumstances.

ARTICLE 5.5
(Determination of kind of duty involved)

In determining the extent to which an obligation of a party involves a duty of best efforts in the performance of an activity or a duty to achieve a specific result, regard shall be had, among other factors, to
- (a) the way in which the obligation is expressed in the contract;
- (b) the contractual price and other terms of the contract;
- (c) the degree of risk normally involved in achieving the expected result;
- (d) the ability of the other party to influence the performance of the obligation.

ARTICLE 5.6
(Determination of quality of performance)

Where the quality of performance is neither fixed by, nor determinable from, the contract a party is bound to render a performance of a quality that is reasonable and not less than average in the circumstances.

ARTICLE 5.7
(Price determination)

(1) Where a contract does not fix or make provision for determining the price, the parties are considered, in the absence of any indication to the contrary, to have

made reference to the price generally charged at the time of the conclusion of the contract for such performance in comparable circumstances in the trade concerned or, if no such price is available, to a reasonable price.

(2)   Where the price is to be determined by one party and that determination is manifestly unreasonable, a reasonable price shall be substituted notwithstanding any contract term to the contrary.

(3)   Where the price is to be fixed by a third person, and that person cannot or will not do so, the price shall be a reasonable price.

(4)   Where the price is to be fixed by reference to factors which do not exist or have ceased to exist or to be accessible, the nearest equivalent factor shall be treated as a substitute.

ARTICLE 5.8
(Contract for an indefinite period)

A contract for an indefinite period may be ended by either party by giving notice a reasonable time in advance.

CHAPTER 6 — PERFORMANCE

SECTION 1: PERFORMANCE IN GENERAL

ARTICLE 6.1.1
(Time of performance)

A party must perform its obligations:
(a)   if a time is fixed by or determinable from the contract, at that time;
(b)   if a period of time is fixed by or determinable from the contract, at any time within that period unless circumstances indicate that the other party is to choose a time;
(c)   in any other case, within a reasonable time after the conclusion of the contract.

ARTICLE 6.1.2
(Performance at one time or in instalments)

In cases under Article 6.1.1(b) or (c), a party must perform its obligations at one time if that performance can be rendered at one time and the circumstances do not indicate otherwise.

ARTICLE 6.1.3
(Partial performance)

(1)   The obligee may reject an offer to perform in part at the time performance is due, whether or not such offer is coupled with an assurance as to the balance of the performance, unless the obligee has no legitimate interest in so doing.

(2)   Additional expenses caused to the obligee by partial performance are to be borne by the obligor without prejudice to any other remedy.

ARTICLE 6.1.4
(Order of performance)

(1)   To the extent that the performances of the parties can be rendered simultaneously, the parties are bound to render them simultaneously unless the circumstances indicate otherwise.

(2)   To the extent that the performance of only one party requires a period of time, that party is bound to render its performance first, unless the circumstances indicate otherwise.

ARTICLE 6.1.5
(Earlier performance)

(1)   The obligee may reject an earlier performance unless it has no legitimate interest in so doing.

(2)   Acceptance by a party of an earlier performance does not affect the time for the performance of its own obligations if that time has been fixed irrespective of the performance of the other party's obligations.

(3)   Additional expenses caused to the obligee by earlier performance are to be borne by the obligor, without prejudice to any other remedy.

ARTICLE 6.1.6
(Place of performance)

(1)   If the place of performance is neither fixed by, nor determinable from, the contract, a party is to perform:

    (a)   a monetary obligation, at the obligee's place of business;

    (b)   any other obligation, at its own place of business.

(2)   A party must bear any increase in the expenses incidental to performance which is caused by a change in its place of business subsequent to the conclusion of the contract.

ARTICLE 6.1.7
(Payment by cheque or other instrument)

(1)   Payment may be made in any form used in the ordinary course of business at the place for payment.

(2)   However, an obligee who accepts, either by virtue of paragraph (1) or voluntarily, a cheque, any other order to pay or a promise to pay, is presumed to do so only on condition that it will be honoured.

ARTICLE 6.1.8
(Payment by funds transfer)

(1)   Unless the obligee has indicated a particular account, payment may be made by a transfer to any of the financial institutions in which the obligee has made it known that it has an account.

(2)   In case of payment by a transfer the obligation of the obligor is discharged when the transfer to the obligee's financial institution becomes effective.

ARTICLE 6.1.9
(Currency of payment)

(1)   If a monetary obligation is expressed in a currency other than that of the place for payment, it may be paid by the obligor in the currency of the place for payment unless

    (a)   that currency is not freely convertible; or

    (b)   the parties have agreed that payment should be made only in the currency in which the monetary obligation is expressed.

(2)   If it is impossible for the obligor to make payment in the currency in which the monetary obligation is expressed, the obligee may require payment in the currency of the place for payment, even in the case referred to in paragraph (1)(b).

(3)   Payment in the currency of the place for payment is to be made according to the applicable rate of exchange prevailing there when payment is due.

(4)   However, if the obligor has not paid at the time when payment is due, the obligee may require payment according to the applicable rate of exchange prevailing either when payment is due or at the time of actual payment.

ARTICLE 6.1.10
(Currency not expressed)

Where a monetary obligation is not expressed in a particular currency, payment must be made in the currency of the place where payment is to be made.

ARTICLE 6.1.11
(Costs of performance)

Each party shall bear the costs of performance of its obligations.

ARTICLE 6.1.12
(Imputation of payments)

(1)   An obligor owing several monetary obligations to the same obligee may specify at the time of payment the debt to which it intends the payment to be applied. However, the payment discharges first any expenses, then interest due and finally the principal.

(2)   If the obligor makes no such specification, the obligee may, within a reasonable time after payment, declare to the obligor the obligation to which it imputes the payment, provided that the obligation is due and undisputed.

(3)   In the absence of imputation under paragraphs (1) or (2), payment is imputed to that obligation which satisfies one of the following criteria and in the order indicated:

  (a)   an obligation which is due or which is the first to fall due;
  (b)   the obligation for which the obligee has least security;
  (c)   the obligation which is the most burdensome for the obligor;
  (d)   the obligation which has arisen first.

If none of the preceding criteria applies, payment is imputed to all the obligations proportionally.

ARTICLE 6.1.13
(Imputation of non-monetary obligations)

Article 6.1.12 applies with appropriate adaptations to the imputation of performance of non-monetary obligations.

ARTICLE 6.1.14
(Application for public permission)

Where the law of a State requires a public permission affecting the validity of the contract or its performance and neither that law nor the circumstances indicate otherwise

  (a)   if only one party has its place of business in that State, that party shall take the measures necessary to obtain the permission;

(b)   in any other case the party whose performance requires permission shall take the necessary measures.

ARTICLE 6.1.15
(Procedure in applying for permission)

(1)   The party required to take the measures necessary to obtain the permission shall do so without undue delay and shall bear any expenses incurred.

(2)   That party shall whenever appropriate give the other party notice of the grant or refusal of such permission without undue delay.

ARTICLE 6.1.16
(Permission neither granted nor refused)

(1)   If, notwithstanding the fact that the party responsible has taken all measures required, permission is neither granted nor refused within an agreed period or, where no period has been agreed, within a reasonable time from the conclusion of the contract, either party is entitled to terminate the contract.

(2)   Where the permission affects some terms only, paragraph (1) does not apply if, having regard to the circumstances, it is reasonable to uphold the remaining contract even if the permission is refused.

ARTICLE 6.1.17
(Permission refused)

(1)   The refusal of a permission affecting the validity of the contract renders the contract void. If the refusal affects the validity of some terms only, only such terms are void if, having regard to the circumstances, it is reasonable to uphold the remaining contract.

(2)   Where the refusal of a permission renders the performance of the contract impossible in whole or in part, the rules on non-performance apply.

SECTION 2: HARDSHIP

ARTICLE 6.2.1
(Contract to be observed)

Where the performance of a contract becomes more onerous for one of the parties, that party is nevertheless bound to perform its obligations subject to the following provisions on hardship.

ARTICLE 6.2.2
(Definition of hardship)

There is hardship where the occurrence of events fundamentally alters the equilibrium of the contract either because the cost of a party's performance has increased or because the value of the performance a party receives has diminished, and
(a)   the events occur or become known to the disadvantaged party after the conclusion of the contract;
(b)   the events could not reasonably have been taken into account by the disadvantaged party at the time of the conclusion of the contract;
(c)   the events are beyond the control of the disadvantaged party; and
(d)   the risk of the events was not assumed by the disadvantaged party.

ARTICLE 6.2.3
(Effects of hardship)

(1) In case of hardship the disadvantaged party is entitled to request renegotiations. The request shall be made without undue delay and shall indicate the grounds on which it is based.

(2) The request for renegotiation does not in itself entitle the disadvantaged party to withhold performance.

(3) Upon failure to reach agreement within a reasonable time either party may resort to the court.

(4) If the court finds hardship it may, if reasonable,

    (a) terminate the contract at a date and on terms to be fixed; or

    (b) adapt the contract with a view to restoring its equilibrium.

CHAPTER 7 — NON-PERFORMANCE

SECTION 1: NON-PERFORMANCE IN GENERAL

ARTICLE 7.1.1
(Non-performance defined)

Non-performance is failure by a party to perform any of its obligations under the contract, including defective performance or late performance.

ARTICLE 7.1.2
(Interference by the other party)

A party may not rely on the non-performance of the other party to the extent that such non-performance was caused by the first party's act or omission or by another event as to which the first party bears the risk.

ARTICLE 7.1.3
(Withholding performance)

(1) Where the parties are to perform simultaneously, either party may withhold performance until the other party tenders its performance.

(2) Where the parties are to perform consecutively, the party that is to perform later may withhold its performance until the first party has performed.

ARTICLE 7.1.4
(Cure by non-performing party)

(1) The non-performing party may, at its own expense, cure any non-performance, provided that

    (a) without undue delay, it gives notice indicating the proposed manner and timing of the cure;

    (b) cure is appropriate in the circumstances;

    (c) the aggrieved party has no legitimate interest in refusing cure; and

    (d) cure is effected promptly.

(2) The right to cure is not precluded by notice of termination.

(3) Upon effective notice of cure, rights of the aggrieved party that are inconsistent with the non-performing party's performance are suspended until the time for cure has expired.

(4) The aggrieved party may withhold performance pending cure.

(5)   Notwithstanding cure, the aggrieved party retains the right to claim damages for delay as well as for any harm caused or not prevented by the cure.

ARTICLE 7.1.5
(Additional period for performance)

(1)   In a case of non-performance the aggrieved party may by notice to the other party allow an additional period of time for performance.

(2)   During the additional period the aggrieved party may withhold performance of its own reciprocal obligations and may claim damages but may not resort to any other remedy. If it receives notice from the other party that the latter will not perform within that period, or if upon expiry of that period due performance has not been made, the aggrieved party may resort to any of the remedies that may be available under this Chapter.

(3)   Where in a case of delay in performance which is not fundamental the aggrieved party has given notice allowing an additional period of time of reasonable length, it may terminate the contract at the end of that period. If the additional period allowed is not of reasonable length it shall be extended to a reasonable length. The aggrieved party may in its notice provide that if the other party fails to perform within the period allowed by the notice the contract shall automatically terminate.

(4)   Paragraph (3) does not apply where the obligation which has not been performed is only a minor part of the contractual obligation of the non-performing party.

ARTICLE 7.1.6
(Exemption clauses)

A clause which limits or excludes one party's liability for non-performance or which permits one party to render performance substantially different from what the other party reasonably expected may not be invoked if it would be grossly unfair to do so, having regard to the purpose of the contract.

ARTICLE 7.1.7
(Force majeure)

(1)   Non-performance by a party is excused if that party proves that the non-performance was due to an impediment beyond its control and that it could not reasonably be expected to have taken the impediment into account at the time of the conclusion of the contract or to have avoided or overcome it or its consequences.

(2)   When the impediment is only temporary, the excuse shall have effect for such period as is reasonable having regard to the effect of the impediment on the performance of the contract.

(3)   The party who fails to perform must give notice to the other party of the impediment and its effect on its ability to perform. If the notice is not received by the other party within a reasonable time after the party who fails to perform knew or ought to have known of the impediment, it is liable for damages resulting from such non-receipt.

(4)   Nothing in this article prevents a party from exercising a right to terminate the contract or to withhold performance or request interest on money due.

SECTION 2: RIGHT TO PERFORMANCE

ARTICLE 7.2.1
(Performance of monetary obligation)

Where a party who is obliged to pay money does not do so, the other party may require payment.

ARTICLE 7.2.2
(Performance of non-monetary obligation)

Where a party who owes an obligation other than one to pay money does not perform, the other party may require performance, unless

    (a)   performance is impossible in law or in fact;

    (b)   performance or, where relevant, enforcement is unreasonably burdensome or expensive;

    (c)   the party entitled to performance may reasonably obtain performance from another source;

    (d)   performance is of an exclusively personal character; or

    (e)   the party entitled to performance does not require performance within a reasonable time after it has, or ought to have, become aware of the non-performance.

ARTICLE 7.2.3
(Repair and replacement of defective performance)

The right to performance includes in appropriate cases the right to require repair, replacement, or other cure of defective performance. The provisions of Articles 7.2.1 and 7.2.2 apply accordingly.

ARTICLE 7.2.4
(Judicial penalty)

(1)   Where the court orders a party to perform, it may also direct that this party pay a penalty if it does not comply with the order.

(2)   The penalty shall be paid to the aggrieved party unless mandatory provisions of the law of the forum provide otherwise. Payment of the penalty to the aggrieved party does not exclude any claim for damages.

ARTICLE 7.2.5
(Change of remedy)

(1)   An aggrieved party who has required performance of a non-monetary obligation and who has not received performance within a period fixed or otherwise within a reasonable period of time may invoke any other remedy.

(2)   Where the decision of a court for performance of a non-monetary obligation cannot be enforced, the aggrieved party may invoke any other remedy.

SECTION 3: TERMINATION

ARTICLE 7.3.1
(Right to terminate the contract)

(1)   A party may terminate the contract where the failure of the other party to perform an obligation under the contract amounts to a fundamental non-performance.

(2)   In determining whether a failure to perform an obligation amounts to a fundamental non-performance regard shall be had, in particular, to whether
  (a)   the non-performance substantially deprives the aggrieved party of what it was entitled to expect under the contract unless the other party did not foresee and could not reasonably have foreseen such result;
  (b)   strict compliance with the obligation which has not been performed is of essence under the contract;
  (c)   the non-performance is intentional or reckless;
  (d)   the non-performance gives the aggrieved party reason to believe that it cannot rely on the other party's future performance;
  (e)   the non-performing party will suffer disproportionate loss as a result of the preparation or performance if the contract is terminated.
(3)   In the case of delay the aggrieved party may also terminate the contract if the other party fails to perform before the time allowed it under Article 7.1.5 has expired.

ARTICLE 7.3.2
(Notice of termination)

(1)   The right of a party to terminate the contract is exercised by notice to the other party.
(2)   If performance has been offered late or otherwise does not conform to the contract the aggrieved party will lose its right to terminate the contract unless it gives notice to the other party within a reasonable time after it has or ought to have become aware of the offer or of the non-conforming performance.

ARTICLE 7.3.3
(Anticipatory non-performance)

Where prior to the date for performance by one of the parties it is clear that there will be a fundamental non-performance by that party, the other party may terminate the contract.

ARTICLE 7.3.4
(Adequate assurance of due performance)

A party who reasonably believes that there will be a fundamental non-performance by the other party may demand adequate assurance of due performance and may meanwhile withhold its own performance. Where this assurance is not provided within a reasonable time the party demanding it may terminate the contract.

ARTICLE 7.3.5
(Effects of termination in general)

(1)   Termination of the contract releases both parties from their obligation to effect and to receive future performance.
(2)   Termination does not preclude a claim for damages for non-performance.
(3)   Termination does not affect any provision in the contract for the settlement of disputes or any other term of the contract which is to operate even after termination.

ARTICLE 7.3.6
(Restitution)

(1)   On termination of the contract either party may claim restitution of whatever it has supplied, provided that such party concurrently makes restitution of whatever it

has received. If restitution in kind is not possible or appropriate allowance should be made in money whenever reasonable.

(2)   However, if performance of the contract has extended over a period of time and the contract is divisible, such restitution can only be claimed for the period after termination has taken effect.

SECTION 4: DAMAGES

ARTICLE 7.4.1
(Right to damages)

Any non-performance gives the aggrieved party a right to damages either exclusively or in conjunction with any other remedies except where the non-performance is excused under these Principles.

ARTICLE 7.4.2
(Full compensation)

(1)   The aggrieved party is entitled to full compensation for harm sustained as a result of the non-performance. Such harm includes both any loss which it suffered and any gain of which it was deprived, taking into account any gain to the aggrieved party resulting from its avoidance of cost or harm.

(2)   Such harm may be non-pecuniary and includes, for instance, physical suffering or emotional distress.

ARTICLE 7.4.3
(Certainty of harm)

(1)   Compensation is due only for harm, including future harm, that is established with a reasonable degree of certainty.

(2)   Compensation may be due for the loss of a chance in proportion to the probability of its occurrence.

(3)   Where the amount of damages cannot be established with a sufficient degree of certainty, the assessment is at the discretion of the court.

ARTICLE 7.4.4
(Foreseeability of harm)

The non-performing party is liable only for harm which it foresaw or could reasonably have foreseen at the time of the conclusion of the contract as being likely to result from its non-performance.

ARTICLE 7.4.5
(Proof of harm in case of replacement transaction)

Where the aggrieved party has terminated the contract and has made a replacement transaction within a reasonable time and in a reasonable manner it may recover the difference between the contract price and the price of the replacement transaction as well as damages for any further harm.

ARTICLE 7.4.6
(Proof of harm by current price)

(1)   Where the aggrieved party has terminated the contract and has not made a replacement transaction but there is a current price for the performance contracted for,

it may recover the difference between the contract price and the price current at the time the contract is terminated as well as damages for any further harm.

(2)   Current price is the price generally charged for goods delivered or services rendered in comparable circumstances at the place where the contract should have been performed or, if there is no current price at that place, the current price at such other place that appears reasonable to take as a reference.

ARTICLE 7.4.7
(Harm due in part to aggrieved party)

Where the harm is due in part to an act or omission of the aggrieved party or to another event as to which that party bears the risk, the amount of damages shall be reduced to the extent that these factors have contributed to the harm, having regard to the conduct of each of the parties.

ARTICLE 7.4.8
(Mitigation of harm)

(1)   The non-performing party is not liable for harm suffered by the aggrieved party to the extent that the harm could have been reduced by the latter party's taking reasonable steps.

(2)   The aggrieved party is entitled to recover any expenses reasonably incurred in attempting to reduce the harm.

ARTICLE 7.4.9
(Interest for failure to pay money)

(1)   If a party does not pay a sum of money when it falls due the aggrieved party is entitled to interest upon that sum from the time when payment is due to the time of payment whether or not the non-payment is excused.

(2)   The rate of interest shall be the average bank short-term lending rate to prime borrowers prevailing for the currency of payment at the place for payment, or where no such rate exists at that place, then the same rate in the State of the currency of payment. In the absence of such a rate at either place the rate of interest shall be the appropriate rate fixed by the law of the State of the currency of payment.

(3)   The aggrieved party is entitled to additional damages if the non-payment caused it a greater harm.

ARTICLE 7.4.10
(Interest on damages)

Unless otherwise agreed, interest on damages for non-performance of non-monetary obligations accrues as from the time of non-performance.

ARTICLE 7.4.11
(Manner of monetary redress)

(1)   Damages are to be paid in a lump sum. However, they may be payable in instalments where the nature of the harm makes this appropriate.

(2)   Damages to be paid in instalments may be indexed.

UNIDROIT Principles

ARTICLE 7.4.12
(Currency in which to assess damages)

Damages are to be assessed either in the currency in which the monetary obligation was expressed or in the currency in which the harm was suffered, whichever is more appropriate.

ARTICLE 7.4.13
(Agreed payment for non-performance)

(1)   Where the contract provides that a party who does not perform is to pay a specified sum to the aggrieved party for such non-performance, the aggrieved party is entitled to that sum irrespective of its actual harm.

(2)   However, notwithstanding any agreement to the contrary the specified sum may be reduced to a reasonable amount where it is grossly excessive in relation to the harm resulting from the non-performance and to the other circumstances.

Finito di stampare nel mese di marzo del 1996 dalla
Capitolina '52 s.a.s. · Roma